Phantom of the Chi

To Lorine & David

With Best Wishes

Feb. 2009

Also by Chi Lo

THE MISUNDERSTOOD CHINA: Uncovering the Truth Behind the Bamboo Curtain

UNDERSTANDING CHINA'S GROWTH: Forces that Drive China's Economic Future

WHEN ASIA MEETS CHINA IN THE NEW MILLENNIUM: China's Role in Shaping Asia's Post-Crisis Economic Transformation

Phantom of the China Economic Threat

Shadow of the Next Asian Crisis

Chi Lo

Foreword by
Nick Lord
Editorial Director, FinanceAsia

© Chi Lo 2006, 2007
Foreword © Nick Lord 2006

All rights reserved. No reproduction, copy or transmission of this publication may be made without written permission.

No paragraph of this publication may be reproduced, copied or transmitted save with written permission or in accordance with the provisions of the Copyright, Designs and Patents Act 1988, or under the terms of any licence permitting limited copying issued by the Copyright Licensing Agency, 90 Tottenham Court Road, London W1T 4LP.

Any person who does any unauthorised act in relation to this publication may be liable to criminal prosecution and civil claims for damages.

The author has asserted his right to be identified as the author of this work in accordance with the Copyright, Designs and Patents Act 1988.

First published in 2006
Paperback edition published 2007 by
PALGRAVE MACMILLAN
Houndmills, Basingstoke, Hampshire RG21 6XS and
175 Fifth Avenue, New York, N.Y. 10010
Companies and representatives throughout the world.

PALGRAVE MACMILLAN is the global academic imprint of the Palgrave Macmillan division of St. Martin's Press, LLC and of Palgrave Macmillan Ltd. Macmillan® is a registered trademark in the United States, United Kingdom and other countries. Palgrave is a registered trademark in the European Union and other countries.

ISBN-13: 978–1–4039–8788–4 (hardcover)
ISBN-10: 1–4039–8788–2 (hardcover)
ISBN-13: 978–0–230–51544–4 (paperback)
ISBN-10: 0–230–51544–4 (paperback)

This book is printed on paper suitable for recycling and made from fully managed and sustained forest sources. Logging, pulping and manufacturing processes are expected to conform to the environmental regulations of the country of origin.

A catalogue record for this book is available from the British Library.

Library of Congress Cataloging-in-Publication Data

Lo, Chi, 1960–
    Phantom of the China economic threat / by Chi Lo.
     p. cm.
    Includes bibliographical references and index.
    ISBN 1–4039–8788–2 (cloth) ISBN 0–230–51544–4 (paperback)
     1. China – Foreign economic relations. 2. China – Economic policy –
2000– 3. China – Economic conditions – 2000– 4. Asia – Economic policy – 21st century. 5. Asia – Economic conditions – 21st century.
6. International economic relations. I. Title.

HF1604.L6 2006
337.51—dc22
                                                                   2005051501

10 9 8 7 6 5 4 3 2 1
16 15 14 13 12 11 10 09 08 07

Printed and bound in China

To the one who makes this book a reality with me

To the one who makes this book's reality with me.

Contents

List of Figures	ix
List of Tables	xi
Preface	xii
Foreword by Nick Lord	xv
Introduction	xvii

1 The New China Threat — 1
- The supply threat — 1
- The demand threat — 6
- Boom/bust growth — 11
- Systemic failure — 13

2 A Conspiracy Theory — 19
- How dependent is Asia on China? — 19
- The conspiracy theory — 25
- Still no way out — 28
- China's labour pains — 32
- It's just rendezvous — 36
- A product-cycle prospective — 38

3 The Outsourcing Threat — 41
- The hollowing-out myth — 41
- The myopic protectionists — 44
- The misguided debate — 46
- The irreversible trend — 51
- The real danger and the ugly face — 54

4 The Next Asian Crisis: Made in China? — 61
- The China trigger — 62
- The China cushion — 65
- A new cushion – agriculture demand — 69
- Fundamentals versus bubble — 73
- Not losing control — 80

5	**The Next Asian Crisis: Self-inflicted?**	**85**
	The fiscal time bomb	85
	Destabilising outlook	89
	Foreign reserves, angel or devil?	93
	The inherent structural weakness	97
	The bad apples fail to turn good	100
	Banking woes, déjà vu	108
6	**The External Stresses**	**111**
	The dark side of capital inflows	112
	The US fiscal time bomb	115
	Forcing the Fed's hand	117
	Asia's irrational exuberance	120
	The need for US dollar realignment	122
	Terrorism – a subtle catalyst	128
7	**The Real Danger Isn't Another Crisis**	**133**
	The crisis cushions	134
	What about the public debt?	140
	And the China trigger?	142
	The real danger	150
	Forcing a China threat	155
8	**What China Threat?**	**157**
	The Chinese reform hype	158
	The competitiveness myth	163
	The growth threat – debunked	167
	The investment threat – debunked	170
	The manufacturing threat – debunked	174
	A China model for development?	180
9	**Hollowing-out, Revisited**	**183**
	Southeast Asia's fate	183
	Breaking up Asia Inc.	185
	Doing it the wrong way	187
	It's not the end of life	189

Notes	194
Bibliography	198
Index	200

Figures

I:1	Chinese import growth	xvii
I:2	China's impact on global markets	xviii
1:1	Gross industrial output by SOEs	3
1:2	China's car output and sales	5
1:3	China's trade balance with Asia	7
1:4	China's real GDP growth	11
2:1	Sign of rising intra-Asian trade	20
2.2	Asian export growth ratio	21
2:3	Asian export-to-GDP ratio	22
2:4	Asian export growth ratio	24
2:5	Asian export growth	24
2:6	Intra-regional trade falling	25
2:7	Import penetration	26
2:8	Net foreign direct investment flows	26
2:9	Real GDP growth	29
2:10	Bank loan growth	30
2:11	China's net trade pattern	37
3:1	US employment/population ratio	42
3:2	China's trade with Japan and the US	43
3:3	US services trade balance	47
3:4	US net income receipt from abroad	48
3:5	US and Japan trade-to-GDP ratios	49
3:6	Non-Japan Asia trade-to-GDP ratio	50
3:7	US trade balance	55
3:8	US export growth	57
4:1	China's primary imports	66
4:2	Japan's exports to China and the US	68
4:3	Japan's export growth	69
4:4	Japan's FDI to China and foreign income	70
4:5	China's import volume growth, 2003	71
4:6	Sown area droppage	72
4:7	Share of grains in total farm output	73
4:8	Consumer price inflation	75
4:9	Gross construction value	76
4:10	Property prices	77

4:11	China's employment by sector	78
4:12	Shanghai A-share index	79
4:13	Change in inventories	80
4:14	Foreign reserve and base money growth	82
4:15	Fixed-asset investment (2004)	83
5:1	Asia's public debt	87
5:2	Asia's growing fiscal gap	88
5:3	Asia's capital inflow growth rates	94
5:4	Ratio of hot money to long-term money inflows	94
5:5	Asia's profit growth	98
5:6	Asian exchange rate and FX reserves	100
6:1	Asian markets' correlation with the US	113
6:2	US external balances	126
7:1	Asia's current account turns around	135
7:2	Asia's FX reserves have soared	135
7:3	Asia's import cover has risen sharply	136
7:4	Asia de-leveraging	139
7:5	Asia's public debt	140
7:6	Creative job destruction	144
7:7	Korea and Taiwan exports to the US and China	152
7:8	Japan and Germany exports to the US and China	153
8:1	China's creative destruction	159
8:2	State sector output and investment	159
8:3	Chinese banks total loans	161
8:4	Real GDP growth	168
8:5	China's balance of payments	172
8:6	China's net asset holding & FX reserves	172
8:7	Current account balances	173
8:8	China's net exports	175
8:9	China's FDI inflow by sector (2003)	177
8:10	China and Asia export growth	179

Tables

1:1	China's import growth	6
2:1	Breakdown of utilised FDI in China, 2003	27
2:2	Government budget balances	29
4:1	China's agricultural output growth	72
6:1	Stock market volatility	114
6:2	Fertility rates (1995–2000)	129
6:3	Working population (15–64 years old)	129
7:1	Asian foreign exchange rate volatility	137

Preface

The rapid ascent of China's economic clout has raised concerns about her potential threat to the world order, and generated much discussion recently about how to manage this rise of the Middle Kingdom. Managing China is tricky because it could be a self-fulfilling process, where if China is prematurely treated as a threat, she will become a threat. What makes many, especially the established powers, uneasy about China's rise is that there is no conviction from history that the ascent of a new power would not spark a global conflict that reshaped the international system.

There have been successful as well as failed attempts to manage a rising power. A notable example of success was Britain's conciliation with the US in the late nineteenth century, when the British effectively ceded the entire Western Hemisphere, except Canada, to the newly risen American power. The US was integrated into the world system and both powers prospered. But the experience of Germany's rise after the 1870s and Europe's reaction to it was quite unpleasant, as it eventually led to World War I. Japan's rise after 1868 also produced two rounds of warfare, first with China and Russia at the turn of the century and later with Britain and the US in World War II.

China sceptics and hawkish politicians argue that China would not want to be integrated into a political and security system that she had no part in shaping and that is not consistent with her ambitions or her own hierarchical principles. Rather, they believe that China would want to reshape the international order to suit her own purposes and to make the world safe for her own rules.

Arguably, these sceptical and confrontational views stem from the rapid rise of China's economic power, which has created envy, fear and suspicion among existing powers. In particular, China clashes hard with the American dream – the Americans admire and are amazed by size, but China is a country that dwarfs the US in many areas. China's 1.3 billion population is about four times the US population; she is also the fastest-growing large economy; the world's largest producer of steel, cement and coal; and the second largest holder of foreign exchange reserves. All this has changed the perception of China as a large but poor country to China as a large and increasingly powerful and threatening country.

Some also argue that China's ascent is raising the odds for another shift in the international order. There have been two major shifts in global power over the past four centuries. The first was the rise of Europe, which became the richest, most ambitious and enterprising region of the world in the seventeenth century. The second shift came with the rise of the US in the late nineteenth and early twentieth centuries, when she became the single most powerful country in the world. Throughout these changes, the world had been dominated by the interests of the Western great powers. China's rise is seen as threatening this 'western order' and, as the sceptics argue, triggering a third shift in the world power balance, perhaps along with the rising weight of India and continued influence of Japan.

The concern of China's potential to wreak havoc on the world order is underscored by the increasing reliance of the global economy on Chinese demand. Cheap imports from China are estimated to have saved the Americans over US$600 billion between 1995 and 2004, contributing to the curbing of US inflation and the rise of American consumers' purchasing power. The world also escaped a recession after the IT bubble burst in 2001 due largely to China's robust growth, which helped boost exports from around the world. By buying US Treasury securities, China (along with other Asian economies) has allowed the US to keep interest rates low, helping to sustain the growth of the world's largest economy.

Crucially, China has followed a very different development strategy from other Asian and emerging economies. She does not just pursue export-led growth and keep her internal market closed, she has also opened herself to foreign trade and investment. This has resulted in much of the world relying on the China market. There is also an increasing concern that the first port of call for the unfolding of the China threat would be Asia's regional economies because of their heavy reliance on Chinese demand for growth momentum and their geographical proximity to the Middle Kingdom. The China threat to Asia, the pessimists assert, would pull off another Asian economic crisis.

Neo-conservatives and Pentagon officials who have sounded the alarms about the China threat recently speak of it only in military terms. They all tend to exaggerate China's capabilities. There has been little economic analysis on the issue. Politics is outside the scope of this book. Rather, it seeks to fill the analytical gap by assessing the China threat and its potential to trigger another Asian crisis from the economic perspectives. The research here diagnoses hidden issues and identifies future trends in China and Asia's economic development (crisis) outlook.

Also, by exposing the political lies behind the rhetoric of China's economic threat and debunking Asia's illusive economic progress, this book warns Asia of the true risk behind its future.

Most observers, whether critics or supporters of China form their informed (or misinformed views) based on partial analysis of China's development. They miss developments in other parts of the global system that are relevant to an understanding of China and Asia. Thus, in many cases, conventional wisdom on China/Asia is often conventional thinking without much wisdom. This book uses a General Equilibrium approach, by enclosing relevant regional and global events, to assess China's integration into the world economy and the likelihood of another regional crisis.

The book is about applied economics diagnosing real world development. The discussions here combine rigorous research, data, facts and economic theories with real world examples and anecdotes to elaborate the arguments. While many of the issues discussed here may be controversial, a critical approach, questioning conventional wisdom at times, is used to assess them so that the discussions are expected to serve as a catalyst for stimulating critical thinking outside the box.

The book represents the thinking and application of analytical tools by economic practitioners. Students of Asian studies seeking to understand China and Asia's economic and financial development, including corporate executives, financial market practitioners and government advisors should find this book particularly useful for brainstorming and developing business, investment and policy strategies.

Foreword

There is only one country in the world where a professional cadre of outsiders build careers watching it. 'China watchers' is a term describing those whose job it is to explain the mysteries of China to the outside world. From Marco Polo on, these people have told a rapt and fascinated audience of the many splendours, terrors and errors of the most populous nation in the world.

Journalists in particular throng to the country, to experience the exotic and try to theorise what China is all about. It is a difficult job, searching for a unifying theory where none really exists. For it is impossible to really explain China in anything other than bland banalities (the most populous nation on earth) or in quite shatteringly complex detail. But that is what makes it enthralling and its quixotic inability to lend itself to easy appraisal makes China watchers of us all.

Added to this mix of journalists, diplomats, adventurers and scribes who watch China professionally, is the growing cast of economists who are trying to highlight the impact of China's burgeoning economy onto a credulous outside world.

Is China a threat or an opportunity? Will it become the world's biggest economy? Are its imports or exports more important? These economic books tend to reflect the rather blinkered focus of their authors, using conventional economic analysis to try to paint the picture of the Chinese economy. But trying to do this with China is like driving a car by only looking in the rear view mirror. Sure you can see what has happened but with a country this large, changing so fast, you will never be able to see what is actually happening nor what might come about.

Chi Lo's latest book is a bold attempt to break from this mould and to use wide ranging economic analysis to answer questions that do not necessarily pertain to the strict application of the dismal science. In this he has done many of his colleagues a favour. By using economic analysis, he shows economically whether or not China's politics should be seen as a threat or opportunity.

For a supposedly communist nation, China has shown that its politics – both external and internal – are driven absolutely by its economic needs. First and foremost, this means the need to keep social stability. This stability is preserved by the constant effort to create economic growth to lift people out of poverty.

These two driving forces of the Chinese economic engine are what also drive Chinese politics. Keeping internal stability by encouraging economic growth has been the overriding domestic policy since Deng took power in 1978. Two successive presidents have continued this policy. And while separate economic and political policies have changed over the years, the end to which they are pointing has remained constant.

For the outside world, understanding this constant gives a measure of constancy to an otherwise contradictory picture. China is on the one hand the fastest growing large nation in the world, yet it is also home to sizeable pockets of abject poverty. It is also one of only four nominally communist countries in the world, but has lifted more people out of poverty in the decade since the fall of communism elsewhere than any other country in history.

It also has an economic impact on the rest of the world that is completely out of kilter with the relative poverty of its own domestic economy. As Lo notes 'a polite burp in Beijing is heard around the world'.

In this book Lo looks to see if the many upcoming economic problems that China faces will turn into political crises for the rest of Asia. In this he follows on the thesis from his previous work on the growing interdependence between China and the rest of Asia, *When Asia Meets China in the New Millennium*. While there are no immediate causes for concern, the potential for crisis from China is a historic norm. And with its growing economic clout, China's neighbours will feel the force. The question is whether these countries can make their economies robust enough to weather the next crisis.

Nick Lord
Editorial Director, FinanceAsia

Introduction

When you lose your job, blame it on China because your company has outsourced jobs to the Middle Kingdom. When your business loses money, blame it on China because the cheap Chinese goods have crowded out yours. When your country loses foreign investments, blame it on China because she sucks in all the foreign capital, leaving other countries starved of capital and retarding their economic development. The China blame game has manifested itself in rising protectionist sentiment in many developed economies, notably in the US in the run up to her presidential election in late 2004. That may be a temporary shift in the US free-trade attitude, due to the misguided pre-election debate. But with weakening globalisation momentum, the negative global sentiment towards free trade, using China as an excuse, does raise the risk of protectionism that will hurt Asia.

It's a shame that after striving for so many years for freer trade, protectionism is returning. But the arguments against outsourcing to China (and other Asian production bases) are flawed, and many views about China's economic development are distorted. It will be a big danger to the global economic well-being if this misunderstanding about China and her relation with the global economy destroys the free trade effort. This book seeks to dispel those myths and expose the lies behind the political rhetoric about China's economic threat.

There is an increasing fear that China's rising competitiveness will eventually overwhelm global manufacturing and gobble up the world economy. And before that eventuality, some fear that China's competitive stress would even trigger another Asian crisis as foreign demand, investments and capital pull out of the regional economies and head to the Middle Kingdom. Remember it was massive withdrawal of foreign capital, which depleted Asia's foreign reserves and raised the fears about a collapsing Asian system, that triggered the 1997–1998 Asian crisis. That financial meltdown started with Thailand's currency devaluation, which unleashed a series of painful currency collapses – across Asia to Russia and Brazil – that spilled over to capital markets of all kinds around the world.

Asia now also fears being drawn too close to the economic benefits that China provides, as the region is increasingly relying on the Chinese market for its exports. This new threat of over-reliance on Chinese demand is adding to the old fears about China 'hollowing out' the regional economies both in terms of jobs and foreign capital. There is also an internal dimension to this perceived new China threat. It stems from China's systemic flaw, which has produced volatile growth cycles. China's economic volatility, the logic goes, will aggravate the danger of the boom/bust cycles dragging the Middle Kingdom's import demand with it, thus adding to the risk of Asia's export growth.

The fear about China's economic threats is intensifying because her impact on the global economy is getting more visible. China's economy has quadrupled in size since 1978. That has pulled more than 220 million Chinese out of poverty. Asia is increasingly pinning its hopes for sustained growth on China's 1.3 billion people being fully-fledged consumers. Indeed, China's surging imports have acted as a major growth engine for Asia by boosting intra-regional trade since the new millennium (Figure I:1).

In absolute terms, China is still a relatively poor economy. But her rapid growth has produced a significant growth dynamic in the global economy. For example, China accounted for an estimated 10% of world GDP growth in 2004, though her GDP size was only about 4% of the world total. She was the second growth driver to the global economy after the US, when the world was struggling in the aftermath of the

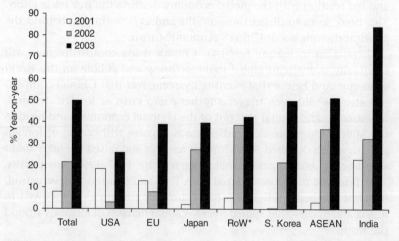

Figure I:1 Chinese import growth
* Rest of the world
Source: CEIC

IT bubble. China's small 4% share in the world's total GDP also masks her significant impact on global industries. For example, global mineral and metal prices surged 57% between 2002 and 2003, when deflationary pressures were plaguing the general business environment, as the Mainland's construction industry consumed huge volumes of cement, steel and other raw materials. Aggregate industry and government data shows that in 2003, China consumed 40% of the world's cement, 27% of its steel and 31% of its coal.

With the world, and Asia in particular, increasingly dependent on Chinese demand, it is not surprising that if China sneezes, the global markets fret that they could catch a cold. The best example can be seen in China's moves in 2004 to cool her overheating economy. Beijing's measures in April 2004 to curb bank lending, limit investment growth and hike bank reserve requirements rattled the global markets. World commodity prices dropped and stock markets fell across Asia and in major centres like Hong Kong, New York and London (Figure I:2). Shares in mining, steel, transport and commodities trading firms from South Korea to Australia and India were among the hardest hit stocks, as those companies had large export exposure to China's demand boom. Gold price fell to a 6-month low as investors worried that Chinese demand would wane. Though other factors, including US interest rate hikes that would slow the world's largest economy and hence its demand for imports, were at play in the markets, China's development appeared to be the catalyst for the global market drop.

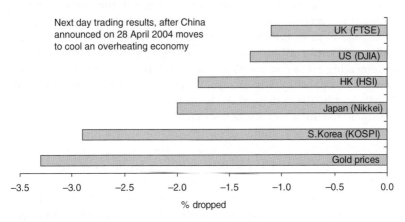

Figure I:2 China's impact on global markets
Source: CEIC

The world's financial and commodity markets were rattled again in November 2004 when China hiked interest rates, by a small 28 basis points, for the first time in nine years. It was the thought that the world's second major growth engine might be tapping the brakes that caused problems for the world markets. The last time when China raised rates in 1995, the rest of the world scarcely noticed. But today China's greater economic weight means that even a polite burp in Beijing is heard around the world.

Then there are concerns about China's structural woes crushing the economy and sending seismic waves across Asia, and even the global economy. Some fret that China might not be able to move fast enough on financial reforms to diffuse the structural time bomb. Numerous attempts to cure Chinese banks' bad debt problem have failed. Worse still, the Chinese leadership seems to lack the vision for an integrated reform plan. After years of restructuring, Chinese banks are still mostly order-takers of Beijing's policy lending decision. The Chinese bond market has remained underdeveloped. The local equity market is mostly a cash-cow for Beijing to support national industrial policy, to subsidise state-owned enterprises' (SOEs) restructuring, but not to allow private companies to raise capital. A mounting fiscal deficit and a rigid foreign exchange regime only reduce Beijing's flexibility to deal with the economic stress stemming from economic reforms.

While China is undeniably exerting economic stress on the global economy, many of the fears are not justified. Worse still, many debates on China's economic development and its relationship with the world are often misguided and distorted. To some extent, the blame game on China is just a cover-up for some economies' inability or unwillingness to change to meet the China challenge. It is unwise to bet on China's collapse.[1] Despite all her economic problems, positive dynamic forces are emerging and a controlled institutional framework will give China a window of opportunity to change. Given the amount of the structural imbalances in the system, there is no reason to believe that a shock-treatment to China's woes is better than the current gradual, learn-from-the-others approach. Building on my anatomy of China's economic myths (see note 1), this book analyses the development of China's competitive power and its potential as a cause for the next Asian crisis.

There are reasons to believe that Asia will not revert to the 1997–1998 crisis mode. Today, most Asian economies have floating exchange rates, so they can adjust more flexibly to economic shocks. Short-term foreign debts are at lower levels now. Crucially, Asian economies have turned their pre-crisis current account deficits into large surpluses. This has resulted in a large build-up in foreign exchange reserves, which provides a powerful cushion against short-term capital volatility. Last, but not least, Asian governments, notably South Korea, China, Hong Kong, Japan, Thailand and Singapore, have entered into multilateral agreements to protect each other from financial crisis contagion by lending each other foreign exchange to fend off currency attacks.

Reflecting the recovery of the regional economies after the 1997–1998 regional crisis, the MSCI Emerging Market Index, a commonly used financial market gauge for the aggregate performance of emerging stock markets, was up almost 40% between 2002 and 2003. This compares with the US Dow Jones Industrial Average, which was up by only 1%, and the Dow Jones Stoxx Index of 600 European companies, which was down 20% in the same period.

However, this does not mean smooth sailing for Asia. The region still has many inherent problems that can push it into another economic crisis if the regional governments do not address them appropriately. The speedy post-crisis economic recovery has also risked breeding investor complacency, which could make the next crisis equally, if not more, painful.

- Fiscal deficit is the number one concern this time around, with many of the regional government deficits running above the comfort range (25%–50% of gross domestic product) defined by the International Monetary Fund.
- Another potential for a financial crisis stems from the build-up of excess foreign exchange reserves by Asian authorities. These excess reserves could feed excessive credit growth, reignite inflation, misallocate capital and eventually lead to financial accidents.
- Insufficient structural reform only rubs salt into Asia's wound by dragging on the region's internal growth dynamics and its flexibility to cope with economic shocks. Despite the reform progress seen in the past few years, reform momentum has faded and there remain significant structural imbalances in the Asian system that could tip the region into another crisis.

There are also stress points coming from outside Asia that could aggravate the regional crisis potential. One can even blame the US Federal Reserve. As the Fed was trying to revive the US economy in the post-IT bubble environment after 2001, it had kept monetary policy looser and longer than usual. The ultra-loose US monetary conditions have spilled over to Asia and created financial bubbles in the global markets.

Any policy or economic shocks, like US interest rate hikes, an oil crisis or a sharp global economic slowdown, could disrupt international capital flows and trigger financial crises in the emerging markets, including Asia.

Subtly, the rise of terrorism is a long-term threat to the global economy, sending periodic shockwaves through Asia. Rather than being a direct cause for another crisis, terrorism could aggravate the crisis potentials, or act as a crisis catalyst, by hitting the regional economies at the wrong time for non-economic reasons. The nerve centres span from the Middle East to Southeast Asia, where the ethnic groups related to terrorist activities are growing.

All this is not to say that another Asian crisis is inevitable. China could be an opportunity for regional growth, helping to diffuse the regional time bomb. More flexible Asian exchange rates, lower foreign debts, large current account surpluses and foreign exchange reserves, and multilateral agreements among the regional governments to fend off currency attacks should also help prevent another Asian crisis. But these positive forces will not last forever, and the China risk could turn bad amid the Middle Kingdom's transition to a market economy.

The point is that after the robust post-crisis economic recovery, Asia might have moved to an unstable equilibrium, with conflicting forces affecting the economic outcome. No one knows what would trigger another crisis. Experience shows that some of the economies that had poor fundamentals managed to escape the worst in the past. A trigger for the next Asian crisis, if it ever emerges, would likely come from outside the region. So watch the global policy development and terrorism. It is easy, but myopic, to blame China for triggering another regional crisis. One should not be blind-sighted by political rhetoric and short-term local developments.

The plan of the book is as follows: *Chapter 1: The New China Threat* analyses the perceived economic threat from various angles. It highlights the fear that Asia's recent increasing reliance on China for growth is too much for comfort. This threat adds to the old fear about China's competitive stress on global manufacturers. The chapter also uncovers a subtle source of economic threat – China's systemic flaw, which causes violent growth cycles. The economic volatility, in turn, aggravates China's boom/bust growth, dragging her import demand with it and thus inflicting an additional risk in Asia's export growth. The discussions evaluate the validity of these fears and question if the China threat is properly debated.

Chapter 2: A Conspiracy Theory assesses the fear that China is using her aggressive industrial expansion to displace Asian exports, cutting off their growth source from the global market so that she could make Asia dependent on China-induced growth as a way to spread influence in the region. Arguably, such fear is not justified because the rising Asian exports to China are a result of the change in the global supply chain structure. This change is in fact mutually beneficial to Asia and China. Further, labour cost in China is rising, especially in the key export regions, so that the fear of China's cheap labour crushing the regional economies is exaggerated. The chapter concludes with evidence showing that China's economic emergence is not different from the development paths of the other Asian economies.

Chapter 3: The Outsourcing Threat exposes the lies behind the political rhetoric that demonises China by presenting evidence and economic truth that some politicians have covered up. The aim is to provide a balanced assessment of the China threat. The discussion also explores the changing structure of international trade and the global supply chain, which are crucial to correctly understand the outsourcing debate. It warns that the real threat comes not from China but from the revival of protectionism, which will be detrimental to everyone if it leads to erroneous policy and business responses.

Chapter 4: The Next Asian Crisis: Made in China? follows on the discussions on the perceived China threat in the previous chapters and assesses the potential of China being a trigger for the next Asian crisis. It argues that while China creates a competitive stress for the regional economies, she also offers economic cushions to help offset the economic risk. The worry about the Chinese authorities losing control of the economy, and thus risking sending a nasty shock to the Asian economies, is also addressed. Special attention is paid to the real estate bubble issue, which has the potential to wreak havoc on the economy. Evidence suggests that the fear of the Chinese authorities losing control of a bubbling economy is more a myth than reality.

Chapter 5: The Next Asian Crisis: Self-inflicted? analyses the idiosyncratic factors within Asia that could lead to another financial crisis. They include the region's mounting fiscal deficits, destabilising debt outlook and excessive accumulation of foreign reserves. More importantly, the chapter argues that Asia's insufficient economic reform and half-hearted restructuring efforts have created an inherent structural weakness. This has not only eroded corporate profits steadily, it has also weakened the region's ability to avoid and weather another economic crisis.

Chapter 6: The External Stresses looks at exogenous factors that would affect the economic stability of Asia. In particular, it examines the dark side of foreign capital inflows to Asia. It argues that America's twin (fiscal and current account) deficit is the most destabilising factor for Asia, as it could force a US dollar crisis as part of the adjustment process. The analysis links the US ultra-loose monetary policy to creating asset bubbles in Asia, and thus contributing to the region's crisis vulnerability. Crucially, the chapter examines an overlooked factor, international terrorism – by analysing the economic dynamism behind the rise of terrorism – as a subtle catalyst for another regional financial crisis.

Chapter 7: The Real Danger Isn't Another Crisis addresses directly the fear factors that could trigger another Asian crisis, including the fiscal and public debt issues and the China threat. But it argues that another Asian crisis is avoidable. There are many economic cushions to mitigate macro instability, and timely policy actions can reduce crisis risk. Rather, the real danger of all these China fears and idiosyncratic flaws in the regional economies is the rise of trade protectionism. It warns that the protectionists' myopic actions could backfire and force the emergence of a China threat, which did not exist in the first place.

Chapter 8: What China Threat? debunks the perceived China economic threat by evaluating the concerns from various angles – growth, reform, competitiveness, investment and manufacturing. It uncovers the overlooked issues that despite years of economic reforms, China's economy is not as efficient as many believe, and that relative labour cost in China is not as low as many fear. These, in turn, argue that the perceived China competitive threat has been grossly exaggerated. Analyses of China's economic growth, trade and investment patterns vis-à-vis the rest of the world also argue that all the fears about China's threat to the world economy have been overstated. China's integration into the global economy is a natural progression of the global economy. Such process is not unprecedented. China could even serve as a development model of the emerging economies.

Chapter 9: Hollowing-out, Revisited concludes the discussion on China's economic threat by evaluating three possible outcomes – optimistic, benign and pessimistic – for Asia under the shadow of China's economic ascent. It argues that to survive an increasingly competitive economic paradigm, Asia needs to uproot many of its old habits by pursuing thorough structural changes. Forming a unified market, like an Asian Monetary Union (AMU) as some have proposed, will not work given the current economic and political diversity of Asia. It could even cause disastrous results to the region. Crucially, an AMU is not a trick for the regional governments to eschew painful structural reforms. The global economy will need careful response and adaptation to the rise of China, but China's economic clout is no cause for panic.

All economic data, data estimates and figures used in this book are based on the databank provided by CEIC Data Company Ltd., unless stated otherwise. Established in Hong Kong in 1992 and acquired by ISI Emerging Markets in 2005, CEIC provides economic, corporate and industry sector time-series data on Asian and other major economies. It has strategic presence in Asia and sources the data from national governments, government agencies and prime releasing entities.

1
The New China Threat

China's rapid economic ascent on the global stage has created a new fear about her threat to the global economy. It is the fear about Asia's increasing reliance on China for export growth, which has been the region's economic growth driver since the 1997/1998 Asian crisis. This new threat of China holding Asian exports hostage is adding to the fear about China gaining export market shares, crowding out global manufacturers, 'hollowing-out' jobs in neighbour economies and sucking up foreign capital at the expense of the rest of Asia.

There is also an internal dimension to the China threat that is often overlooked. This dimension is rooted in China's systemic flaw, which has manifested itself in volatile growth cycles. The resultant violent economic swings, in turn, aggravate the threat that China's boom/bust growth will drag her import demand with it, inflicting an additional risk profile in Asia's export growth. Some even worry that China would trigger another Asian crisis by either hollowing-out the region's economic and financial resources, leaving it with nothing but economic chaos, or pulling the region along with her own economic implosion.

The supply threat

Beijing started pushing for exports as a growth policy in the early 1990s. It has successfully attracted foreign investments to help build a critical mass in the export industries by the mid-1990s. The combination of local cheap labour and the availability of foreign capital has boosted China's competitiveness significantly, with rapid export volume growth compressing global export prices. China's entry to the World Trade Organisation (WTO) has intensified her competitive threat further, as WTO accession has acted as an external discipline for reforming China to become super-competitive. Given the Mainland's vast production capacity, its competitive stress on Asia will remain a dominant force in the years to come.

Let us not deny the benefits for other economies of China's entry to the WTO. Major commitments made by China to other WTO members include cuts in tariff and non-tariff barriers on industrial goods, agricultural trade liberalisation and opening up of major services sectors to foreign investment. But China's integration with the global economy is a two-edged sword, as it creates more competitive stress in the global trading system too.

Some see the direct benefits that China gets as a WTO member as a big threat to other exporting economies, as they give China access to the North American and European markets, especially for textiles and apparel in which China has a strong comparative advantage. More subtly, the external discipline of the WTO for pushing Chinese economic reform will combine with technology transfer and capital goods imports to raise China's competitiveness by improving the efficiency of resources allocation via increased specialisation, faster capital accumulation and productivity growth.

ASEAN countries,[1] excluding Singapore, fear China the most because they have an endowment structure similar to China's (i.e. abundant labour but scarce capital resources). Their exports compete head-on with China's labour intensive products. This means that some ASEAN economies, like Indonesia, the Philippines and Thailand, will lose significant export market share to China if they do not upgrade their export structure in the coming years.

China's domestic reform is already creating a formidable competitive force that makes other Asian economies feel uneasy. In the gradual creative destruction process, Beijing has destroyed old inefficient state firms in sunset industries and replaced them by new ones in sunrise sectors. Since the Asian crisis, the number of state-owned enterprises (SOEs) has declined steadily from about 40% of total enterprises in the system to 17% in 2004, while the share of private firms has risen from less than 10% to over 40%. If foreign enterprises are included, the private sector share has gone up to almost half of the total. In terms of output, Chinese SOEs now account for less than 15% of total industrial output, down sharply from over 80% in the early 1980s (Figure 1:1).

Chinese labour productivity has soared along with creative destruction and increase in investment by foreign firms in China. A US economic think tank, the Conference Board, estimated in a 2004 report that productivity growth in China surged by an average 17% a year between

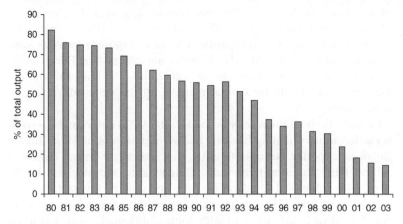

Figure 1:1 Gross industrial output by SOEs
Source: CEIC

1995 and 2002. Continued economic restructuring, with a structural shift to services, should lead to more productivity growth and rising per capita income in China. The study also found that the advances in productivity were broad-based, with 36 of the 38 leading industries experiencing surging productivity growth in the period. In fact, 27 of the 38 industries saw annual average productivity growth of over 10%, compared with about 4% in US manufacturing in the same 7-year period.

Even developed economies, notably Japan, fret about the China stress. Nowadays, some Japanese still call China the workshop of the world and warn of her economic threat. Indeed, China has displaced Japan as the nation with the largest trade surplus with the US since 2001. The implications of China's rapid economic ascent are felt far beyond Asia. In the western hemisphere, economic dislocations attributed to Chinese competition have stretched from Mexico in the south to as far north as the French-speaking Quebec province of Canada, where Noranda (a premier Canadian mining company) was forced to close a major magnesium plant in 2003 in the face of competition from low-cost Chinese imports.

Yet, what has perhaps not been fully grasped is the extent to which China will compete effectively, not only in basic manufacturing but also in more sophisticated manufacturing. While retaining her basic manufacturing pre-eminence, China is also developing impressive competencies in areas such as engineering, high tech and services. Evidence is seen in the movement of the regional semiconductor industry, especially from Taiwan to Shanghai and the surrounding area. Further down China's eastern coast, highly skilled and educated Chinese workers are steadily displacing western expatriates. More and more knowledge work is being done on the Mainland, bypassing places like Hong Kong. Although most of these tech jobs are still of mid- and low-value nature, the trend is certainly for China to move up the value-added ladder, albeit slowly.

China's climb up the economic ladder after WTO entry can be seen in her auto industry. Beijing has long had an ambition of making China a global car exporter. But until recently, that was only a dream. Protected behind tariff and non-tariff walls, China's auto industry was inefficient, with sub-global standards on price and quality. Few factories had economies of scale. Though labour cost was low, car components were not. According to industry estimates, some China-made parts were up to 40% dearer than world prices. More disturbingly, Chinese joint-venture partners have a preference for local suppliers. Their strong bias for *guanxi* deals[2] has stifled competition. If opaque relationship deals were not enough to impair foreign confidence, the abundance of pirated car parts certainly acted to raise suspicion about components and their quality sourced in China.

That was in the recent past. Things have changed, particularly after China's WTO entry in 2001. The domestic car market has become increasingly competitive, as foreign car makers have piled into China recently. Since WTO entry, import tariffs have dropped sharply. Car output has soared to meet rising sales (Figure 1:2), which doubled to 2.8 million in 2003 from 1.4 million in 2000. Improving economies of scale have cut prices so that cars and most car-parts made in China are not much dearer than elsewhere in the world now. At the same time, quality and safety requirements are rising to meet world standards. Beijing is promising support, with tax breaks and low-interest loans, for car and component exporters. Car-parts export is already jumping ahead, with export value soaring by over one-third (or more than US$3 billion) between 2002 and 2004. Beijing has set an annual export target of US$70–$100 billion in car-parts by 2010. That is an aggressive target, which roughly equals the total US$75 billion in car-parts imported by the US in 2003. But that also shows Beijing's confidence in pushing China as a major player in the world auto market.

The fear of China's rising production clout in the value chain is best illustrated by the concern of Morris Chang, chairman of the world's largest computer chip manufacturer, Taiwan Semiconductor Manufacturing Company (TSMC). In September 2003, Mr Chang alarmed

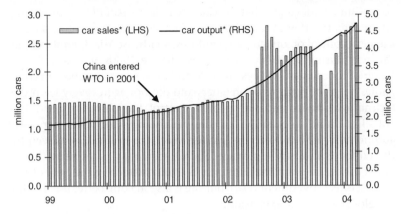

Figure 1:2 China's car output and sales
* Series in 12-month rolling sum
Source: CEIC

the semiconductor industry by predicting an industry-wide recession before 2007, caused by China's rapid rising chip output capacity. Underscoring Mr Chang's worry is Beijing's policy to make China self-reliant on semiconductor manufacturing, and enable the nation to source its own chips locally for everything from tape recorders to computers.

Whether Mr Chang's prediction will turn out is another matter. The threat is Beijing's funding of what is being seen as reckless expansion in semiconductor fabrication plants, or 'fabs'. Like its support for the car industry, Beijing has set China on pace to provide the world with a quarter of its capacity in the coming years in the made-to-order chip industry (or foundry). It is providing subsidised-interest loans, tax exemptions and even direct investment for the industry. From virtually nothing a few years ago, Chinese fabs now hold about 10% of the foundry market's capacity. They are expected to make 25% of the world's computer chips by end-2005.

According to analysts, this volume is enough to cause a serious glut that will drive down prices, squeeze profits and suppress return on equity. The volatility of the semiconductor industry could make Mr Chang's worry worse. From a robust 30% growth in 2004, the global semiconductor industry is expected to record only 10% or less growth a year in the next few years. The China factor would worsen the supply demand imbalance and tilt the industry into recession.

Sheer production capacity aside, it is the way that China pursues her industrial policy that is aggravating fears about her economic threat.

Some China critics argue that the Chinese policy is part of her self-serving and pragmatic attempt to rapidly push for technology transfer and management control of foreign joint ventures. Southeast Asia did not expand this way during its boom, they argued. In the 1980s and early 1990s, Filipino, Indonesian, Malaysian, Thai and even some Singaporean companies let go of control to foreigners and did not aggressively learn the technologies or demand management control. But China is quite different. Her rapid acquisition of the technology to build her own autonomous auto industry in just ten years, for example, was seen by the critics as industry espionage. Such a view may be extreme, but it underscores the point that not only is China attracting the bulk of the foreign direct investment (FDI), but she is also making better use of it for her global economic expansion.

The demand threat

In addition to the competitive threat stemming from the supply side, another fear about China's economic threat to Asia has arisen recently. It stems from the region's increasing reliance on China as a growth source. Indeed, China's demand for Asian exports has grown rapidly (Table 1:1). For example, her import growth from ASEAN jumped from an annual rate of 3% in 2001 to 52% in 2003. Her imports from South Korea were even more dramatic, surging from almost nil in 2001 to 50% in 2003. This should be good for Asia because at any given level of imports, a rise in Asian exports to China adds directly to the region's gross domestic product (GDP) and, hence, economic growth.[3]

Table 1:1   China's import growth (YoY %)

	2001	2002	2003
Total	8.0	21.5	50.0
ASEAN	3.0	37.0	51.5
EU	13.0	8.0	39.0
India	23.0	32.5	84.2
Japan	2.0	27.5	39.8
RoW*	5.0	38.5	42.5
S. Korea	0.5	21.5	50.0
USA	18.5	3.0	26.0

* Rest of the world

Source: CEIC

As a share of GDP, China already imports more than Japan from Asia, though her economy is only about a quarter the size of Japan. China has been running a trade deficit with Asia since the turn of the millennium (Figure 1:3). Her import appetite is likely to grow, as continued economic liberalisation and free trade rules under the WTO will open more doors for Asian exports to the Mainland.

Already, China's rapidly growth is strengthening her economic role in Asia. Rubber plantations in southern Thailand are filling demand for tyres as China's auto industry growth soars by over 70% a year. Rice farmers in northern Thailand now ship half of their premium jasmine-rice exports to China and Hong Kong. China is now the largest customer for Japanese and Korean steelmakers. Huge demand from the factories of coastal China, which now assemble vast quantities of electronics, are boosting exports from computer-chip plants in Taiwan, Korea and Malaysia. As the Middle Kingdom seeks to diversify its sources of energy to meet its huge demand for power, it is tapping oil and gas fields in Indonesia and Australia.

Arguably, China is gaining economic importance at the expense of the US and Japan. She has replaced the US as the largest growth market for Asian exports. For example, at least 50% of all export growth in South Korea, Japan, Taiwan, the Philippines, Malaysia and Australia in 2003 came from Chinese demand. In absolute dollar terms, the US is still the largest market for Asia exports. But who knows, in ten years' time, China

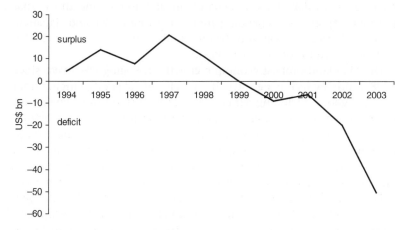

Figure 1:3 China's trade balance with Asia
Source: CEIC

may challenge the US as the largest continental market for Asia. As for Japan, while she consumed almost a quarter of Asia's exports a decade ago (down to 10% now) and provided a third of the region's bank loans, China is taking over that economic role, buying over 30% of Asia's exports and is preparing to become a source of regional funding. Overall, China has become the largest contributor of export growth in Asia in recent years.

Even for Japan, the world's second largest economy after the US and the wealthiest economy in Asia, her economic well-being is increasingly tied to China's demand. Indeed, China has risen to become the single biggest contributor to trade growth for Japan. According to Japan's Cabinet Office, total trade (imports plus exports) in goods and services accounted for about one-third of Japan's 2.7% growth rate in 2004. While exports to the US, Japan's traditional leading market, have been flat, exports to China have been rising in recent years at a rapid rate of about 30% a year.

Of course, China is still far from supplanting the US in Japan's mind, even in economic terms. Japan has far more money invested in the US than in China. From 1951 to 2002, total Japanese investment in US factories, companies and other direct investment amounted to over 43 trillion yen, compared with only 2.8 trillion yen in China, according to Japan official statistics. Japan also holds US$720 billion of US Treasury bonds, larger than the entire foreign reserves of China as of early 2005. But the point is that Japan is already learning about the downside of her reliance on China's import demand. In addition to the threat that Japanese exports are depending more on Chinese demand, Japanese exports of machine tools and steel to build factories in China will ultimately be used to compete with Japan.

The Mainland's robust economic growth, averaging 8% a year since 1998, is driving its buying spree. It buys all sorts of goods, ranging from resource goods, including agricultural products, foodstuffs, chemicals, minerals, metals and textiles, to manufacturing goods, such as electronics, machinery, equipment and instruments. The surge in China's equipment imports was the most important factor in the revival of Japan and South Korea's exports in 2003. Equipment exporting economies in Europe also benefited significantly from the surge in Chinese demand.

The overall product mix of Asian exports to China has also changed. Between 1995 and 2003, according to research by the Asian Development Bank, Asian exports (from Hong Kong, Indonesia, Japan, South Korea, Malaysia, Philippines, Singapore, Taiwan and Thailand) of precision instruments and electrical machinery to China soared six-fold, while their exports of machinery, chemical products and transport equipment to China surged three-fold. However, shipments of agricultural goods and food, textiles and apparel, as well as leather goods and shoes to China grew only slowly. This means that there has been a structural shift in major Asian exports to China from low value-added to high value-added sectors in recent years. Hence, a wide range of manufacturers and exporters have benefited from China's import demand, and their reliance on the Chinese market has been rising swiftly.

However, this is not all positive, as relying heavily on the Chinese market has also made Asia vulnerable to Chinese economic shocks. Notably, problems in China will be transmitted more easily to the rest of Asia. Many regional governments are also not buying China's portrayal of her rising economic clout in Asia as entirely benign. Since the late 1990s, Beijing has been forging diplomatic ties with its Asian neighbours and weaving trade links that have started to shift Asia's centre of economic gravity. It has projected this engagement as mutually beneficial, driven by idealism instead of self-interest. In his meetings with Asian leaders, Chinese Prime Minister Wen Jiabao often likes to pitch China as a 'friendly elephant' which creates 'win–win' ties with, and poses no threat to, Southeast Asia.

But many Asian neighbours still find China too friendly to embrace. They are worried about being too dependent on China's economy. Such a worry has, in turn, brewed a fear of political dominance by China. Cambodia, for example, who has built a spawning web of economic and political agreements with China in recent years, now frets that she is being drawn too close to China. The Cambodian government signed a military agreement with Beijing in November 2003, under which China would provide its army with funding and training. China lent Cambodia more than US$45 million between 2001 and 2003, mostly on interest-free terms, for development. Cambodia also accepted Chinese aid for building a railway for access to the sea via the Chinese Yunnan province. China also has a high cultural profile in Cambodia, helping to build new schools and promoting the study of the Chinese language. But such a close tie with China has created a sense of insecurity for many Cambodians, who think China has gained a strategic foothold in their country as a buffer against Vietnam at the expense of Cambodian autonomy.

Burma has a similar concern. Rangoon signed 24 pacts on economic and technical cooperation with Beijing in March 2004. The Chinese also granted Burma US$200 million low-interest loans. But China's keen interest in building ties with Burma has led some regional analysts to suspect that Beijing now has a big say in Burma's domestic issues. Indeed, it was reported that Hu Jintao, now Chinese president but was still acting president when he met with Burmese junta leader Than Shwe in Beijing in January 2003, had urged the Burmese leader to consider speeding up political change in Burma. The move was seen as a sign of China spreading her influence to Burma's domestic affairs.

Even more developed ASEAN economies, such as Thailand, have started to worry about the impact of their close ties with China. The devil is in China's recent move to sign bilateral deals with her Asian neighbours. The regional economies have no problem with signing a multilateral free-trade agreement with China because it does not put China's economic weight at the centre of the region's economy. But when China signs bilateral trade pacts with an individual economy, that creates jitters as the unequal economic clout between the Middle Kingdom and the Asian partner becomes obvious.

For example, under the 2003 Sino-Thai trade agreement, which applies to fruit and vegetables, cheaper Chinese pears, apples, garlic and onions have flooded into Thailand, especially from the nearby Yunnan province. Northern Thailand's farming economy has been seriously damaged due to its proximity to Yunnan. Meanwhile, Thailand has had a tough time selling her durians (a smelly exotic fruit favoured by most Southeast Asians) and mangosteens in China, due to marketing problems and invisible trade barriers, like lengthy quarantine procedures, in the restricted Chinese market. The Thais knew they might not benefit from the agricultural deal with China, but still hoped to use it as a sweetener for China to consider an open-skies agreement to increase air-cargo traffic and simplify customs procedures for Thailand. But after many rounds of negotiations, Beijing has only agreed to study the proposals. That only makes the Thais feel unequally treated and more insecure.

The threat of Asian growth being too dependent on China's demand has also created a sense of insecurity in international politics. For sure, China's win–win rhetoric is for real, as she is strategically committed to ensure Asia benefits from her robust growth. But some are worried that if China continues her growth and political trajectories, she would eventually seek a pattern of engagement with Asia similar to that adopted by the US. Long ago, Washington discarded engagement on a multilateral level in favour of a series of bilateral agreements with individual economies, a strategy known by the Americans as 'hub-and-spoke arrangements'. And China has already started to move in this direction, notably in the military area. For example, President Hu Jintao announced at the perennial Boao Forum, held in the Chinese resort of

Hainan Island, in April 2004 that China would seek 'security dialogue and military-to-military exchanges' with other Asian countries.

Boom/bust growth

China's history of volatile economic growth only aggravates the region's concern of being too dependent on Chinese demand, as it adds more risk to Asian, and global, exports. After surging growth in the late 1990s, there was a concern in late 2003 and 2004 that the Chinese economy might be overheating. And the global markets were rattled when China announced tightening measures in late April 2004 to fan off potential overheating in the economy. In the next few trading days after China's announcement, commodity prices fell and stock markets across Asia and in major centres, like New York and London, slumped (see Introduction, Figure I:2). It was the first-ever major global shock inflicted by China. Why the panic?

It was the thought that Chinese authorities might have to slam on the monetary brakes to curb China's growth that caused the financial ripple across the region. China's record of boom/bust growth intensified the fear that policy errors could tip the economy into a hard-landing,[4] killing the world's growth engine. There have been three violent economic cycles, each with a swing in GDP growth of over 10 percentage points (Figure 1:4), since China began her economic reforms in 1978. The previous cyclical

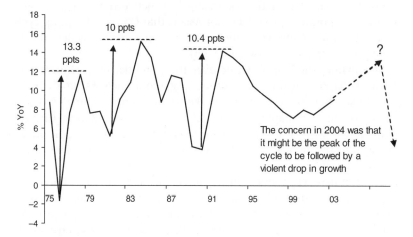

Figure 1:4 China's real GDP growth
Source: CEIC

peaks were 1978, 1984 and 1992. The concern in 2004 was that it might be the peak of the fourth cycle to be followed by a violent drop in growth.

GDP growth soared to 11.7% in 1978 when paramount leader Deng Xiao-ping started China's economic reforms by initiating a series of industrialisation projects. That pulled the economy out of a recession in 1976, when growth was −1.6%. But the economy crashed back down to 5.2% in 1981, when Beijing failed to sustain the runaway growth with public spending. The investment fever returned in 1984, pushing GDP growth to over 15% before it slumped back down to less than 3% after the Tiananmen incident in 1989.

Anxious to reboot economic growth by creating wealth, Mr Deng revived fast development plans in 1992 by encouraging the growth of the non-state sector. GDP growth surged by 14.2% as a result. But the relaxation of years of economic suppression also brought rampant inflation, when the retail price inflation rate soared to 26% a year. This prompted former premier Zhu Rongji to hit the monetary brakes in 1994 to fight inflation. GDP growth fell back down to 7% in 1999.

But then Beijing panicked over the potential impact of the Asian crisis on China's economy, and embarked on pump-priming GDP growth with public investment and monetary expansion in 2000. The drastic policy swing pushed economic growth back up to 9.1% in 2003. China's boom/bust economic cycles, depicted in Figure 1:3, looks like a roller coaster with swings violent enough to make even the most adventurous rider throw up. Given the increasing link between the region's and China's economies, the concern for Asia is that China's abrupt up-cycle could transmit inflationary shock to the region while her violent downswing could drag the region along with it.

Meanwhile, the world's panic over the potential of a Chinese economic collapse only underscores the rising importance of China's role in the global economy. Take the oil market as an example. China's growing thirst for oil is reshaping the global energy market. Robust Chinese demand for oil was seen as a major force pushing up world oil prices, aggravating the problems of bottle-neck supply and the threat of terrorism, in 2002 and 2003.

To stimulate economic growth after the 1997–1998 Asian crisis, Beijing had invested billions in infrastructure, encouraged bank lending and relaxed curbs on home purchases and auto production to boost domestic spending. These measures sparked explosive sales in real estate and cars – growth that filtered through the rest of the economy with a multiplier effect, and led to quantum leaps in oil use.

Surging oil demand made China the world's number two petroleum user after the US in 2003, surpassing Japan. The International Energy Agency expects Chinese oil imports to double to some 4 million barrels a day by 2010, and to 10 million barrels a day by 2030, roughly equal to current US imports. Meanwhile, China's domestic oil output has hit its capacity constraint. Such an outlook has prompted oil companies from Houston to London to Moscow to secure market share in China, as the Middle Kingdom roams the world looking for oil fields to develop. Of course, the downside is that a collapse in Chinese demand will set off a negative domino effect on the world's oil market.

The impact of China's oil demand has gone beyond economics to politics, which has helped create a geopolitical threat for the global economies. Some are wary of a Beijing that could begin to feel boxed in by its energy needs. They fear China, which does not have large strategic reserves of fuel, might grow so desperate for oil that she might battle the US for influence in the Middle East, or even trade weapons technology to alleged terrorist states for access to oil.

Chinese demand is already making geopolitical waves in the US. In US Congressional debate sessions in late 2003, the US–China Economic and Security Review Commission, a committee of congressional appointees, flagged the potential threat of how China's thirst for oil would affect US access to energy supplies. And earlier, the Pentagon was alerted of the China threat by a study on the implications for US national security if China and Saudi Arabia grew closer. Nevertheless, others believe that Beijing will come to share the US interest in ensuring the Middle East as a reliable oil supplier. In the long run, this confluence of interest might draw Beijing closer to the US.

The point is that the flip side of growing Chinese oil imports is increasing the economic vulnerability for the rest of the world. The lack of conviction for the impact of China's oil demand reflects the essence of market fear – uncertainty. The geopolitical impact may turn out to be positive or negative. But for global business and political leaders, this is one uncertain aspect of the China threat on their radar screens until the clouds are cleared.

Systemic failure

In the West, where election for the head of the state is held once every four years, the business cycles of these democratic nations are closely related to the election cycle due to pre-election spending boosting GDP growth prior to the election. Though China does not have democratic elections for her leaders, her business cycle also tracks the country's political cycle closely due to the same incentive but in a different form. The Communist Party convenes its national congress every five years; the latest one was held in 2002. Each congress determines leadership changes both at the top and at the provincial level. Hence, central and provincial elites eager to demonstrate their ability and secure their jobs are motivated to turn in the best possible growth in what is China's closest equivalent to an election year in the democratic countries.

In an economy like China in which the ruling party controls the state, which in turn controls about half of the government's capital spending, the impact of such political calculations on GDP growth can be quite substantial. Chinese official data show that the growth rate in the year when a party congress is convened is sharply higher than in the preceding year. There were six Communist Party congresses between 1977 and 2002. Except for 1997 (perhaps due to the negative impact of the Asian financial crisis), the average annual growth rate in the years when there was a party congress was about 4 percentage points higher than in the preceding year.

Experience shows that sizzling growth in the 'congress years' sparked rampant inflation, prompting the authorities to rein in capital spending at once or after a lag of a few months. Growth slowed sharply as a result, but an economic soft-landing was not assured. Since job security and promotions of provincial chiefs rest on their economic performance, in terms of growth and tax revenue, new appointees have strong incentives to spur capital spending in their jurisdictions to raise growth and enlarge the tax base. Research by the Massachusetts Institute of Technology Sloan School of Management found that when a new party boss and a governor were appointed in a province in the same year, fixed-asset investment (the bulk of which is accounted for by public spending) in that same province would soar by an average of 36% from the previous year.

Provincial leaders can significantly raise fixed-asset investment mainly because they have access to bank credit and other forms of capital. The state nominally owns the four state banks (which account for 80% of the total banking assets), but in reality provincial authorities dictate their decisions. Managers in the provincial branches of the state banks owe their jobs not to the bureaucrats in Beijing, but to local party bosses who control their political future. Few would dare to deny credit to the pet projects picked by the local officials.

Practically, China's violent economic swings are rooted in politics, which often results in policy conflicts and errors that aggravate the economic cycles. Fundamentally, the problem of policy errors in China stems from the Communist Party leadership's control of the nation's financial system. While these small groups of people think that they make better decision about finance than the markets, the fact is that they make much cruder judgements. And the institutional set-up facilitates this political fault in the system.

Strict capital controls are forcing household savings into the hands of politicians, albeit indirectly, as every legal saving avenue is looped under government bureaucracy. The problem with this system is that bureaucrats are always tempted to push for excessive investment, in the name of boosting growth and employment. But when that investment leads to economic overheating, the politicians cannot help but slam on the brakes hard. This results in a harsh impact on the economy because there is no effective market mechanism in China to regulate the economy before it gets too hot.

Worse still, China's monetary tools are rustic despite gradual progress in modernising the system in recent years. This means Beijing needs to hit the brakes even harder to cool an overheated economy, thus raising the risk of an economic hard-landing. To see this, consider a move to raise banks' reserve requirements – the portion of deposits that banks must keep with the central bank. Normally, this will help tame reckless lending. But it does not work properly in China because capital controls have flooded banks with deposits. Making them park a bit more money with the central bank has little impact on their lending ability. Crucially, state control of banks means most bank lending is still based on policy decision, which overrides any market-based policy moves like changing the reserve requirements and/or interest rate levels.

Meanwhile, China's unofficial, but de facto, policy of pegging the renminbi (RMB) to the US dollar since 1994 is also depriving Beijing of economic management flexibility. Whenever there is capital inflow, putting appreciating pressure on the RMB, the People's Bank of China (PBoC), China's central bank, needs to sell RMB (and thus increase domestic money supply) to keep the exchange rate from rising. Such a move will add fuel to the cyclical upswing if the economy is already overheating. On the other hand, when there is capital outflow, putting downward pressure on the RMB, the PBoC needs to buy RMB (and thus shrink domestic money supply) to prevent it from falling. This will aggravate the downswing if the economy is already slowing down.

The key problem in China's monetary control is that Beijing wants to commercialise the banking system in a command framework. This results in a hybrid system in which Chinese banks have no autonomy over interest rate setting, but they also face no serious competition. Even the WTO requirement for China to open the finance sector to foreign investors by 2007 will not likely raise competition rapidly because the invisible barriers to compete will linger. Yet the banks are very liquid, and they keep lending in the hope of growing themselves out of insolvency. Thus, China's malfunctioning financial system may not collapse because it is awash with cash,[5] though it is not sustainable in the long-term if nothing is done to fix it. All this makes it much harder for Beijing's economic management to achieve the desired results. As and when the authorities resort to hash policy measures to regulate economic activity, boom/bust cycles result.

Aggravating the systemic flaw are Beijing's conflicting objectives and the lack of policy coordination between the central and local governments. Chinese politicians are trying to achieve multiple policy objectives. They include boosting growth, creating millions of jobs, raising farmers' incomes, keeping social stability, curbing inflation, restructuring the corporate sector and cutting bank bad debts. But these policy objectives are often in conflict with each other. It is doubtful if an optimal policy mix ever exists for Beijing, especially in the short-term. A lack of common policy objectives between the central and local governments, especially when the benefits and costs are unevenly distributed among the localities, only makes the problem worse.

The top policy priority, which both the central and local authorities share, is to keep economic growth strong enough to create millions of jobs to absorb the surplus labour from economic restructuring. China's true urban unemployment rate is estimated to be well over 10%, though the official rate is about 5%. But the common macroeconomic policy goal stops here.

The central government is responsible for overall macroeconomic stability. It is thus concerned about rising inflation and the stability of the banking system. But policies that may be good for the macro economy may not be good for the local economy. For example, inflationary pressures may not be evenly distributed among the provinces. Hence, an interest rate hike by the central authorities to fight inflation could hurt those localities that do not have high inflation. Meanwhile, these local authorities may be pursuing pro-growth policies to boost local employment. There is thus often a tension between the central and local governments as to how the trade-off between local and national, and growth and other policy objectives should be made. Such tension will be especially striking in the coming years, as China's economic transformation will continue to create shocks with cross currents that will cause policy conflicts and confusion.

Further, with multiple policy objectives, the central government's policy response will also be multidimensional. And this could easily lead to policy inconsistency, aggravating the boom/bust economic cycle. The problem lies in whether the policy response to challenges in one aspect of the economy aggravates the challenges on other aspects. For instance, to clamp down on run-away investment in a few economic hot spots will inevitably increase banks' bad debts and worsen unemployment.

Beijing may want to avoid boom/bust economic cycles, but the lack of an effective policy transmission mechanism almost ensures the risk of sharp economic swings. China is still in transit from a planned economy to a market driven system. The current hybrid economic nature will remain for some time. This system will likely pose increasing challenges to Chinese policymakers, who are themselves also transiting from being central planners to market regulators. As the central government remains sceptical about the effectiveness of market-based policies in the hybrid system, it will rely on administrative measures to regulate economic activities, thus increasing the odds for policy mistakes and amplifying their impact on the economic cycle.

Until recently, China's economic cycles were not terribly important for the outside world. But since the turn of the millennium, the scale of the China boom has sucked in unprecedented imports from the rest of the world – up by 50% in 2003 after jumping 22% in 2002. Justified or not, these reported numbers by the media are enough to raise concern that if China's economy collapses, it could trigger a global recession by cutting off an important source of demand.

Whether China goes boom or bust is becoming more important for the global markets. Her growth affects other Asian nations whose economic and financial market recoveries have been heavily dependent on sales to China. It affects the bottom lines and stock prices of large multinational companies, ranging from US consumer goods giant Wal-Mart to British mining giant Rio Tinto, who benefit significantly from China's huge appetite for finished goods and raw materials. The Chinese growth effect goes beyond the goods market to as far as foreign exchange where seemingly remote currencies, such as the Australian and Canadian dollars, are affected due to their commodity-based economic nature. Last but not least, it affects investor expectations of the future outlook for industrial sectors, such as cars, power, steel and metals.

18 Phantom of the China Economic Threat

China's economic threat is like a pair of pliers, clamping down on the global economy on both the supply side (via her manufacturing clout) and demand side (via her rising import demand). No wonder the global markets fret when China sneezes. However, it is not clear if the world's fear about the China threat is all that justified. It is even doubtful if the potential of the China threat is properly debated.

2
A Conspiracy Theory

When one looks at Asia's increasing reliance on China's import demand on the back of her rising production clout, it is easy to theorise a conspiracy for the China threat – that China's aggressive industrial expansion beats her Asian neighbours in exports, and cuts off their growth source from the global market so that she can make Asia rely on China-induced growth as a way to spread influence in the region. Such a conspiracy theory has been exploited by many politicians, both within and outside Asia, to promote their political interest often at the expense of the economic truth (see next chapter for more). Let us examine the two fears of the China threat – Asia's over-dependence on China and China's stress on the global supply chain – in detail to evaluate this conspiracy theory.

How dependent is Asia on China?

A demand threat from China has been bothering Asia recently. As Asia enjoys a big economic boost from the Mainland's robust demand for its imports in recent years, it is also becoming clear that the regional economic growth is being held hostage by the Chinese demand. Naturally, Asia's worry about China's demand threat has intensified, as its reliance on China as a major export market has risen. The question is how dependent is Asia's economic well-being on China? Is this worry a result of too many people talking about an exaggerated China threat, or is it real?

Asia's fears about being dragged into a China demand trap and the regional economic growth being held hostage by the Chinese stem from a structural change in the international trade flows in recent years. Evidence shows that Asia is depending less on its traditional Japanese and American markets for export growth. Meanwhile, China has emerged as the region's most important growth market for exports. The switch of economic dependence from the developed markets to China has made many regional governments fret that their economies may be over-exposed to China.

Some have argued that there has been a rise in intra-regional trade within Asia in recent years. That should be good news because if Asia is trading more among its member economies, it is a sign of regional integration creating growth dynamics without relying too much on out-of-the-region demand, including that from the developed markets and China. To see the amount of intra-regional trade, deduct from the aggregate exports of Asia's major trading economies[1] (known as MTEs below) their shipments to the developed markets, namely Japan and the US, the remainder is a proxy for intra-Asian trade. All other markets outside Asia, Japan and the US are presumably piecemeal. Thus, a rise in the share of this intra-regional exports in the MTEs' total exports will suggest that trade is redirected to domestic markets within the region. Indeed, evidence shows that there has been a marked rise in Asia's export share to markets outside Japan and the US since 2001 (Figure 2:1).

Further, if Asian exports are relying less on the developed markets, its export growth to these markets should be slower than its export growth to the other markets. In other words, the ratio of Asia's export growth to the developed markets to its total export growth should fall below 1. The decline in this ratio means that Asian exports have found new markets

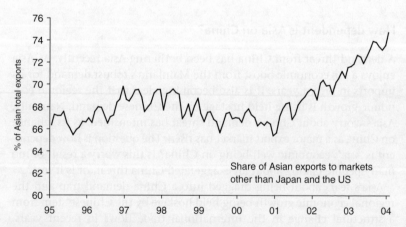

Figure 2:1 Sign of rising intra-Asian trade
Source: CEIC

outside Japan and the US, and are thus less dependent on the import demand from these developed markets. On the other hand, if Asian exports to the developed markets grow at the same rate as, or faster than, its total exports, the ratio should have a value of 1 or higher. This in turn means that Asian exports are tightly tied to, or increasing dependent on, the developed markets' demand changes. Evidence shows that after the 1997/1998 Asian crisis and after the bursting of the global IT bubble in 2001, Asia's export growth to the developed markets has indeed fallen relative to its total exports (Figure 2:2). The decline in the export ratio after the 1997/1998 Asian crisis might be distorted by the sharp contraction of the regional economies, which also grounded export production to a halt. But the steady decline in the ratio to below 1 since the global IT bubble burst in 2001 is evidence that Asian exports have found new export markets outside the developed world.

If Asia's foreign trade is redirected to domestic demand of the regional economies, there should not be a worry about the region's growth being held hostage by Chinese demand. Indeed, Asia should be switching from its traditional export-led growth model to a domestic consumption-based growth model to survive the new economic paradigm of prolonged disinflation with periodic deflation, due to rising competition and constrained pricing power.[2] Some have argued that the rapid expansion of Asia's middle class, which is defined as someone with a

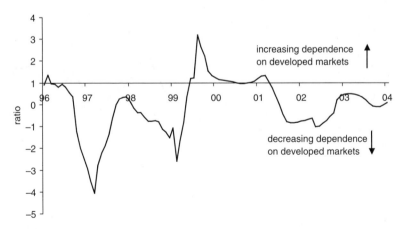

Figure 2.2 Asian export growth ratio (developed market exports-to-total exports: six-month moving average)

Source: CEIC

minimum income level of US$5,000 person per year,[3] has indeed set the stage for Asian private consumption to expand. The point is that the rise of the middle class translates into broadly based growth in domestic demand. Mass middle class demand, in turn, provides both economies of scale and scope. These conditions are crucial for creating new opportunities for small and medium size businesses to emerge. New and generally better employment opportunities in the services sectors, in turn, bolster the growth of the middle class, making the consumption creation process a self-reinforcing virtuous circle.

Thus, if the recent trend of decreasing export dependence on the developed markets is a reflection of Asia diverting trade to the regional economies due to expansion of their domestic demand, that should be good news. But evidence shows that Asia has continued to rely on exports for growth after the 1997/1998 regional crisis. The aggregate export of the MTEs has risen steadily from 45% of GDP to 60% since the mid-1990s (Figure 2:3), with some MTE members recording quantum leap in their export ratios. For example, Korea's exports have soared from 23% of GDP in the early 1990s to 54%, Malaysia's export ratio has jumped from 75% to 115% and Thailand's ratio has risen from 38% to 70%. A large part of this reliance is due to insufficient structural reform, which has dragged on domestic demand growth and forced the region to export its way out.

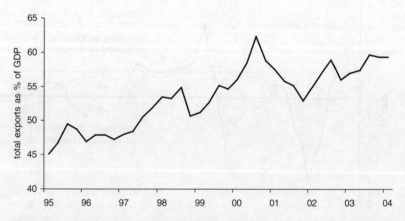

Figure 2:3 Asian export-to-GDP ratio (Korea, Taiwan, Malaysia, Indonesia, Philippines, Thailand)

Source: CEIC

Arguably, strong export growth is a symptom rather than strength of Asia's growth model. This is true even before the 1997/1998 Asian crisis. The region's chronic problem is over-saving and under-consuming. This has resulted in a large build-up of capital stock that yields low return on assets. A natural remedy to this excess saving problem is to consume more. Over-reliance on exports for growth also puts Asia in direct competition with China. This will erode the region's growth momentum if it fails to move faster and deeper on structural reforms, as China has formidable comparative advantage in manufacturing for a long time to come. Consumption-driven growth will also reduce Asia's economic vulnerability stemming from export volatility. So contrary to what many optimists see, Asia is still export-dependent with the domestic sector lagging as a growth driver. Insufficient structural reforms forced the region to rely on exports as the key growth source. This begs the question of where Asian exports have gone, given that export growth to the developed markets has slowed?

China is where the bulk of Asian exports have gone in recent years. How do we know? Remember Figure 2:2 shows that Asia's export dependence on the developed markets has fallen in recent years, as reflected by the decline in the ratio of Asia's export growth to the developed markets to its total export growth. But when we add the MTEs' exports headed for China to their exports headed for Japan and the US, the MTEs' dependence on these China-plus-developed markets has risen noticeably to above 1 since late 2002 (Figure 2:4). This is consistent with the observation that China's recent strong economic growth has taken in a lot of imports, including those from Asia. It also suggests that China has been the key source of export growth for Asia in recent years, though she is still smaller than Japan and the US in terms of absolute market size.

To drive home the point of Asia's dependence on China trade, let us examine Asia's export growth trends. The region's total export growth has risen faster than its export growth to the developed markets in recent years. But when exports to China are added to the exports to the developed markets, Asia's total export growth moves in tandem with export growth to the combined China-developed markets in recent years (Figure 2:5). This is evidence that China has replaced Japan and the US as the key export growth market for Asia.

China's role in boosting Asian export growth also has an implication for intra-regional trade, and this implication in turn ties back to the perceived China demand threat. If trade among Asian economies is really significant, China's role should not affect the intra-regional trade trend. Let us check this. Let us deduct Asia's exports to China, Japan and the US

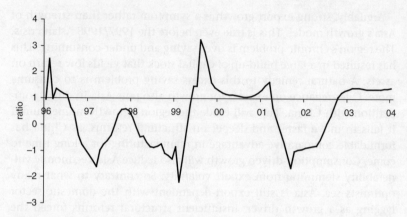

Figure 2:4 Asian export growth ratio (China + developed mkt exports-to-total exports: six-month moving average)
Source: CEIC

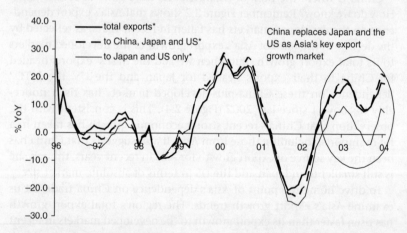

Figure 2:5 Asian export growth
* Three-month moving average
Source: CEIC

altogether from its total exports. Note that this is just building on what we did for calculating the intra-regional trade in Figure 2:1 by taking away the region's exports to China together with those to the developed markets.

Alas, the share of Asian exports outside these three major markets has fallen (Figure 2:6). This, in turn, means that intra-regional trade has in

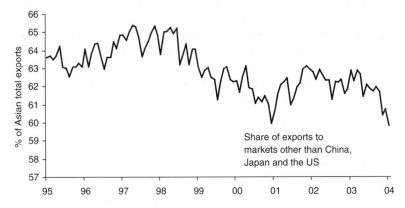

Figure 2:6 Intra-regional trade falling
Source: CEIC

fact dropped, not risen, in recent years when China is not in the equation. The corollary is that Asia has grown more dependent on Chinese demand for their exports, and hence the fears about the China demand threat.

The conspiracy theory

Complementing this view of the perceived China threat is the Middle Kingdom's significant import penetration in the global markets (i.e. growth of China's import share in the developed world's total imports), which is often seen as at the expense of the rest of Asia. The combination of Asia's dependence on Chinese demand and China's rapid import penetration has given rise to a conspiracy theory: On the one hand, China is pursuing ruthless industrial expansion to out-compete her Asian neighbours in exports, thus cutting off their growth source. On the other hand, she is giving them China-induced growth by making them overly dependent on Chinese demand. This economic tactic, the sceptics charge, allows China to plant her influence in the region. The growing sense of insecurity has prompted ASEAN members to propose to form an ASEAN Economic Community (AEC) to counter China's economic threat. The AEC aims at creating a single market for goods, services, capital and skilled labour by 2020.

Indeed, since the 1990s, most Southeast Asian economies have lost export market shares in the developed world while China's import penetration has more than doubled. Notably, US imports from ASEAN fell from over 7% of total imports in 1994 to 6% in 2003, while China's import penetration rose from 5.4% to 12% in the same period (Figure 2:7). Further, net foreign direct investment (FDI) inflows to China have risen sharply since the early 1990s, but FDI flows to ASEAN have fallen (Figure 2:8). All this seems to underscore the claim that China has gained export market shares and foreign capital at the expense of the rest of Asia.

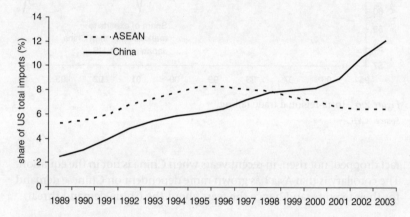

Figure 2:7 Import penetration (US imports from ASEAN and China as % of total US imports)
Source: CEIC

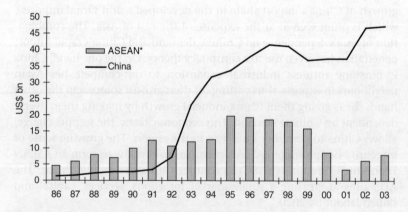

Figure 2:8 Net foreign direct investment flows
* Indonesia, Malaysia, Philippines, Singapore, Thailand
Source: CEIC

The conventional wisdom is that with an average monthly manufacturing wage of about US$100 and rising productivity, China is sucking in investment resources and gobbling up export market share because she can produce almost everything cheaper than the others. If the rest of Asia wants to compete, the logic goes, they have to compete on price. But higher labour cost and cut-throat competition imply a painful process of deflationary adjustment, profit erosion, falling exchange rates and prolonged economic disruption for the rest of Asia.

So much for this conventional thinking, but it does not have much wisdom in it. Price is not everything. Invisible costs, such as red tape, corruption, local protectionism and distribution problems, all add to the bottom-line cost. Further, low labour cost is not going to last forever in China (see below), and it is not China's monopoly. Micro comparative studies of low-income ASEAN economies often finds that there is little difference between their and China's total labour-related outlays. So what makes China more attractive than ASEAN? It must be something more than labour cost comparison.

We can get a clue by looking at the composition of China's FDI inflows. Table 2:1 shows the breakdown of China's FDI that is actually utilised. Less than a third is invested in export-oriented sectors, like light manufacturing and electronics; together they account for 28% of all utilised FDI. The rest is aimed at China's domestic (mostly non-tradable) sectors, like auto, machinery and equipment, retail, real estate, catering, chemicals, mining and energy. This means foreign investors are attracted by China's large, rapid-growing domestic market but not, or not only, her ability to produce cheaply.

The small share of utilised FDI in the export sectors also suggests that price is not of sole importance for making China a formidable economic

Table 2:1 Breakdown of utilised FDI in China, 2003

	% of total
Other manufacturing	40
Services	18
Light manufacturing*	15
Electronics*	13
Property and construction	14
Total	100

* Export-oriented

Source: CEIC

force. Rather, a large local market potential is needed for breeding success in export markets. Surveys of export manufacturers in China suggest that logistics infrastructure, proximity to suppliers and commercial stability top their considerations in locating production bases. And all these factors are fostered by a sizeable domestic economy. Relative labour costs appear very low on the list. In a nutshell, to compete with China in attracting investment resources, an economy needs more than just a cheap labour force; it also needs to offer a large domestic market.[4]

Still no way out

The corollary is for Asia to develop large domestic markets to reduce its dependence on China. Thailand is doing it and initial signs show that the policy has been successful. Thai Prime Minister Thaksin started a two-pronged economic strategy in 2001, after the burst of the global IT bubble that dragged down the world economy, to boost growth by pushing exports and domestic spending at the same time. He has put particular emphasis on the latter to lessen Thailand's dependence on exports. This so called 'Thaksinomics' has got Thai consumers spending, banks lending and asset markets booming. Thai real GDP growth averaged over 6% a year in 2002 and 2003 while other Asian neighbours' growth averaged only 4%. Attracted by Thailand's positive growth outlook, FDI inflows to Thailand jumped by 44% in 2003 to US$1,244 million from US$862 million in 2002.

This has got many Asian authorities thinking about following Thailand's approach. Unfortunately, Thaksinomics is not all applicable to other Asian economies. First, large government budget deficits, especially in Southeast Asia, (Table 2:2) will prevent these regional governments from boosting their domestic sectors by aggressive fiscal expansion like Thakin. Attempting to recreate the Thai strategy could risk worsening the fiscal and debt burdens and destabilising the whole economy.

Second, Thailand (along with Korea and Indonesia) went through a painful consumption and investment adjustment during the Asian crisis, while the other Asian economies did not suffer as much. This is seen in GDP growth and bank lending (Figures 2:9 and 2:10), where the three Asian-crisis economies of Thailand, Korea and Indonesia all contracted more sharply than the rest of Asia (excluding China, India and Japan). But Thailand (and Korea and Indonesia) also came out of the crisis with more aggressive economic restructuring under the International Monetary Fund (IMF) bailout programmes than the rest of Asia. Arguably, Thailand is now reaping the benefit of both a sharper economic cleansing process

Table 2:2 Government budget balances (% GDP)

	2002	2003
Singapore	−1.6	6.4
Korea	3.4	0.8
Thailand	−3.1	−1.6
Indonesia	−1.2	−1.6
Taiwan	−4.3	−4.0
Philippines	−5.3	−4.6
Malaysia	−5.6	−5.3

(minus = deficit)
Source: CEIC

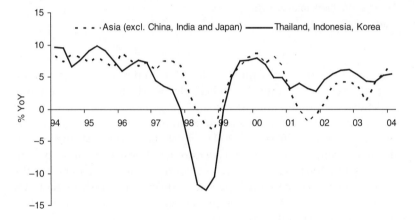

Figure 2:9 Real GDP growth
Source: CEIC

during the Asian crisis and deeper structural reforms after the crisis. Her stronger growth experience is not likely to be repeatable in many other Asian economies because they had suffered less and gone through less structural changes. The point is that Asian economies are quite different from each other. There is no one set of panacea policies for the region. Asia's dependence on China is inevitable. But China is not swallowing up the world because her growing economic importance is just a natural evolution like any other Asian economy (see the section 'It's just rendezvous' later).

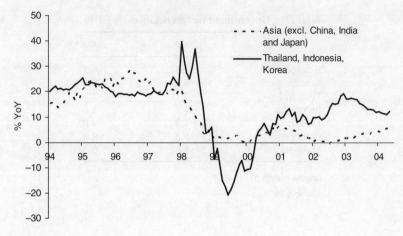

Figure 2:10 Bank loan growth
Source: CEIC

As far as the threat of China holding Asia in demand hostage is concerned, there is a significant cyclical element in it. Asia has certainly depended on Chinese import demand for generating growth in recent years. But that has also been a result of China's robust growth, averaging over 8% between 2000 and 2003, which has created strong import demand. Chinese imports may have recorded almost 40% annual growth in 2003 and 2004, but that is certainly not a sustainable trend for the future. As China's economic cycle slows down, so will her demand for imports. This means that the perceived threat of Asia as overly dependent on Chinese demand should also fade.

If Asia wants to balance its increasing reliance on the Chinese market for exports in the long-term, it has no choice but to join together and create a large, unified market with ample resources. This is the motivation behind ASEAN's idea to create the AEC. The trouble is that the idea is very far away from implementation. ASEAN is highly fragmented, in terms of geographic, economic, political and cultural diversities, with relatively closed borders to labour and capital flows. These obstacles are the reason why only an estimated 20% of total ASEAN trade is conducted between ASEAN partners, compared with an estimated 40% of inter-provincial trade in China and over 50% in the EU and the US.

The problem with ASEAN economic integration is already seen in the difficulty for the formation of the ASEAN Free Trade Area (AFTA), a similar but less grand step prior to achieving the AEC. Despite the progress seen in tariff reduction, as required by AFTA rules, the free trade area is not quite what it is supposed to be. Several of its members have refused to cut tariffs on certain critical products to meet the agreed deadline in 2003. Notably, Malaysia still insists on protecting her state-owned carmaker, Proton, to the dismay of Thailand, which has a fast-growing auto industry. The Philippines, after cutting tariffs on petrochemicals initially, later thought better of it and raised them again. Rice, the region's biggest crop, is excluded from the pact together, mainly due to Thailand's resistance.

More seriously, there is failure to implement the tariff cuts that have already been agreed. There are no records for what proportion of intra-ASEAN trade has taken advantage of the Common Effective Preferential Tariff (CEPT) scheme under AFTA. Some private estimates put the share at 5% of total trade. Some anonymous officials at the ASEAN Secretariat argued the share should be higher, but were unable to give any estimates with proof. This is because member countries have not bothered, or unable, to give the secretariat any persistent relevant data, largely due to the tedious reporting system and paper work that have deterred implementation.

The problem of ASEAN's diversity is also evident. There is not much incentive for economies with already low tariffs to push the CEPT, since the tariff rate difference between it and their own rate is small. For economies with high tariffs, these are reluctant to cut into their customs revenue by implementing the CEPT. While ASEAN leaders are trying to address these problems by pledging to cut red tape, adopt common product standards and set up a monitoring system and a dispute-settlement mechanism, their effort has so far not been real enough to solve the ASEAN diversity problem.

For example, in their ACE initiative, which is modelled after the European Union concept, ASEAN leaders have made it clear that they would not tolerate any reduction in sovereignty for the sake of deeper economic integration. They have even rejected the idea of a common customs union and a shared external tariff, since that would force the member countries to make dramatic changes to their economic policies. Meanwhile, many members are pressing ahead with bilateral trade agreements to pre-empt, or even undermine, collective negotiations. For example, Singapore has concluded trade agreements with Japan, Australia, New Zealand and the US.

This divergence over trade pacts suggests a deeper rift within ASEAN's economic goals. Relatively open members, like Singapore and Thailand, see the grouping as a means to raise external competitiveness and to attract foreign capital to survive the Chinese competition. But the other less developed members want grouping mainly to promote trade and investment within ASEAN, but not with outsiders. This fundamental difference in thinking will keep ASEAN members' economic interest from aligning so that any grouping effort will be rendered ineffective.

China's labour pains

For those who fret that China's unlimited cheap labour supply will crash the regional economies by taking over global manufacturing, exporting deflation and attracting all the foreign investment, they should be relieved to know that the tide is changing, albeit gradually, against China's labour advantage. In autumn 2004, the Chinese government reported for the first time that factories around Shanghai and the Pearl River Delta (PRD), China's two great export powerhouses, were suffering from severe labour shortages (of some 2 million workers), and had significant difficulties in hiring additional resources and expanding capacity.

The emergence of labour shortage in China will certainly turn established economic wisdom on its head, as huge numbers of underpaid migrant workers have been the driving force behind China's export success and, hence her economic threat as some see it. For years, China's 900 million-strong rural population is seen as an inexhaustible pool of cheap labour for the coastal factories to tap. This unbeatable competitive advantage, the argument goes, would suck in foreign investment for years and fuel decades of rapid growth for China at the expense of the rest of Asia.

But with 1.3 billion people, how can China suffer from labour shortages? On detailed examination, there is indeed no shortage of labour in China. What's going on is that China's labour market is maturing, albeit at a very slow pace and in an unevenly distributed pattern with some cities maturing faster than others. Hence, manufacturing wage pressures are on the rise in the cities with fast maturing labour market. This wage trend will continue over the longer-term as a natural economic evolution process. This should also dispel the myth of unlimited cheap Chinese labour supply and the conspiracy theory of China displacing the world's manufacturing.

Of China's 1.3 billion population in 2003, some 900 million are classified as agricultural, and almost 800 million are registered in rural villages (with the rest registered in small towns). Within the rural population, there are about 500 million people of working age between 15 and 59 years old. Some analysts estimate that China only needs 100 million people working in the farms to support the current agricultural output levels. This means that four-fifths of the 500-million strong working-age rural population are surplus labour with insufficient or no work at all. This surplus labour can be hired elsewhere. And many of them do find jobs elsewhere, notably in manufacturing and services in more developed areas, like Guangdong, Fujian, Zhejiang and Jiangsu provinces, as migrant workers. Indeed, Chinese census data shows a 'floating' rural population of 100 million. This still leaves about 300 million working-age rural labour unemployed or under-employed;[5] that is 300 million potential new workers for manufacturing and services. So where is the shortage?

This estimate for China's surplus labour pool shows not a shortage problem, but rather a combination of a labour market maturing process and labour immobility that pushes up costs. Skilled manufacturing labour has been in short supply since early 2002, and wages for skilled labour have been rising faster than overall economic growth since then. But the perceived shortage of unskilled labour is unprecedented. The root of the problem lies in the structure of the labour market.

Given the abundance of young workers, most textile, toy and electronics manufacturers do not hire old rural workers. In fact, they hire mostly young female workers. A Ministry of Labour study in 2004 found that some 75% of the factories surveyed hire only females between 18 and 26 years old. In the more laborious sectors like construction, there is a similar focus on hiring young men in the same age group. But how many in the 100 million floating rural workers are between 18 and 26 years old? No one knows, but presumably a large share. According to Chinese census data, about 100 million rural residents are aged between 18 and 26.

However, the disturbing trend is that the remaining supply of men and women under 26 years old is falling. This is largely a result of China's strict population control policy since the late 1970s. The so-called one-child policy has led to a declining growth rate in both the population and the labour force since the 1980s. Meanwhile, manufacturers have been mean on providing worker welfare. Most light manufacturing firms are used to a workforce willing to work for 12 hours a day and live in crowded dormitories for a monthly salary of RMB600. If they hire worker in their 30s or older, that means dealing with families, housing and health care needs and, hence, higher cost.

The poor working conditions have become really a problem as the younger workers move up the education ladder fast. They are demanding higher pay and better employment terms and working conditions. Due to demographics, China has seen a sharp rise in the proportion of students going beyond the nine-year compulsory education ending in junior high school. This has important implications for the manufacturing sector, which relies heavily on junior high school graduates for its labour force. The more education people get, the less likely they are to seek a factory job; or they will demand higher wages and better working conditions. This also means the supply of unskilled labour has shrunk. Hence, although the labour pool remains large, labour cost is rising.

Meanwhile, Chinese factories have been spoiled by a seemingly endless supply of young rural workers. Many manufacturing regions have not seen wages increase for years. For example, the average monthly salary for an unskilled worker was about the same (RMB 600–700 range) at the end of 2003 as it was around 1998. This stagnation was made possible by the low subsistence wages until recently. This subsistence wage is the migrant workers' income from farming, which represents the opportunity cost for them to move from the countryside to work in the cities. In other words, the subsistence wage is also the minimum for manufacturing wages because workers will not move from their farms to the factories if they cannot earn more than their farm income.

So if farm incomes are low or stagnant, there is no need for factory wages to rise to lure workers. And this was what happened in China. Between 1992 and 1996, farm incomes rose 150% to RMB200 a month from RMB80. But then there was no growth in the following years. As of 2001, monthly rural incomes were still hovering at about RMB212, barely increased from the levels five years previously. That was why the subsistence wage was low and stagnant too. The farm sector suffered badly between 1996 and 2002, when China's economic growth fell sharply under former premier Zhu Rongji's austerity programme to fight inflation. Agricultural prices fell by an average of one-third during that period, as a result of weak domestic demand and rising agricultural yields. But what was a disaster for the farm sector had turned out to be a big boon to the export manufacturers, who enjoyed a combination of rapid overseas, especially US, market growth and cheap and flat wages at home.

But the Chinese farmers' fortunes have changed since 2002. Farm prices have recovered strongly since then, boosting farm income growth, due to a sharp rise in grain prices and agricultural subsidies paid directly to farmers and the cut in agricultural taxes. This has resulted in fast rural income growth, which has outpaced urban income growth since early 2004. Thus, with rising prices have come rising wages as the farmers' subsistence wage rises.

This will have profound implications on China's labour cost going forward. China used to be in a situation where there was an essentially unlimited supply of labour. In economics terms, China's labour supply curve was flat. This means as factory and construction demand for workers rose, there was a seemingly infinite reserve of young rural workers willing to work at the prevailing wage. Not anymore; China's labour supply curve has turned to a normal upward-sloping one. This means rising wages are needed to lure the supply of labour. With rising farm prices and incomes, and a tighter supply of single, under-26 years old workers, the marginal cost of hiring new young workers is rising.

The days of cheap wages and flat wage growth in China are probably gone for good. Farm prices are expected to have embarked on a secular up-trend (see Chapter 4, pp. 69–73) and labour market dynamics are pointing to a tightening supply of unskilled workers in the coming years. Many of the available unemployed and/or underemployed workers are older and have families, meaning that they are not as readily or as cheaply mobile. The inevitable upshot of rising labour cost will squeeze profit margins, but the short-term impact on China's competitiveness will still be limited. An increase in export-oriented manufacturing wages from US$80 to US$110 over the next few years, as seen by many observers, would not make a dent on China's cost advantage vis-à-vis other Asian economies like India, Indonesia and Vietnam. Further, China has many other short-term advantages, like infrastructure support, huge domestic market potential, stable political climate and proximity to suppliers. But in the longer-term, China will inevitably lose competitiveness to other low-end export economies. That will be a natural economic development process. It should ease fears about Chinese cheap labour crashing the regional economies and creating economic chaos.

Manufacturers and investors are reacting to combat rising labour cost in China by moving from the dearer coastal areas to the cheaper interior provinces. With improved transport and pro-business local government, second-tier cities like Wuhan and Chengdu have attracted increasing investment flows from both foreign and domestic investors. FDI data also shows a relocation trend. Once the darling of FDI, the Pearl River Delta region is under increasing competitive pressure. Indeed, FDI in Guangdong, Hainan and Fijian all saw double-digit decline in 2004. In contrast, the once ignored areas like Yunan and Shanxi provinces recorded more than two-fold increase in FDI inflow in 2004. Together with Southwestern Guangxi Autonomous Region and the northeast coastal provinces of Shangdong and Liaoning, they made up the top five FDI gainers in China in 2004, with annual FDI growth rates all over 100%.

It's just rendezvous

The fears of China gobbling up the world economy have also been misplaced. This is because China's economic emergence is not different from the development paths of the 'Asian Tigers'.[6] Hence, the conspiracy theory does not stand up for scrutiny. China's impact on the global economy has been exactly what the theory of international trade predicted. As a low-income and labour-rich economy, China has focused on making low value-added goods for global consumers. There is no doubt that this shift in manufacturing power in China's favour has had some impact on shifting relative prices for raw materials and finished goods in the global markets. But to some critics, the most worrying part is China's entry to the world economy in a drastic way, taking over industries like autos, shipbuilding, semiconductors, biotech and even high-end capital goods when the rest of the world is totally unprepared. They fret that China is quantum leaping in the global value-added chain and striking at the heart of the developed world's livelihood.

If these critics were right, we should have seen China taking over the world's high value-added manufacturing exports, such as high-end electronics and machinery. But evidence does not support this view. Over the past 20 years, China has evolved according to her comparative advantage. On a net basis, she has been importing raw materials and high value-added goods, such as heavy machinery, and exporting labour-intensive goods, notably light manufacturing (Figure 2:11). The evidence also shows that China's light manufacturing exports only took off since the mid-1990s, when her export industries achieved a critical mass.

Granted, the electronics sector may be China's fastest growing export segment, accounting for about 30% of total shipment. But on a net basis, she is still importing more electronics goods than exporting them. Meanwhile the domestic value-added component of her electronics exports is still focused on processing, assembly and low-end parts. In a nutshell, China's overall foreign trade pattern clearly reflects her low-income status, evolving according to the law of comparative advantage. This indeed suggests China will compete with other emerging markets, but not with the developed economies and hence will not gobble up the global economy.

Though the Mainland's development pattern is similar to that of the Asian Tiger economies, it is the biggest and fastest-growing economy of them all. So could things be different as China enters the global system? From an economic development point of view, the two Tiger economies of South Korea and Taiwan are the best comparables. In Korea, per capital annual income reached US$1,000 in 1977. That was

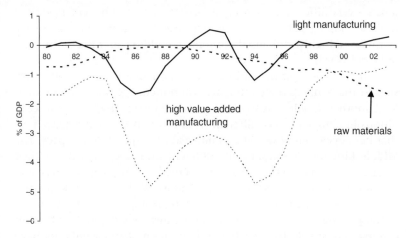

Figure 2:11 China's net trade pattern (net exports, in 3-year moving averages) Negative = net imports (or trade deficit)
Source: CEIC

the time when the Korean economy looked very much the same as China today, with rising net exports of labour-intensive consumption goods, a growing electronics export segment and large net imports of capital goods and raw materials.

But it is crucial to note that it took Korea another decade to move markedly up the value-added chain, get out of the low-end exports and move into sophisticated electronics. That happened in 1987, when per capita Korean income reached US$3,500 a year. Then it took another ten years for Korea, whose per capita annual income rose to US$10,000 in 1997, to become a net exporter of heavy machinery and high value-added electronics. Evidence shows that Taiwan followed pretty much the same development pattern as Korea, with the major industrial shifting points occurring at roughly similar income levels. In particular, Taiwan moved out of labour-intensive manufacturing into electronics in the late 1980s, and only became a net capital goods exporter by 2001.

What about Japan? Does her large economy not make a better comparison with China? Not really. Japan's per capital annual income was US$1,000 in 1965, the same as China today. But Japan's experience is quite unique. From the start of her industrialisation, Japan was already a large net exporter of heavy industrial equipment and a declining exporter of light manufacturing goods. By the early 1970s, Japan's net trade pattern had more or less reached what it had become 30 years later. Hence,

Japan is very different from every Asian economy that has emerged from their developing status via step-by-step structural shifts. She is more like Germany, a highly capitalised economy rebuilding after the destruction of World War II.

So, if the development paths of Korea and Taiwan are a guide, they suggest that China's trade influence will not change dramatically for at least another decade. But sceptical souls still charge that economic conditions in China are very different from those in Korea and Taiwan, so that her development would also move at a sharply different pace. The Middle Kingdom is indeed quite different from the other Asian Tiger economies, but not in the way most observers see. Arguably, China could take much longer to make the kind of industrial shift seen in Korea and Taiwan, not to mention the fast developing Hong Kong and Singapore.

The driving force behind Korea and Taiwan's structural shift is an external cost shock. The two Tiger economies probably would not have moved out of light manufacturing so fast in the second half of the 1980s if their wage differentials with the developing ASEAN economies had not become economically significant. In other words, the advent of an external low-wage shock was the key factor to force Korea and Taiwan's structural changes. China's competitive stress only came in at the later stages to accelerate their moves up the value-added ladder. But such an external shock is unlikely to hit China anytime soon, due to her own huge supply of cheap labour in the medium-term. China's labour-intensive industries are more likely to move inland than overseas as and when labour cost in the current industrial hubs becomes too expensive. The recent overseas expansion by some Chinese industries is driven by a desire to capture market share rather than to reduce cost, and this will be the case for many years to come.

What about China's undervalued currency and state-subsidised funding costs? Wouldn't these artificial policies give China an unfair competitive edge to grow her high-tech and capital intensive industries and eventually overwhelm the global market? These are certainly policy issues subject to debates. But they had also existed in the rest of Asia for the past two decades, and had not really affected the development pace of the tiger economies. This is thus not a reason to expect China to move any faster than her Asian neighbours in her industrialisation process.

A product-cycle perspective

China's elevation to the world's manufacturing house is in fact a natural evolution of the global product cycle. The product cycle model is an elaboration of the basic international trade tenet, comparative advantage. But it is powerful enough to dispel the conspiracy theory of the China economic threat.

Many manufactured goods, like television sets, video recorders, DVD players, semiconductors and automobiles, go through a product cycle in which the inputs used change over time. When these goods are initially produced, there is a great deal of experimentation in both the characteristics of the final product and its manufacturing process. Hence, this first stage of the product cycle needs to be supported by a high-income market, where consumer feedback, market information and money are available. On the input side, research and development in design and manufacturing require scientific and engineering inputs, together with skilled labour and entrepreneurs willing to risk failure and an initial period of little or no profits. Typically, the first stage of the product cycle takes place in the rich industrialised economies.

Over time, the manufactured product enters the second phase when it becomes standardised in size, features and manufacturing process. Experimentation with basic new design begins to wane, as product development shifts to incremental improvements in a basic design. The price of the product begins to fall, squeezing the manufacturers' profit margin in the rich countries where it is made. At this stage, production begins to shift to countries with low labour costs, as standardised production routines allow the usage of unskilled and semi-skilled labour in assembly-type operations.

Prices have fallen further in the final stage of the product cycle. Consumption in the rich countries begins to exceed production of the product. Making the product in the rich countries has also become uneconomical due to their high labour costs and margin squeeze. Thus, an increasing share of the rich world's manufacturing output is being moved to developing nations where labour cost is kept low by the abundance of unskilled and semi-skilled workers. In this late stage, the rich countries will quit producing the product and turn to development of new products. A new product cycle for the new products will start all over again.

The core of this product cycle model is all about opportunity cost. As manufacturing processes become standardised, they can be performed by unskilled labour. This is because the blend of inputs changes over time, from highly skilled scientific, engineering and marketing elements to basic unskilled and semi-skilled labour. Hence, the opportunity cost of production in developing countries, like China, becomes lower than the cost in the rich countries, like Japan and the US. This change in inputs, in turn, reflects the shifting of an economy's comparative advantage over time.

Advances in transport and communications have played a crucial role in facilitating this product cycle development, which in turn has driven a structural change in international trade in recent years. Jet aircrafts, container ships, fax machines, satellite systems and emails have enabled firms in Japan, Europe or the US to relocate their production far from their home base of operations. Goods produced in China's Guangdong province can be monitored from a home base in Osaka or Birmingham or Detroit. Since unskilled labour is abundant in China, rich countries' manufacturers can cut their production cost sharply by relocating assembly and manufacturing processes there. In general, this is a process of 'international labour arbitrage', where rich countries take advantage of cheap labour outside the domestic economy by relocating production to other lower wage economies.

Meanwhile, by setting up a factory in China, an American or Japanese manufacturer may find it easier to secure a better and reliable flow of quality inputs by going through a foreign subsidiary rather than buying the inputs from wholly independent foreign firms. It may also find it cheaper to work with distributors that it owns than with independent firms. From these perspectives, the massive influx of foreign capital to China is a natural result of the product cycle development.

The development of China's high-tech industry relating to telecommunications and computing (data processing) is a good illustration of the product cycle. These Chinese exports originate in assembly operations, many of which have been set up with foreign capital. A telephone manufacturer, for example, decides to take advantage of low wages by producing a standardised product in China. Once the assembly plant is built, only a handful of skilled workers are needed to run the plant. Most workers can be quickly trained to assemble the product and perform simple diagnostic tests on it. The result is that China exports telecommunications equipment and appears to have been developing a fast-growing high-tech sector that threatens some manufacturers. But this is not true because there is no design, research or industrial engineering taking place in China's assembly workshop.

Similarly, some decades ago, radio receivers and plastics were exclusively products of industrial countries. As their manufacturing process became standardised, the production migrated to places where unskilled labour was relatively more abundant. In sum, China's successful export drive and her ascent to become the world's dominant manufacturing base has been the result of two forces: a shift towards her comparative advantage and the product cycle. There is no conspiracy theory to take over the world economy.

3
The Outsourcing Threat

The fear about the China economic threat has led many opportunists and politicians to jump on the China-bashing bandwagon. The blame game has revived protectionist sentiment. The most notable example is the hot debate on the damage of cross-border outsourcing on the US economy, especially in the run-up to the US presidential election in 2004. Though the debate was misguided by pre-election rhetoric, it may have a profound impact on shifting America's free trade attitude. With weakening globalisation momentum, the negative sentiment towards free trade does raise the risk of protectionism that will hurt Asia. Arguably, such a risk is more imminent and real than the perceived China threat to the global economy.

The hollowing-out myth

Cross-border outsourcing occurs when a company in one country contracts out part of its production process to another company (or companies) in another country to exploit cheaper production (typically labour) cost overseas. This practice in effect amounts to a *global labour arbitrage* process, and it has been intensifying in recent years. Notably, the information technology (IT) sector has acquired an international dimension rapidly, as US firms find it more profitable to contract IT software and services out to developing economies, such as China and India. A study by McKinsey, an international consulting firm, in 2004 estimated that every dollar spent on cross-border outsourcing resulted in a 58 US cents cost saving for US businesses.

Corporate outsourcing is a key survival strategy in today's highly competitive world. The process refutes the integrated production model – keeping everything in-house in pursuit of economies of scale – that

Figure 3:1 US employment/population ratio (adults 16 years old and above)
Source: CEIC

business school has taught. Instead, production chains are broken up, with specialisation taking place across the globe, exploiting opportunities for the lowest costs. Cross-border outsourcing is representative of the essence of economic efficiency, which is a never-ending quest for cost reduction. The companies that produce at the lowest cost venues are the ones that prosper.

Many Americans have blamed US corporate outsourcing, to China in particular, on US job losses in recent years. In 2003, some 15 states in the US, including Maryland, Indiana, Florida, Michigan, New Jersey, New York and North Carolina, introduced anti-outsourcing bills. Though none of these were passed, thanks to the strong opposition from big US businesses, the blame game has not stopped. But contrary to perception, cross-border outsourcing has not curbed American job growth. The US employment-to-population ratio has risen steadily through the years (Figure 3:1), suggesting that outsourcing has not been an obstacle to job growth. It could even be a job-creating machine by allowing America to cut costs and increase its production capacity via the growth of international trade.

The view that China has stolen manufacturing jobs from the developed world does not stand up for scrutiny. Economic maturity and productivity gains in the advanced countries explain a large part of the job losses. By some estimates, Japan and the US (who have frequently pointed fingers at China and other Asian economies for stealing jobs) saw a total of nine million manufacturing jobs lost in the past ten years.

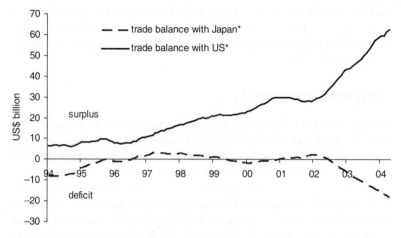

Figure 3:2 China's trade with Japan and the US
* Series in 12-month rolling sum
Source: CEIC

If those jobs had gone to China, they should show up in a massive expansion in Chinese manufacturing capacity for exports. Given China's low labour cost, this should, in turn, be reflected in a big growth in China's trade surplus with Japan and the US. The Mainland's trade surplus with the US has indeed grown, but it has actually run a trade deficit with Japan (Figure 3:2).

Despite China's trade surplus with the US, the bulk of the job losses in the US (and also Japan) have nothing to do with China's trade. Rather, it is a result of economic maturity, due to productivity gains in the manufacturing sector and a natural move of jobs into the service sector from manufacturing. Productivity gains mean fewer workers are needed to make the same amount of goods. But rising labour productivity (defined as output per labour hour) is a two-edged sword. On one hand, it raises America's GDP growth. On the other hand, it reduces the effect of faster economic growth on job creation. In other words, increased labour productivity has boosted economic growth by creating fewer new jobs.

Meanwhile, as the US economy becomes richer, demand for lifestyle-enhancing services, like travel, education, healthcare and restaurants, rises. This has prompted a change in the structural demand for labour, and hence a migration of jobs from manufacturing to services. Since the rate of job creation by the services sector is slower than the rate of labour-shedding by the manufacturing sector, unemployment rises.

Labour immobility also bars a smooth job transition from manufacturing to services. Overall, productivity gains have combined with the change in the structural labour demand to account for much of the job losses in the developed world.

The myopic protectionists

The fear about the hollow-out process is understandable. Manufacturing is not the only sector facing cut-throat competition, and it is not just blue-collar jobs that are moving offshore. Even service sector jobs are being lost; some of them are high skills, notably in software engineering. Critics of outsourcing fret that nothing will be left for the Americans soon.

Those politically-driven alarmists who argue that China and India have threatened the US economy by hollowing-out American jobs are ignorant about basic economics. The trend of international competition spreading to services is nothing new. Offshore outsourcing is all about the simple economic principles of comparative advantage and specialisation. These economic dicta argue that an economy should focus on making what it is good at (and hence cheaper) so that the resultant cross-border trade of goods and services at lower prices, and hence higher purchasing power, will raise global economic well-being. It is all about better resources allocation.

Companies that have outsourced are able to remain competitive by cutting costs and prices. This, in turn, has benefited consumers in the advanced economies with cheaper goods and services. Meanwhile, the manufacturing work that has gone to poorer, cheaper, economies has helped spur their economic development, as evident in Mexico, China and India in recent years, and the Asian Tiger economies of Hong Kong, Singapore, South Korea and Taiwan in the 1980s and early 1990s. This is how gains from trade is achieved.

True, the US experienced a jobless economic recovery after the burst of the 2001 IT bubble. Despite rising profits and output, US firms were not creating many jobs. This reflected the reality of the outsourcing process. But this is part of the creative destruction process for making America more competitive in the long-term. Experience shows that GDP had grown steadily, in both rich and poor countries, along with outsourcing. This was made possible because workers who were in the sunset industries were absorbed into other parts of the economy. The key to growth is economic (labour market) flexibility, not trade protectionism.

To most of the business community in the developed world, the value of corporate outsourcing lies in cheaper wages for labour-intensive manufacturing. But this is only part of the benefits, as some leading US companies can attest that offshore outsourcing can do a lot more than just cutting costs. The progressive companies are taking advantage of the distinctive skills and high performance offered by developing Asia to enhance their own operating performance. By moving manufacturing operations from their higher-cost home base to China, some major US electronics companies have tripled manufacturing productivity and cut cycle times and defect rates. This is only one of the many examples showing the ability of offshore firms to combine low labour cost with distinctive skills to benefit US firms.

The reason why these firms can benefit so much is that the real gains of outsourcing come not just from low wages, but also from combining cost savings with the availability of skills. Indeed Asia possesses many skills that are even more abundant than the US. For example, China produces 350,000 graduate engineers a year, compared with 90,000 from US engineering schools. Industry sources also say that most leading Indian IT-sourcing firms operate at a higher level of expertise than the internal IT departments of many US firms. Meanwhile, low wages allow offshore companies to hire more middle managers, who can devote more time to build the skills of their employees and to improve the operating environment to the benefit of the US companies that have outsourced.

Contrary to the common perception that Asian firms lack managerial efficiency, those that have gained the confidence of, and hence the outsourcing business from, US firms show that the combination of low wages and availability of skills has enabled them to use managerial practices more effectively than many US companies. This is because in the US, high labour cost has pushed companies to cut layers of middle management to raise the operating span of the remaining managers, who are forced to work outside their core competence and into excessive administrative and supervisory duties. The problem with downsizing is that a company can only do so much cutting. Fats can easily be cut in the beginning. But once the optimal manager-to-worker ratio is reached, further cost cutting will backfire on operating performance. In other words, severe downsizing pressure has pushed many US companies into diminishing returns. But in Asia, due to low labour cost and ample skills, the manager-to-worker ratio is higher so that they can operate more effectively. The higher manager-to-worker ratio allows companies to pay greater attention to identify and implement process improvements that enhance their operational performance.

Expanding outsourcing initiatives into adjacent higher value-added activities can also allow companies, especially those with production costs largely related to manufacturing, to realise greater value. For example, US Original Equipment Manufacturers (OEMs) at first only moved relatively simple assembly operations offshore by farming them out to electronics manufacturing services. But in recent years, they have increasingly relied on cross-border outsourcing for higher-value services such as product design, sourcing and inventory management.

Outsourcing can also help companies expand new product lines. Consider the way US computer manufacturing firms are expanding into consumer electronics. Gateway has swiftly established leadership in the US plasma TV market. Hewlett Packard has carved out a 6% market share in digital cameras, which is reasonable enough for it to keep expanding in this market. Dell Computers is also targeting televisions and smart phones. All these have happened despite stiff competition from market leaders like NEC, Fujitsu, Canon and Nikon. These American OEMs are using their knowledge of and relationship with Asian original-design manufacturers (that had earlier helped them design and make computers and peripherals) to lessen the risks of entering what were once for them inaccessible consumer electronics markets.

In a nutshell, barring cross-border outsourcing will not bring back the lost jobs. Protectionist measures will only hurt US companies by depriving them of a new source of efficiency and, thus, eroding their competitiveness.

The misguided debate

Many critics do not seem to understand that cross-border outsourcing is a dynamic, but not static, process. These alarmists and pessimists think that Asian companies can only do low-skilled production jobs, and that these same companies would never be able to develop the marketing expertise needed for success in developed markets. Hence, they feel threatened by China's low-cost production capability and accuse her of stealing jobs from the developed world.

Populist US politicians have been exploiting this concern to score political points in Capitol Hill. They have misguided the debate on outsourcing towards protectionism with lies. In international trade accounting, outsourcing is entered as US import of services. Thus, if outsourcing had hurt America, as these critics have charged, the US should have suffered from a serious services trade deficit as American firms buy more (via outsourcing) from abroad than they sell. But contrary to this claim, US official data shows that the country has gained far more than

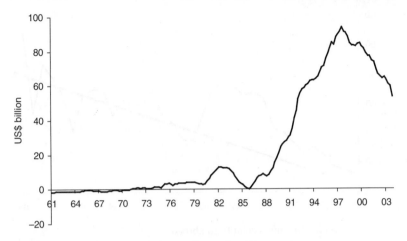

Figure 3:3 US services trade balance (4-month rolling sum)
Source: CEIC

its trading partners in outsourcing. US exports of white-collar work, such as legal, banking, telecom, computer programming and back office work, have been outpacing its imports of such work. This is seen in America's persistent surplus in the services trade account since the mid-1970s (Figure 3:3). The decline in the surplus since 2000 is a result of robust US demand for services imports but not a result of outsourcing.

At the corporate level, US firms' net income receipt from abroad has also risen steadily (Figure 3:4), suggesting that outsourcing has not hurt American companies. In fact, America had never recorded one single year of deficit income receipt over the past 30 years, despite all the complaints about hollowing-out and outsourcing. In general, for companies in the developed world, cross-border outsourcing can lead to better performance (even in highly skilled activities) and a better platform for entering new product markets. This, in turn, should generate new revenues, as underscored by the evidence of rising US net income receipt from abroad. The outsourcing-induced business expansion should also give these corporates the confidence in keeping a competitive edge in the developed markets, even if they move design and technology elements to China and other parts of Asia.

All this means that the US Congress' effort to curb US firms outsourcing could backfire. The anti-outsourcing moves are also self-defeating, if they provoke trading partners' retaliation. The crucial point is that trade

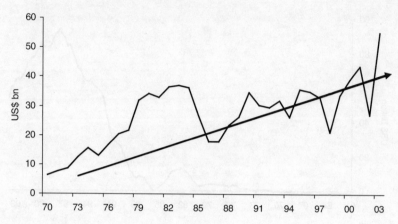

Figure 3:4 US net income receipt from abroad
Source: CEIC

protection will not save jobs. If they are not outsourced, automation and rising productivity will still eliminate them eventually.

While international labour arbitrage does not affect overall employment level, it does alter the pattern of employment. This is desirable, just as it was desirable for the industrial revolution in eighteenth-century England to change employment patterns that resulted in subsequent efficiency gains. But the undesirable micro impact on the US labour market needs to be attended to. The focus of public policy should be on providing a transitional safety net for those adversely affected and ensuring adequate long-term public and private investment in skills and education to match the new job requirements. Any policy debates that steer towards anti-globalisation are totally misguided and dangerous.

There is a serious misunderstanding of the outsourcing process behind the misguided political debate on its impact. Generally, if industries in the developed world are outsourcing significantly to China to the extent that the process hurts their economies, we should see evidence for their production capacity migrating to the Middle Kingdom. One clue for this is a sharp rise in the developed world's dependency on international trade. This is because when a developed economy is outsourcing instead of producing at home, it should be trading more for what it wants. Hence, its trade sector relative to the size of its economy should grow over time. But evidence does not support this.

Take the Japanese and American cases. If they were outsourcing industrial capacity and creating job losses at home, their trade-to-GDP ratios

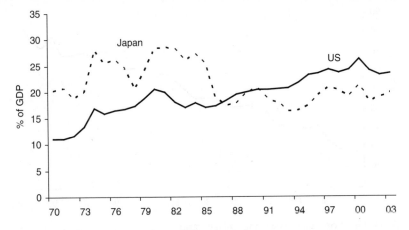

Figure 3:5 US and Japan trade-to-GDP ratios
Source: CEIC

should have risen sharply over time. Country data shows that this is not true. The US ratio has risen very slowly, from 11% of GDP in 1970 to 24% in 2003, averaging an increase of 0.43 percentage points a year in the past 30 years, while Japan's ratio has shown no rising trend at all (Figure 3:5). This sluggish growth in the US and Japanese trade sectors shows either that the US and Japan are not outsourcing a significant amount of industrial capacity, or that outsourcing has led to a sharp rise in GDP growth so that the trade-to-GDP ratio has remained stable. Either way, outsourcing is not an evil.

Meanwhile, the non-Japan Asia trade-to-GDP ratio has grown by leaps and bounds, rising by over 4-fold in the past 30 years (Figure 3:6). This divergence between non-Japan Asia's rapid trade sector expansion and the US and Japanese sluggish trade sector argues that the real story is not that outsourcing has hurt Japan and the US, but that outsourcing has been a natural economic evolution process that helps expand the gains from trade. Here is how the process works.

In the 1950s and the 1960s, Japan began to rebuild and grow after World War II, using an export-oriented policy as the key growth strategy. Back then, Japan was an emerging economy, with comparative advantage on labour-intensive production. Hence she dominated light manufacturing, shipping toys, electronics and sporting goods to the European and American consumer markets. Around the same period of time, Europe and the US were shedding labour-intensive industries, due to rising labour costs as their economies matured. Hence, they outsourced

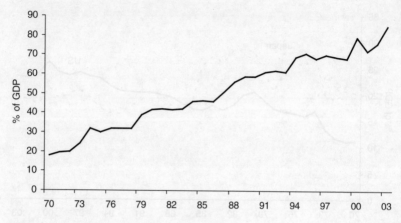

Figure 3:6 Non-Japan Asia trade-to-GDP ratio
Source: CEIC

low value-added production to Japan and focused on high value-added production.

By the 1970s, it was high-income Japan's turn to outsource low-end manufacturing activities. The 'tiger economies' of Korea, Taiwan, Hong Kong and Singapore were all too willing to step in Japan's old shoes and develop labour-intensive exports. This started the so-called 'Asian production chain', where the tiger economies became the world's manufacturing houses. In the two decades of the 1970s and 1980s, Europe, Japan and the US focused on high value-added production like capital machinery and high-tech products, while the Asian Tigers took over downstream processing and assembly functions.

As the economic evolution went into the late 1980s, China and Southeast Asia joined the production chain by taking over capacity from the tiger economies, which had climbed the value-chain and became dear for low-end production. So the outsourcing route shifted from the Asian Tigers to China and Southeast Asia. While the developed world continued to focus on high-end production and capital equipment, the tiger economies moved into providing IT inputs and machinery, leaving most of the labour-intensive processing and assembly functions with China and Southeast Asia, notably the less developed ASEAN[1] economies like Indonesia, Thailand and the Philippines.

The outsourcing chain will shift again in the next decade or two, particularly as China's manufacturing wages rise. Low-end light manufacturing like toys, textiles and sporting goods will migrate to new low-cost production bases, such as Vietnam, Bangladesh, Cambodia and Pakistan. China and the richer ASEAN economies, like Malaysia, will move up to higher value-added production, developing domestic capacity in electronics and consumer brands.

The importance message from outsourcing is that every time another economy joins the Asian production chain, the trade volume grows without hurting the upstream economies. This is possible because every economy specialises according to its comparative advantage along the outsourcing chain and gains from the resultant trade. For example, Japan, the US and the EU sell high-end, tech foundry equipment to Korean and Taiwan, who in turn make semiconductors and other upstream components. These are then shipped to China for processing, making cases, monitors, connectors and other computer parts. The end products are then exported back to the developed markets that outsourced in the beginning. The production costs and the end-product prices are lower in this process than they would have been if there were no outsourcing, no specialisation and no trade.

This evolution of outsourcing explains why non-Japan Asia's trade sector has grown so much faster than the developed world's trade sector since the 1970s. China has been the catalyst in the latest round of this outsourcing process. Hence, rather than being a culprit of inflicting damages in the developed economies by changing/breaking the rules of the game, China is only following the economic evolution path that other economies went through. The perceived China outsourcing threat that has generated so much attention in recent years is no different from the Asian Tiger outsourcing story of the 1970s and the subsequent Southeast Asia outsourcing story of the 1980s. The latest outsourcing wave is part of the global economic evolution and it will continue with Asia being the driver of the process. The China force is far from being spent. The outsourcing stress from China will be here for some time and critics will continue to exploit it to score political points. But this is far from proving that China has posed a significant threat to the world economy.

The irreversible trend

The fact that foreign competition now impinges on services as well as manufacturing raises no new issues of principle whatever. If a computer can be made cheaper in China, it should be. If a telephone enquiry can be processed more cheaply in India, or a travel package booking can be done less costly in Thailand, they should be. All such transactions raise real incomes on both sides, as resources are better redeployed, with added investment and growth in the exporting economy (i.e. the receiving end of outsourcing) and lower prices in the importing country (i.e. the outsourcing country).

All this is made possible because international trade is a positive sum game. Cross-border outsourcing is just international trade elevated to a higher level. Some politicians are trying to raise legislative barriers to stem the flight of jobs from the US. Yet they should note that while legislation and negative publicity about unpatriotic companies may slow outsourcing, the process is irreversible. The search for comparative advantage will continue to underpin this modern production-migration trend, just as it had in the beginning of the US industrial revolution when American entrepreneurs defied Britain's technology-export ban and transferred the technology to set up textile mills in New England. In the past, those mills moved from England to the American south in search of cheaper labour. In recent decades, textile and garment manufacturers have left the US to seek even lower costs in China. An icon of America's garment industry – Levi Strauss – closed its last US plant in January 2004 in favour of production in China and other cheaper Asian bases.

However painful, further manufacturing job losses will only represent the continuation of a process that began some three decades ago. Indeed, even the outsourcing of call-centre jobs is the culmination of a trend over a decade ago that has seen these functions move from high-cost metropolitan centres to smaller towns, then to rural America and now to India and Thailand. While workers in manufacturing should have understood that they are exposed to the challenge of competition from low-cost China, workers in services hitherto have yet to wake up to this reality.

Foreign competition is spreading fast to the service sector, which traditionally has been shielded from external forces. What was formerly deemed non-tradables are not spared from being outsourced. Education is a recent example. Schools in the US desperate to improve their students' maths grades are hiring Indian tutors across the border but without having them physically teaching in US soil. Thanks to IT advancement, these Indian tutors sit in New Delhi, Mumbai or Bangalore, helping American pupils with their maths homework of reviewing lessons via telephones, video-conferencing or the Internet.

This new form of outsourcing underscores the irreversible trend for one simple reason – lower cost. US tuition companies, known as supplemental education service providers, are expensive. Those big and reliable ones charge about US$40 an hour because the cost of hiring tutors is high. Using the same logic as firms in the corporate sector that have outsourced their back-office work to cut cost, these providers are now outsourcing tutoring to qualified Indian education service providers at about half the cost they pay to American tutors. While education outsourcing is still a recent development, those in the business believe that it is only a matter of time before Indians offer online tutoring to any English-speaking country where there is a need, and not just in maths but also in other subjects.

Rising competition also makes the service sector ripe for outsourcing on a global scale. According to the international consultancy firm McKinsey, almost 90% of the value of services output in the US is produced within the providing firm. But this share is expected to fall to 60% in ten years, suggesting that significant outsourcing from the service sector is on the way. High-tech firms like IBM are now outsourcing software programming to India. China is catching up fast in the technology ladder and will become another key high-tech outsourcing destination in the not-too-distant future.

So, some fear that the service sector in the advanced economies will be hollowed-out soon. But if the experience from the manufacturing sector is any guide, this will not be true. Outsourcing has broken up the manufacturing process from vertically integrated structures to highly fragmented ones. Fifty years ago, Detroit's River Rouge plant snapped up iron and coal for churning out cars, all within one chain process. Now, auto firms source component parts from a vast array of domestic and foreign suppliers. Has US manufacturing disappeared? No, manufacturing output has risen by 40% over the past decade, despite the dramatic changes. Despite lower wages abroad, foreign firms still have chosen to make cars in the US, including Honda in Ohio, Mercedes-Benz in Alabama, BMW in South Carolina and Toyota in California.

It is true that the share of the US manufacturing workforce has dropped steadily in the post-war period. But that is mostly because of large gains in productivity and a structural change in labour demand from manufacturing to services output. A shrinking manufacturing workforce is also a global phenomenon. Between 1995 and 2002, China, Japan, Brazil and many other economies lost more manufacturing jobs than the US, according to private sector research such as one by the US investment firm Alliance Capital in early 2004.

International trade development will certainly reshape the service sector. But just as low-wage China has not taken all of the US manufacturing capability, low-wage India is not going hollow-out America's service sector; nor will China in the future. Rather, US services producers will become more specialised, just like their manufacturing counterparts. No doubt there will be pains in this creative destruction process and the existing players will have to seek new ways for improving their efficiency and productivity.

Politicians fighting the irreversible outsourcing trend are denying both their own and the global economies the benefits of specialisation and gains from trade. With outsourcing, local consumers will be provided with cheaper services they want, while many local firms can also buy cheaper services and pass on the lower cost to consumers. US goods and services producers will also benefit from the extra export income prompted by outsourcing. Since outsourcing to China is counted in the US balance of payments as services import, the US must export something, and thus generate export revenues, to pay for such services. Meanwhile, the US dollars spent on China by the US firms to buy these services imports will eventually go back to America, either in the form of increased Chinese demand for US goods (American exports to China) or Chinese investment in the US. This is seen in the fact that services providers in low-wage China and other Asian economies require US high-tech equipment, computers and other high-value hardware and software. Further, they also buy legal, financial and market services from the US.

Despite the fears about the cross-border outsourcing threat, the US is still a major exporter of services, accounting for about a fifth of the world's services trade. Services amount to nearly 30% of the value of all US exports and are a key income earner. In 2003, for example, when the US had a US$550 billion goods trade deficit, she racked up almost a US$60 billion surplus in services trade. Indeed, the US services trade with the rest of the world is always in surplus, while her goods trade is in chronic deficit (Figure 3:7). The latter is a result of many factors, including foreign trade barriers, but also because of the insatiable US consumer demand for imports in recent years. Outsourcing to China and other Asian economies is not the culprit.

The real danger and the ugly face

It is a fact that the US remains economically and technologically well ahead of the developing world. Thus, the question is not whether outsourcing will erode America's competitive power. American politicians have to realise the massive changes in the global economy and adopt forward-looking policies to keep the US global economic and

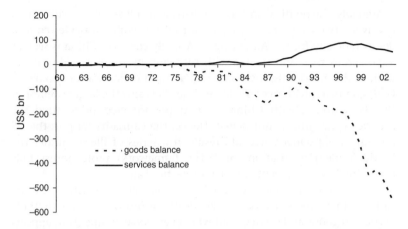

Figure 3:7 US trade balance
Source: CEIC

technology leadership, rather than inward-looking to demonise Chinese workers. Penalising firms for outsourcing is myopic. If outsourcing to China helps US firms to become more efficient, then forbidding them from doing so when their rivals are free to do it will only handicap the US competitive power.

The real danger of the misguided thinking and debate on cross-border outsourcing is not China's threat to hollow-out the US and other developed economies. It is the threat of the revival of protectionism. It is unfortunate to see the US, after promoting free trade for so many years, going back on her globalisation initiatives. Worse still, America's lead in the crooked discussion on the China threat could act as a pace setter for reviving anti-free trade/anti-outsourcing sentiment. This certainly does not help the globalisation effort, which is losing momentum already.

In the 1980s, a rising US trade deficit with Japan fuelled protectionist pressure in Congress. The then Regan administration introduced the so-called 'voluntary export restraints' (VER) on Japanese steel and cars. Under the VER, Japan 'voluntarily' agreed to limit her exports to America for some period of time. The agreement was reached after prolonged negotiations, in which Japanese exporters might have been threatened with much more severe restrictions if they did not limit their exports to the US. Given the element of coercion, it is indeed hypocritical to call these restrictions 'voluntary'. The Regan team also abandoned its laissez-faire currency policy, and engineered a sharp drop in the US dollar to help boost American exports.

Arguably, the political and economic risks are bigger today with China involved. Twenty years ago, Japan, for all her faults, was viewed as a democratic ally for the Americans in Asia. By contrast, China is seen as a dangerous rival and treated with suspicion by the Bush administration. In the mid-1980s, the US current account deficit was only 3.5% of GDP, compared with over 6% today. The US is also the largest debtor in the world today, with China as an important creditor to fund the American current account deficit. Hence, the China-bashing in the US presents a big danger. It could result in a series of illegal (under the World Trade Organisation, or WTO, framework) protectionist bills becoming laws, propagating global protectionism.

Many critics who attack outsourcing to China are hypocritical. On the surface, they are globalisation advocates wanting to remove trade barriers in goods and services. But whenever global competition appears to hurt their interests, they turn protective either through heavy subsidies (as is evident in the heavy US farm subsidies) or by creating other kinds of trade barriers, such as labour standards, patent rights and environmental laws. These measures are justified by nature. But the ways they are being exploited for implementation go against the spirit of free trade and the goals of globalisation to enhance aggregate economic well-being.

Crucially, they send the wrong signals to economies like China, which have undertaken a number of liberalisation measures and pushed ahead with structural reforms to integrate with the world system. Instead of pulling the world closer together, protectionist measures and the distorted motives behind them could put pressure on China and other Asian economies to create roadblocks for free trade negotiations and demand the application of a uniform policy for all WTO members. This will only lead to deadlock in trade negotiations.

These critics have also completely missed the real issue of the need to correct inequalities in bilateral trading relations and to address issues of market access. They are totally wrong-headed to restrict the ability of US companies to utilise the advantages offered by countries like China. Protectionism will only deprive American companies and, hence, the US economy, of international competitiveness. Open markets have proven to be beneficial for US firms; witness the sharp rise in American exports to China, which has jumped by 75% since China's entry to the WTO. US exports to China have also grown four times faster than her worldwide exports (Figure 3:8). Going back on the free trade initiatives will only deny the global system the benefits of expanded economic opportunities.

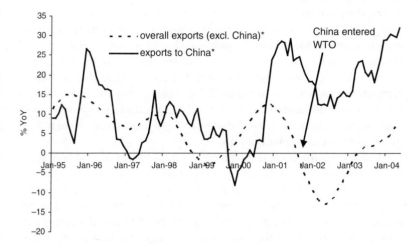

Figure 3:8 US export growth
* Series are based 12-month rolling sums
Source: CEIC

The damage on the US will also be far-reaching. Today's competitive environment requires companies to manage complex global supply chains where products often pass through a series of countries in a tightly organised process. This should help contribute to US global competitiveness because, as many US multinational corporations' CEOs can tell, US companies are leaders in supply chain and global organisational management. Barring them from organising themselves in the most efficient way possible, via outsourcing, will erode their competitive edge, drive them out of business and accelerate job losses in the economy in the end.

No one should dispute the commitment of lawmakers to long-term prosperity and job creation. But protectionism is not the answer. The inward-looking measures that many politicians have proposed are wrong for achieving those goals. The focus should be on promoting American goods and services in foreign markets and addressing market access barriers. In particular, the focus should be on pressing China to continue to open her markets and honour her WTO promises, but not to shut her off from the global market.

Some critics are hostile to free trade but they have also, ironically, ruled out protectionist solutions. Why? Presumably, they are trying to hide the fact that they have no solutions to offer. The poverty of free-trade critics is that they fail to bring any constructive ideas to the table. A careful look at the US official data makes one wonder that even these critics recognise that trade is not the problem. For example, in 2003, the US Bureau of Labour Statistics (BLS) reported that only 3% of the 1.2 million workers displaced as a result of extended layoffs were due to import competition (which accounted for 2% out of the 3%) and overseas relocation (which accounted for the rest of 1%). Another BLS survey on outsourcing in early 2004 showed that only 2.5% mass layoffs were related to the overseas movement of jobs.

Those who think trade is the problem for manufacturing should learn from the experience from the agricultural sector. The long-term decline in the share of agricultural employment in the US over the past decades was mostly due to productivity gains, not import competition. But distorted analysis and bad policy prescription have imposed a heavy cost on the US economy, in the form of massive agricultural subsidy. When the agriculture sector started shedding jobs due to its productivity gains, the US government levied a total US$40 billion of taxes from various sources to pay for the subsidies to US farmers. That is about 20% of gross farm income in 2003, according to the Organisation for Economic Cooperation and Development, and represents a hefty burden on American taxpayers and consumers.

Those critics should also heed the huge benefits accrued to the US economy of deregulation and trade liberalisation in the 1980s and 1990s. The US administration delivered the North American Free Trade Agreement (NAFTA), the Uruguay Round, China's entry into the WTO and free trade agreements with Singapore, Chile and Australia. US markets were thrown wide open as a result. Imports came rushing in, with Americans buying a record US$1.9 trillion from other countries in 2004. That amount was 16% of US GDP, almost double the 8.5% of a decade ago. Nevertheless, the US economy continued to strengthen. Output has grown by an average of 3.3% a year since 1994 when these free efforts started to accelerate. Despite a recession, the economy added almost 16 million jobs, and unemployment has been low. US productivity has surged under rising competition and technological improvement. No other major economy matches America's economic performance during this period of surging imports.

There is no doubt that foreign competition harms some American industries. However, imports are not poison to the overall economy. In fact, they have helped America grow and succeed. Bargain imports from China and other countries directly lower the US cost of living. This raises the average American's buying power, enabling them to spending on more goods and services with a given amount of money and thus benefiting local business. Meanwhile, cheaper inputs and components have helped US producers lower their costs. More crucially, competing against China and other low-cost rivals forces the US producers to cut cost and bolster efficiency. This explains the crucial link between rising imports and surging productivity.

Many critics have raised legitimate and crucial issues about wages and job creation in the US. So the debate should focus on strengthening workers in an increasingly competitive labour market. But instead, these critics seem more content on bashing the idea of free trade, picking on China and other low-cost Asian production bases, than on coming up with constructive solutions to the problems they identify. Rather than thinking hard about labour market policy, they go the easy way of putting the blame on China and putting forth reasons why free trade does not work because some conditions do not hold.

The hostility towards free trade and fears about China's threat are not only misplaced, they also prevent critics from coming up with positive ideas about how to improve economic performance. The focus on outsourcing and hollowing-out to China as a reason for the bad domestic labour market has not only distorted the economic truth, it has also led to a wrong diagnosis of the problem and misled policymakers to consider ill-advised solutions. The erroneous measures to save jobs that involve closing markets will only harm the US and global economies in the long run.

From a monetary perspective, the protectionist myopia presents a new danger to the American economy, which also has a far reaching impact on the global economy, given the importance of the US on the world stage. Cheap imports have helped keep inflationary pressure at bay in recent years. Since the 1997–1998 Asian crisis, when massive production capacity has been unleashed from China and other Asian economies, prices of many traded goods have fallen in the US: almost 90% for computers and peripherals, 70% for video equipment, over one-third for toys, 20% for women's outerwear, 17% for men's shirts and jumpers. Prices of non-tradeables have fared better: tuition fees up 52%, cable and satellite television up 41%, dental services up 38% and prescription drugs and medical supplies up 37%.

The point is that America could not have kept overall inflation low at an average of 2% in recent years without imports. Prices tamed by competition gave monetary policymakers more leeway to keep interest low to boost economic growth. Stifling imports, including outsourcing, would rob the US of their beneficial impact on inflation. Protectionism forces consumers and producers to pay more for foreign goods. Domestic firms raise their prices as import competition slackens.

Whatever fuels inflation heightens the need for monetary restraint. With the US markets open, inflation has been reasonably contained. If protectionism were to unleash inflationary pressures, the US Fed would have to fight back with tighter monetary policy, resulting in higher interest rates and a likely dampening of economic growth. Imports are not the enemy of jobs and growth; protectionist impulses are. A misdiagnosis of the modern economic paradigm and inward-looking policies can backfire to a detrimental outcome. The harmful impact will not be limited to the US, but also spread to the rest of the world if the largest economy runs into trouble.

4
The Next Asian Crisis: Made in China?

China's opaque system is not helping others to understand her role vis-à-vis the global economy. Even in basic economic information like GDP reports, China has failed to give a clear picture for assessment. For example, the national GDP growth data that Beijing announces every year never tally with the aggregate provincial growth data. Total provincial GDP is always higher than the national GDP. The disparity has grown by an ever-wider margin since 1995. In 2002, the provincial total output was reported 14% larger than the national output, and in 2004 that disparity grew to over 16%. As a result, the GDP growth rate of the provincial total is also higher than the national rate.

Hence, many people doubt the reliability of China's growth data. Is her growth really that robust to have dragged Asia into over-reliance on Chinese demand for growth? Is China's competitive stress really that strong to cause chaos to the regional economies? Or is she plagued by inherent economic woes masked by the inflated growth rate? Confusion and information inaccuracy have stretched Chinese officials' credibility in economic management. This mystery about China breeds fears about the potential eruption of China's hidden economic woes dragging the rest of Asia into another financial crisis. It also reinforces the worry about China's manufacturing clout overwhelming the world.

While it is possible for China to start a financial contagion, it is equally likely for any other large economy to trigger a regional or even global financial crisis. China, meanwhile, can be an opportunity to help Asia avoid another crisis. There are many other factors, both internal and external to Asia, which could bring about another regional crisis (see next chapter). Further, the fears about the explosion of China's economic woes, due to Beijing losing control of economic management, have been exaggerated.

The China trigger

Policymakers and industrialists are paying more attention to China not only because of the concern about Beijing's militarism or human rights records or the opening of the Chinese markets. They also fear that China's manufacturing clout is about to explode with accelerating vitality when the rest of the world is not prepared for it. Anecdotes are easy to find to support such jitter.

Those CEOs who visited manufacturing plants in the Pearl River Delta (PRD), one of the faster-growing regions in China, can attest that work ethics there is aggressive and often ruthless just for the sake of economic survival. For example, in an electronics manufacturing plant that I visited a few years ago, it hired over 30,000 workers, all young women who did not wear eyeglasses. Out of curiosity, I asked the manager if they had any workers with bad eyesight. He replied bluntly that he fired them when their eyesight went bad, noting that they could find other jobs elsewhere. The manager could not care much about the workers since there were lots of people wanting to work for the factory.

Such brutal practice is astonishing in the eyes of the industralised nations, and it would not be tolerated by the labour laws. A comparable precedent can only be found some 40 years back during Japan's postwar economic boom, or in Dickensian England (the dawn of the industrial revolution), or the 'robber baron' era in America, when cheap labour was exploited to work with new technology. But in Chinese boom towns like Shenzhen, Suzhou, Dalian and even Shanghai, where hundreds of millions of people eagerly flock to urban jobs from the rural areas, such practices are commonplace.

China not only has a glut of cheap and educable workers that gives her a strong competitive power, Chinese industrialists are also eager to learn and are uninhibited by complacency. They are like the eager Japanese executives back in the 1970s and early 1980s, who confronted every formidable challenge when they cracked the US market by pursuing persistently the ways to produce, innovate, and market. Today, many Japanese entrepreneurs have become complacent, and have tried to reckon all the reasons why they fail to achieve and put the blame on the economy and the government for their woes.

But the Chinese have picked up where the Japanese left off. They are developing innovative competitive businesses in a wide range of goods, such as vitamin supplements, foods, apparels, watches, consumer electronics and appliances, footwear, plywood and electronic and mechanical components. In the PRD, there are more than 60,000 electronics components suppliers sophisticated enough to make 'just in time' delivery of their wares to the local Japanese and Taiwanese manufacturers. In a nutshell, China is rapidly displacing industries that took other Asian countries 15 years or more to build.

What's more, within China, provinces compete against each other for foreign investment and markets. This inter-provincial competition will sustain, and even speed up, China's economic expansion beyond expectation. The world will have no choice but to expand trade with China, as consumers want China's affordable goods and producers need inexpensive components. This trend is already accelerating, as discussed in Chapter 2.

While this means that the global economy should be better off from trading with China, pessimists see China as a fierce economic competitor, perhaps the fiercest one since the US economic ascent at the turn of the last century. To them, the increasing economic weight of China, her inherent economic woes and Asia's increasing reliance on China for growth momentum are all crisis recipes for Asia with China acting as the catalyst – from both the demand and supply sides (see Chapter 1). Some even predict that the next Asian crisis would be 'made in China', and that it would be more severe than the previous one because unlike currency speculators who triggered the 1997–1998 crisis but left Asia swiftly, China will not go away.

Underscoring the pessimists' concerns is research by the US Cleveland-based Manufacturing Performance Institute (MPI), released in late 2004, which shows that China is closing manufacturing gaps with the West at a rate much faster than many believe possible. In some cases, the MPI argues, China is overtaking US plants in research, innovation and productivity. A notable piece of evidence comes from the rise of Shanghai-based Baoshan Iron & Steel (or Baosteel as it is locally known) to the global stage. A decade ago, the steel maker concentrated on making basic construction materials. Now it is making a sophisticated calibre of metal for car doors that even some global producers are not yet able to make. So foreign auto makers, like Volkswagen AG and General Motors Corp., are buying from Baosteel cold rolled steel plate for their vehicles.

Virtually the same thing is happening across China's many other industries. From clean coal to car doors to lingerie, Chinese companies have been investing in top-flight technology to climb the value chain, distancing themselves from low-cost producers elsewhere. In the brassiere industry for example, Chinese companies such as Top Form International Ltd are making curvy foam-padded bras from moulds for Victoria Secret and Playtex. These products are more technologically advanced than traditionally labour-intensive bras using hand-sewn padding inserts. Chinese firms' achievements in many other areas are equally impressive. With 21% of the world's output in personal computers, over 50% of the world's cameras and 30% of televisions, China's manufacturers are no longer trailing behind the West.

The MPI research found that Chinese manufacturers' on-time delivery rate was 99%, 3 percentage points higher than their US counterparts, and 98% of Chinese manufacturers' products met specifications on the first try, compared with 97% for US firms. Part of China's edge, the MPI report cited, is her low wages for engineers, so that companies can hire many of them around the clock to monitor and boost production.

However, on detailed examination, the MPI findings were distorted. China has become the world's leading site for manufacturing investment, everyone knows it. But what is often overlooked is that she is undergoing the same transformation from an agricultural to an industrial economy that Europe underwent some 150 years ago and that the Asian Tiger economies went through in the decades after World War II. But since China is industrialising at a time of globalisation, she is making a quantum leap that raises fears (and envy) of her seizing global industrial leadership. Critics thus charge that the world would soon be dominated by super-competitive Chinese firms. The latest MPI report seems to lend support to that view. But this is just not true.

The implications from the MPI report are crooked. First, the study compared a selection of Chinese firms, certified by the ISO 9001 quality standard, with much broader sample of US manufacturers. Of course, the results show China is better because the study compared apples (the leading edge of Chinese manufacturing) with oranges (the US average firms). Second, one-third of the Chinese manufacturers in the sample were joint ventures or wholly foreign-owned companies, while the US manufacturers in the study were local entities. More crucially, three-quarters of the surveyed factories in the US were over 20 years old, while over 75% of the Chinese plants were under 20 years old, with the bulk less than 10 years old. This makes the comparison not meaningful because the newer Chinese plants must have better information technology than the older US plants.

Hence, the survey does not really show that China's manufacturers are overtaking their US counterparts in efficiency gains. What the results show is the fact that the Chinese and American manufacturing sectors are at different stages of development. China's manufacturers are operating in a fast growing developing market and focus on adding capacity. But the US manufacturers are operating at high cost in mature markets and focus on improving efficiency by cutting costs. China is well on her way to become a manufacturing giant, but this does not mean she is overtaking the world.

The China cushion

There is no doubt that China's competitive stress is here to stay. But what those crisis mongers have ignored is the other side of the China story, namely her role as a cushion to any potential crisis. This cushion, ironically, stems from China's large demand for Asian exports. There can hardly be a globally-oriented investor who has failed to notice China's sharp import growth in recent years. With an average import growth rate of over 20% a year since 2000 (40% in 2003 and 36% in 2004), the Mainland has been one of the key drivers in world demand for steel, crude oil, cement, iron ore, and a host of other commodities and basic materials.

China's huge import demand is a result of a combination of her rapid economic growth, Beijing's trade liberalisation (which allows more imports to come into China) and limited domestic capacity expansion (until recently). All this has led to a steady increase in imports in China's major raw materials and material processing sectors. For minerals, chemicals, metals and fuels, import shares in China's total import demand (also known as import penetration) have risen sharply since 1994 (Figure 4:1). In aggregate, China's imports of raw material and fuels averaged a large 20% of total Chinese imports over the last decade, with the bulk of the increase in demand coming after 1998 when the Chinese economy outperformed the rest of Asia in the post-Asian crisis environment. But the agriculture sector has remained a laggard, though it will likely be a huge opportunity for foreign agriculture exporters in the coming years (see below).

Critics who fear that 'giant sucking sound' of jobs going to China would do well to heed the benefits of China, which could turn things around beyond imagination. Take for example the events in Minnesota, USA, in early 2004. When its EVTAC Mining Co. went broke in early 2003, costing hundreds of jobs, China came as an unexpected saviour. The company was re-opened in late 2003 as United Taconite under the part ownership of Lai-Wu, a Chinese steel company.

EVTAC, which produced iron ore pellets, was operating at less than 50% of its capacity before shutting down due to a lack of business. The iron ore industry in Minnesota, which supplies steelmakers, was suffering from demand deficiency. On the other hand, China was facing exactly

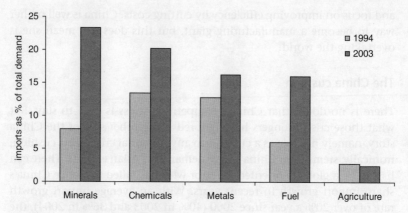

Figure 4:1 China's primary imports
Source: CEIC

the opposite problem – excess demand for raw materials. The Middle Kingdom's robust growth has left its producers unable to meet demand for minerals like iron ore.

But when East meets West, the supply–demand imbalance is resolved. Lai-Wu has agreed to take EVTAC's full production of pellets for the next ten years. More subtly, this also means the traditionally isolated US mining industry is shifting its orientation towards a global marketplace. China still wants iron ore from the US though she can get it from home and other closer suppliers like South Korea. That is because her demand is so huge that she needs whatever supply is available. China imported about 140 million metric tons of high-grade ore in 2003, according to industry estimates. That amount was more than double what all six mines in Minnesota and two mines in Michigan could produce in full capacity.

The moral of the story is that Chinese growth is not necessarily a threat to other economies. Rather, it can create jobs and profits for them. The China-benefit all comes down to one simple fundamental issue – the US comparative advantage in producing high-grade ore. According to industry research, China need higher-grade ore than her domestic mines can produce. While Chinese ore is mostly between 30–40% iron, US taconite pellets may run to 65%. China's steel industry was largely self-sufficient until its producers realised that they could meet the rapid rising demand for steel by importing high-grade iron ore that would smelt better in existing blast furnaces. This should prompt the US producers to focus on greater value-added products. This case also shows that China's rising economic weight will give foreign suppliers an incentive to move up the value chain and make high-end goods.

Over to Japan, it is a similar story. China has given Japanese manufacturing a big lift instead of just hollowing it out. If the pessimists were right, you would not expect Hitachi Construction Machinery Co. to be hiring more workers to make power shovels in Japan, where labour cost is sky-high and demand for construction has dwindled due to the prolonged economic slump since 1990. Indeed, the company posted a loss in 2001, cut its work force and started to move production to China. But things were dramatically different in 2004, when Hitachi Construction's two factories were so busy that it had boosted overtime and added workers. The company turned in a profit in its 2003 fiscal year, which ended in March 2004. The reason for its turnaround was China – the same force that critics see pulling jobs away from Japan.

In general, China has not only offered an expanded market opportunity to Japanese manufacturers, her competitive stress has also pushed many Japanese firms to restructure for greater efficiency. On the demand side, robust Chinese growth is creating such a construction boom that Hitachi Construction cannot make enough power shovels in its plants in China. So it has to ship them from its factories in Japan. On the restructuring side, Chinese competition has prompted years of cost-cutting in Japan, allowing many Japanese firms to keep high-value manufacturing at home. Big manufacturers, like Hitachi Construction and consumer-electronics giant Matsushita Electric Industrial Co., have boosted efficiency and can now make complex goods as economically in Japan as they can overseas.

Meanwhile, Japanese firms producing in China are reaping double gains. As they set up factories there to make everything from mobile phones to clothes irons, fans and rice cookers, almost half of the goods are sold to China's domestic market, and the rest are exported. But the equipment and components used in these China-based factories mostly come from Japan, creating demand for more Japanese products (exports).

Like most advanced economies, Japan is losing manufacturing jobs, as they migrate to the service sector and overseas. But all is not doomed for manufacturing. Although simple manufacturing work, like circuit boards for mobile phones, are being made in China, high value-added work, like multilayer boards for advanced handsets, still stay in Japan. Large Japanese manufacturers are trying to keep in Japan the production of hard-to-make key parts that needs constant upgrade. On a positive note, the perceived China threat is a blessing in disguise, as it forces Japan to change and focus on production where her comparative advantage lies. That China threat has also acted as an external discipline to force Japan to overcome thick domestic reform inertia and push through the much needed creative destruction, which will probably be very difficult to carry out without the China shock.

Increasing trade and investment with China are giving Japan additional growth sources. This structural change in Japan's external environment could be a rejuvenating factor for sustaining Japan's long-term economic growth. China has become an increasingly important export market for Japan. Japan's export share to China (as a percentage of her total exports) has double to almost 20% since the early 1990s, while the export share to the US market has fallen to 24% from almost 40% (Figure 4:2).

Some may wonder if Japan's exports are just shifting to China from the US market, so that the total export cake is not growing for Japan. Japan's total exports and trade surplus have been growing at an average of 3% and 5% a year, respectively, since 1990. At the same time, the share of trade with China has been rising. This suggests that Japan's exports to China are not substituting for exports to other major markets, especially the US. It is estimated that exports to China contributed to almost all of Japanese export growth in 2003, and accounted for a third of Japanese GDP growth that year.

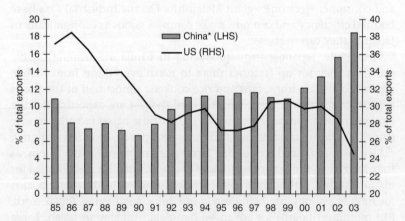

Figure 4:2 Japan's exports to China and the US
* Includes Mainland China and HK
Source: CEIC

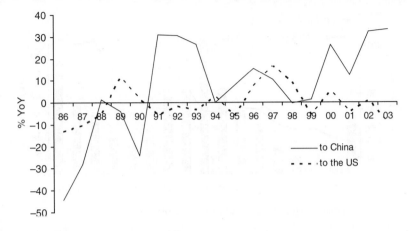

Figure 4:3 Japan's export growth
Source: CEIC

Further, most of Japan's growth of exports to China is linked to Chinese exports to third markets. This is reflected by the divergence between the export growth to China (which has been rising steadily) and the US (which has been stagnant with a downward bias) (Figure 4:3). This divergence suggests that a substantial share of exports, like electronics and electrical goods, are headed for China for reprocessing for final export markets like the US. This also means the vulnerability of Japan's export, and hence economic growth, has been reduced by China serving as a conduit for Japan to sell into the global market at competitive prices.

Meanwhile, the competitive stress from China has forced many Japanese corporations to become adaptive about investing in China. Indeed, Japanese direct investment in China has been growing again after its first wave in the 1990s, and income from overseas investment has kept rising (Figure 4:4). The progression of production outsourcing to China has spurred many Japanese firms to invest locally in creation of high-tech products. Both increased trade and investment with China suggest that Japan has found a new source of growth and income, underscoring Japan's transformation to sustainable long-term growth.

A new cushion – agriculture demand

It is very likely that China's agriculture sector will provide another big benefit for Asian and global exporters in the coming years, reinforcing

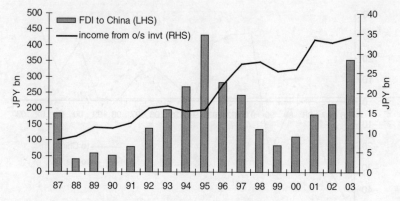

Figure 4:4 Japan's FDI to China and foreign income
Source: CEIC

China's role as an opportunity for Asia rather than a trigger for another crisis. Currently, the agricultural sector remains closed to outsiders, with imports of foreign agricultural products accounting for less than 3% of total domestic consumption in the past decade (see Figure 4:1 above). China's agricultural imports even seem to be insensitive to cyclical demand. For example, during the peak of the recent growth cycle in 2003 when robust demand should have sucked in massive imports, the volume of total agricultural import grew by only 12% on a year-on-year basis. This is much less than the 30% average growth rate for other commodity, basic materials and fuel items (Figure 4:5).

There are two main reasons for China's sluggish agriculture imports. First, throughout China, and until recently, the regional governments have pursued self-sufficient food policies. They have kept most land in agricultural use and boosted grain output via subsidies and minimum grain prices above market clearing levels. Second, most of the demand growth in recent years has come from capital investment in steel, semiconductors, energy, construction, and other growth industrial sectors, or household spending on durables such as household and autos. As income and wealth rise, increasing demand is being shifted to non-subsistence goods so that food (or in general agricultural) demand has lagged overall income growth by a wide margin.

But the laggard situation in China's agricultural imports is about to change fairly rapidly. China could well emerge as a potent driver in global agricultural markets in the coming years. The strong rise in farm product prices and rural income since 2003 is no coincident. It is likely

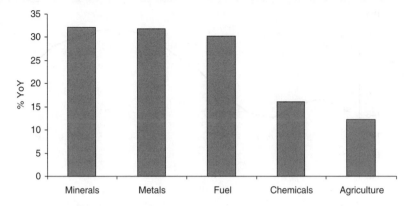

Figure 4:5 China's import volume growth, 2003
Source: CEIC

the beginning of a new long-term trend. Secular forces, including rising demand, falling supply and trade liberalisation in the agricultural sector, are pushing up agricultural prices. There has been a marked shift in Chinese demand towards higher-calorie foods in recent years, driven by rapid income growth. Per capita consumption of meat and dairy products has soared. Demand for processed foodstuffs, such as snack items and fast food, has also risen. All this means much higher usage of feedgrains and vegetable oils, items that China needs to import.

On the back of this long-term rise in demand for better foods is falling net supply of agricultural land. Liberalisation of land-use policies and rapid urbanisation have been taking land away from agricultural use at an accelerating pace in recent years. This has resulted in a steady drop in sown acreage since 1999 (Figure 4:6). Meanwhile, the shift in food consumption patterns, due to rising income, has led to a sharp reallocation of the remaining agricultural land supply away from land-intensive grains and towards higher value-added activities such as dairy, animal husbandry, fruits and vegetables (Table 4:1). The share of gain crops in the total sown area has thus dropped steadily since the late 1990s (Figure 4:7).

These trends of declining supply of arable land and falling grain output are likely to continue in the years ahead. They imply that food prices in China will rise further, suggesting further rise in rural income and, hence, sharp acceleration in agricultural imports. The experience of agricultural import development in other economies may shed some light on how much China's agricultural imports will grow in the coming years.

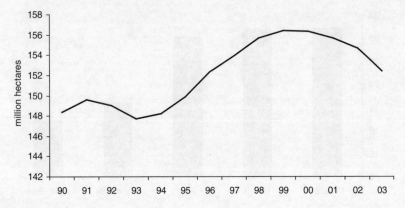

Figure 4:6 Sown area droppage
Source: CEIC

Table 4:1 China's agricultural output growth (year-on-year change, 2003)

milk	88.6%
rapeseeds	31.2%
fruits	28.4%
meat	21.5%
sugarcane	14.4%
beans	13.5%
corn	11.0%
cotton	5.6%
rice	−20.0%
wheat	−29.8%

Production focusing on less land-intensive and higher value-added products.

Source: CIEC

It is normal for emerging markets to have low agricultural imports at the early stage of economic development, due to their governments' self-sufficient food policy and low income weak demand. China is no exception. The Middle Kingdom's agricultural imports account for about 4% of domestic agricultural output. This is similar to the share in India, Indonesia and Brazil. However, the share in developed economies is far larger; about 36% in the EU and the US and 65% in Japan.

What this means is that as an economy moves from a developing to developed stage, demand for agricultural products and imports will rise due to higher affordability of more and better foods. China is expected

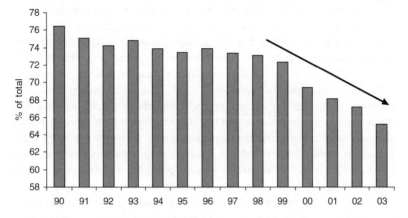

Figure 4:7 Share of grains in total farm output
Source: CEIC

to see a sharp rise in agricultural imports in the coming years, with a rate of increase much faster than normally expected. This is because she has the highest rate of urbanisation and industrialisation growth among emerging economies. It will not be surprising to see China begin to move towards the import shares seen in the developed economies in the next couple of decades.

To put some numbers in the perspective, assume China significantly increases her foodstuff and agricultural imports in the next 20 years, say by 5-fold from the current 3% or so to 15% of total domestic consumption. This share is higher than a typical emerging market economy but still much lower than those seen in the developed economies. If China's GDP grows by a trend rate of 7% a year, some industry estimates project that China's agricultural imports would grow by over 30% through the end of this decade. And this import demand should be focused on grain crops, like wheat, rice and corn. The projection is subject to uncertainty and only time will tell how things will turn out. But with rising demand, tightening supply and market opening for commodity imports, it seems very likely that China's agricultural imports are set to embark on an accelerating trend in the years to come. As and when that happens, the world's exporters are certainly going to benefit.

Fundamentals versus bubble

Many also fear that the Chinese authorities have lost control of the economy, so that its inherent woes will erupt one day, dragging the rest of Asia into chaos. In particular, some fear that China had built up a stronger-than-ever economic bubble in 2003, paving the way for an economic disaster to happen later. To clearly understand this concern, one needs to distinguish between economic overheating and a bubble. The former refers to an unsustainable growth pace, which will eventually slow down but with no economic crash. The latter means that asset prices or economic capacity have risen way above the underlying fundamentals so that a collapse will become unavoidable. Judging from the surging investment growth rates and surging property prices in some key cities, it was likely that the Chinese economy was overheated in 2003 and early 2004. But there was no proof for a bubble that would burst and send seismic waves across Asia in the coming years.

Those who are concerned about China building a bubble economy argue that the Middle Kingdom's investment as a share of GDP has risen higher than the 1993–1994 peak, with a particular surge in 2003 when fixed-asset investment soared by 28% year-on-year. This compared with an average of 13.3% a year between 2000 and 2002 and 9.3% a year between 1997 and 1999. But just looking at the soaring investment growth does not necessarily point to a bubble. Other than the lack of justification by economic fundamentals, another pre-condition for a bubble is that there is a prevalent surge in economic and/or financial activities across the system. However, nearly all the surge in the investment-to-GDP ratio from 1997 to 2003 came from government infrastructure spending and housing construction and a few other sectors like steel, cement, aluminium, autos and petro-chemicals. The bulk of the economy remained cool, with some sectors like manufacturing still suffering from excess-capacity. This suggests that the investment surge in recent years was not broadly based.

A broad-based demand surge that creates speculative behaviour is the classic determinant of an economic bubble, where demand diverges sharply from underlying fundamentals for a sustained period. A typical gauge of speculation is asset price inflation, though surging goods price inflation is also reflective of rampant speculation behaviour. But China has not had inflation since mid-1998. In fact, retail prices fell every year between 1998 and 2003. Overall consumer prices just emerged from deflation in October 2003 after almost six years of falling prices. The recent revival in inflation is mild, averaging 2.8% between 2004 and early 2005, and is nowhere near the frenzied inflation rates seen in the 1990 peaks (Figure 4:8). Moreover, unlike the last bubble periods, consumer prices in this cycle are being pushed up by food and raw material prices, but not pulled up by excessive money growth feeding surging demand.

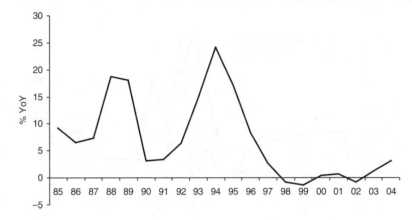

Figure 4:8 Consumer price inflation
Source: CEIC

One big worry about China's economic bubble is property prices, which have been surging at high double-digit rates in some cities since 2003. Yet, a detailed examination shows no evidence for a national property bubble. The overheated spots are concentrated in a few cities, notably Shanghai and Qingdao. If there were a bubble, property prices should be surging with little fundamental support. Like in the early to mid-1990s, there was a real estate mania driven by rampant speculation in high-end office buildings, hotels and shopping centres. There was virtually no residential market then since housing was not privatised until the housing reform in 1998.

While official property price data are not available for the nation before 1998, we can approximate property market activity with the gross output value of construction. Evidence shows that there was indeed a sharp surge in building activity in the early 1990s (Figure 4:9), with construction surging 43% a year in 1993 from just 3.7% in 1990. But in the recent 2002–2005 cycle, construction output has averaged only 18% a year since 2000, about the average seen in the 1980s.

Even in Shanghai, the city's building data shows that the increase in construction output has been nowhere near the frenzied rates seen in the mid-1990s (Figure 4:9). While the gross construction value may have risen sharply through the years, so has GDP, so that the construction value-to-GDP ratios for both the nation and Shanghai have risen at a reasonable pace (13 percentage points altogether in the past 24 years). Further, Shanghai's 49% cumulative gains in property prices between

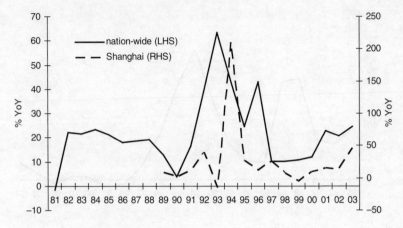

Figure 4:9 Gross construction value
Source: CEIC

2002 and early 2005 were not out of line with other major markets, with UK prices up by 49%, Spain by 53%, Australia by 56%, Canada by 33% and the US by a lesser extent of 30% in the same period.

Meanwhile, there is no evidence for an excessive rise in property prices on a national basis. For example, while property prices in Shanghai and Qingdao had outpaced the national average between 2001 and 2004, in particular rising at an annual average of 22% and 17% respectively, in 2003 and 2004, nation-wide property prices had only risen by an average of 7% a year in the same period (Figure 4:10).

Recall that an asset bubble is defined as a rise in asset prices in excess of fundamental support. But there are stronger fundamental reasons for the strong rise in property prices in the 2002–2005 cycle, so that even in the context of Shanghai where property prices have risen the fastest, it is not sure if a bubble can be properly defined.

This time around, activities are focused on the residential market, as home ownership is now clearer and property rights are better defined than in the early 1990s. Hence, both buyer and seller behaviour is more rational. Beijing launched the housing privatisation programme in 1998 and fully implemented it in 2000. This is a long-term boost for housing demand. Underscoring housing affordability is strong income growth. Between 1993 and 2003, per capital GDP soared by 209% while per capital saving (as measured by the saving deposits in the system) surged by 524%. In Shanghai, strong income growth (which has outpaced the national growth rate by an average of 3 percentage points since the

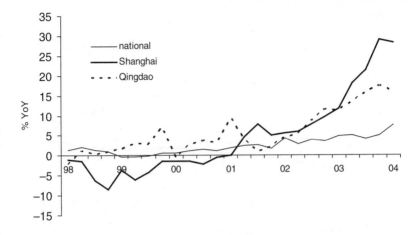

Figure 4:10 Property prices
Source: CEIC

mid-1990s) has provided a strong support for property demand, justifying at least part of the faster-than-average rise in its property prices.

Income growth is expected to remain robust in the medium-term, as the market segment of the economy continues to grow and boost employment and private sector income. Indeed, private sector employment (private + foreign enterprises + self employed) has grown steadily over the past decade, while the state sector has declined (Figure 4:11). There are now over 52 million people working in the private sector, accounting for over 20% of the total urban workforce and up from 7% ten years ago. This group of people has been the major buying force of property.

Crucially, financial liberalisation is enabling mortgage lending for the first time. From near zero a few years ago, mortgage lending has grown swiftly, doubling every year on average between 1997 and 2003. Despite its robust growth, the mortgage market is still in its infancy, representing less than 9% of total lending, well below other countries. Both regulators and Chinese banks will remain keen on growing mortgage lending because of its low risk and stable return. Most of those taking out a mortgage are first-time borrowers, and delinquency rates are low at about 0.5% compared with at least 25% of corporate default rates. All this means that there is a long way for the Chinese mortgage market to grow, lending a long-term support to property demand.

Those who are concerned about a property bubble should also note that China's full real estate demand has yet to peak because the country's rapid industrialisation has not led to a correspondingly rapid

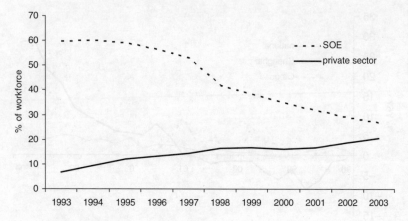

Figure 4:11 China's employment by sector
Source: CEIC

pace of urbanisation. The current urbanisation rate, estimated at about 40% (up from 28% ten years ago), is low by international standards. It is a legacy of Beijing's restrictive *hu kou* system, which requires everyone to register at their birthplace. People who leave their places of registration are usually denied all social benefits and deemed illegal residents in their new location.

In the last decade or so, however, the central government has gradually relaxed *hu kou* restrictions, and some localities have made it easier for migrants to gain benefits and even residency status. The thriving private sector, which provides jobs and benefits, also encourages people to leave their birthplace by offering higher compensation and better prospects. There were about 99 million rural residents working in urban jobs in 2003. By 2020, the World Bank estimates that some 300–400 million rural workers are expected to have moved to China's cities and towns. As China's urbanisation speeds up, so will housing demand.

All these suggest that there are solid reasons for supporting a strong property market, and bubbly conditions are confined to some cities only. What about financial asset prices? Here, we do not see excessive price increases either (Figure 4:12). After rising in the late 1990s, and despite the strong run-up in property prices in some cities in recent years, the domestic A-share stock index has not seen a sustained ascent. In fact, the stock market (as represented by the Shanghai A-share index) fell by 30% in autumn 2004 from its high point reached in mid-2001. So there is no evidence for a financial market bubble.

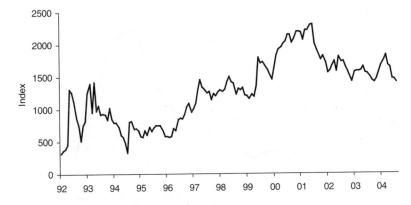

Figure 4:12 Shanghai A-share index
Source: CEIC

Bubbles could also be seen in real economic activity, not just in asset prices. If there an economic bubble had developed in 2002–2003, as many feared, we should have seen substantial excessive capacity build-up, as happened between 1992 and 1995, which led to widespread industrial glut, layoffs and a sharp fall in profits in the second half of the 1990s. A gauge of capacity creation is the changes in inventory. The last upturn (1992–1995) saw a big rise in inventories across the economy. But in this cycle there is hardly any evidence of excessive inventory build-up (Figure 4:13), except in a few sectors like steel, chemicals and autos. The RMB1.85 bn of inventory increase in 2003 amounted to only 0.02% of GDP, the smallest rise in more than 20 years.

In a nutshell, there is a big difference between China's economic activity in this economic cycle and that of a decade ago. The soaring growth rates in the 1990s were boosted by uncontrolled credit creation, which led to excessive demand growth and rampant inflation. There was not as much underlying fundamental support then as there is today – income growth, wealth accumulation, growth of the middle class, accelerating urbanisation, housing reform and financial liberalisation. Hence, when once all the excess capacity came online and Beijing started to clamp down on the runaway demand growth, the economy came crashing down.

However, genuine demand growth supported the 2002–2003 economic upturn and accounted for the lack of rampant speculative prices and economic behaviour in this cycle. Economic liberalisation in recent years has created solid demand growth. Rapid urbanisation and wage

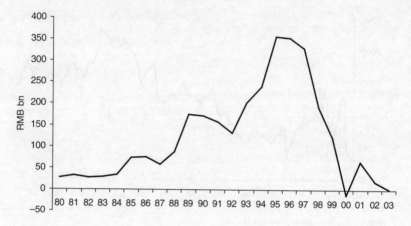

Figure 4:13 Change in inventories
Source: CEIC

growth has sharply increased the size of the domestic consumer market. Privatisation of housing stock and infrastructure construction and the introduction of consumer finance markets have created wealth and expanded individual demand for autos and housing. Finally, exports now account for a much bigger share of GDP (40% today compared with only 15% in the early 1990s), providing a bigger external boost to aggregate demand for China's economic growth.

Not losing control

The point is that China's economy is not as imbalanced today as it was in the 1990s. But there are still concerns about the authorities losing control of the economy, which will eventually lead to economic chaos infecting the rest of Asia. The most common fear is significant hot money inflows flooding the Chinese banking system in ever-increasing amounts, and the People's Bank of China (PBoC), the central bank, is unable to contain the resultant surge in domestic liquidity.[1] When banks are flooded with cash, the worry goes, they would be free to entertain local government demand for inefficient investment projects through rampant credit growth.

While capital flows into China did rise sharply in 2003 and 2004, largely due to mounting speculation on RMB revaluation, there was no evidence that they were flooding into the economy in uncontrollable amounts. China keeps formal restrictions on capital movement.

This does not mean that the capital controls are air-tight, but it does suggest that there are practical limits to the size and number of informal capital transactions. Experience also shows that the controls are effective when the Chinese authorities strictly enforce the rules.

Some argue that the large portfolio inflows for speculating on RMB revaluation in 2003 and 2004 had fuelled China's real estate bubble, stretching the authorities' ability to control the economy. This hot money was parked in Chinese assets including bank deposits and property assets. Once the speculative fever was over, massive withdrawal of hot money could crush the real estate market, creating a domino effect on the economy.

Hot money inflow was estimated at US$172 bn in 2004 (up 421% from 2001). Some industry players estimated that about a third of this hot money (or US$57 bn) were put into property speculation. This would be equivalent to about 40% of China's total real estate investment in 2004. But this amount is most likely to be overstated. It is simply impossible for overseas speculators to account for 40% of China's real estate transactions. Chinese property agencies admitted that such a huge amount of speculative fund was wishful thinking. Meanwhile, the big jump in bank deposit growth suggested that a lot of money was parked in liquid funds for pure RMB speculation. For example, time deposits in Chinese banks grew by an average of almost 30% a year and savings deposits by almost 20% a year in 2003 and 2004. These were about 10 percentage points higher than their long-term average growth rates. In a nutshell, currency speculators are unlikely to put their funds in the less liquid real estate market.

More fundamentally, the PBoC has not lost control of monetary policy. It if had, we should see China's monetary growth surging out of control under the current RMB regime. This is because foreign exchange reserves are part of a country's monetary base. Under China's de facto fixed exchange rate system, any capital inflow that swells the foreign reserves should lead to surging domestic money growth (see note 1). But this has not been the case in China; rapid foreign reserve accumulation since 2001 has not resulted in surging base money growth (Figure 4:14). Foreign exchange has been rising at an annual rate of 30% since 2001, so in principle this should push up money supply growth by the same rate. But it has not. The reason is that the PBoC has 'sterilised' most of the foreign exchange inflows through domestic monetary operations, or sales of government bonds.[2]

Bond issuance is only one of the sterilisation tools the PBoC uses, and it is not necessarily the most crucial one. Private analysts estimate that

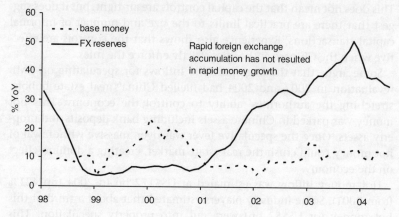

Figure 4:14 Foreign reserve and base money growth
Source: CEIC

bond issuance roughly accounted for about one-third of the PBoC's sterilisation operations in recent years, while reserve requirements increase accounted for another one-third. The rest is a combination of other measures, such as allowing the outstanding refinance credit to the banking system to mature and moral suasion to influence credit growth and allocation.

Beijing has also relied on administrative measures to fine tune the economy, hitting the overheated sectors with selective tightening measures while sparing the other parts. For example, a series of selective measures were used to slow the uneven economic boom in 2003 and 2004. The PBoC raised capital requirements for new property development projects and investment in the steel, cement and heavy chemical sectors. It also raised interest rates on loans for buying properties other than primary residences and investment in the other overheated sectors, like steel, aluminium and autos.

Beijing's reliance on administrative means to control the economy reflects the fact that the market mechanism is not fully functional in allocating capital and investment in China. Arguably, the administrative measures are proper economic management tools as long as China has a hybrid economic system (with the coexistence of command and market mechanisms). This can be seen in the composition of China's fixed-asset investment, which was the major economic growth driver between 2001 and 2003 with excessive growth rates. About 60% of fixed-asset investment came from the state-owned enterprises (SOEs)

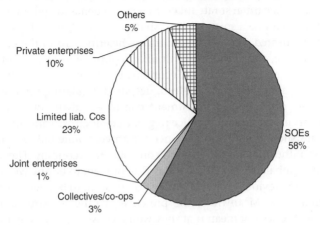

Figure 4:15 Fixed-asset investment (2004)
Source: CEIC

(Figure 4:15). These investments were not sensitive to interest rate movement under market conditions, since they were mostly politically driven. Only administrative curbs, such as capital rationing, discriminatory capital requirements and moral suasion, can have a real impact on their growth. Beijing's selective tightening efforts to cool the economic hot spots between 2003 and 2004 had shown effective results, as both GDP growth and loans to the overheated sectors had fallen from their excessive growth rates in late 2004 and early 2005.

Meanwhile, the PBoC is committed to a strategy of gradual financial liberalisation to improve demand management policy. In October 2004, it abolished the upper limits on the interest rates for bank loans and allowed commercial banks to set deposit rates according to market conditions. The move was a strong signal to begin the transition from administrative measures to a greater role for market-based tools such as interest rates. With interest rates in the policy tool kit, which are more flexible in terms of timing and magnitude of adjustment, future policy adjustments should be less blunt and should, thus, help reduce economic volatility.

The removal of the lending rate ceiling is clearly a sign of the authorities' commitment to market-based pricing of credit as a structural goal. But the PBoC is still not in a hurry to rush policy liberalisation since it takes time for the state to cede control of the economy. As long as the state sector is driving non-market demand and generating uneven inflation pressures in China's diverse economy, relying on market-based policy tools, like interest rate hikes, to regulate demand and inflationary pressures would be a mistake. Any sharp rate hikes to cool the policy-driven overheated sectors would hurt the healthy parts of the economy as well. Hence, the authorities will likely continue to rely on administrative measures to fine tune the economy until the market segment has grown to a dominant force. Indeed, despite deregulating interest rates, Beijing has not removed investment controls, and the PBoC has not stopped its moral suasion practice to guide credit growth and allocation.

In a nutshell, there is no evidence for an economic bubble, and the Chinese authorities are still in good control of the economy. The macro-economic imbalances in China today do not seem to be any worse than those in the previous cycles, and they do not seem to be aggravating the structural woes. Meanwhile, the presence of inherent structural economic woes does not mean that they would cause the economy to crash in the adjustment process.

The US has many economic problems too, the most prominent one being her chronic and huge current account deficit (standing at over 5% of GDP since the turn of the millennium, over 6% in 2004[3]). Many analysts have been predicting for a long time that an adjustment of the deficit would involve sharp contraction of the US economy, sending a negative shock to the world economy. But the prediction has failed to materialise because there are also structural improvements that help keep public confidence in the US economy.

Granted, the comparison between the Chinese and US economies is a loose one, since they are in different development stages. But the point is that as long as there is structural progress that is being recognised, the economic cleansing process does not have to end with dire consequences. The US current account deficit may never go back to zero for the adjustment process to be completed, as other positive aspects in the US economy can keep investors' confidence high in US assets. Likewise, China's structural woes may not go away in the medium-term but the structural adjustment does not have to end in an economic disaster, as many pessimists have argued. The fear of a made-in-China Asian crisis has been exaggerated, and the conspiracy theory of China taking over the global economy and triggering another financial crisis does not stand up for scrutiny.

5
The Next Asian Crisis: Self-inflicted?

Many Asian economies are plagued by internal structural faults, which could trigger, or act as a catalyst for igniting, a financial crisis in the medium-term. One big worry is Asia's fiscal problems, which are similar to almost all emerging market crises in recent history. Another concern is the massive foreign exchange reserves that Asian central banks have built up since the 1997–1998 regional crisis. Far from being a sign of economic strength, the Asian Development Bank (ADB) warned in 2004 that Asia's foreign reserves accumulation had reached unhealthy levels that could trigger another financial crisis. If and when significant capital outflow happens, that resultant loss of foreign reserves will erode public confidence in the country's ability to repay its debts. This will, in turn, worsen the inherent fiscal woes, deepening and prolonging the crisis.

That is not all, as despite some reform efforts after the 1997–1998 regional crisis, Asia's economic restructuring has, arguably, been insufficient relative to the amount of structural faults in the system. The 'V' shape output rebound in the two years after the regional crisis had either masked the urgency for structural reforms in some Asian economies or eroded the reform resolve in others after their good start. As a result, many Asian economies are stuck with weak domestic growth dynamics, which only make them vulnerable to the outbreak of another crisis.

The fiscal time bomb

Many investors and policymakers in Asia still focus on anticipating or preventing a crisis of the type that happened in 1997–1998. They are missing something crucial. The next Asian crisis, if it hits, could be quite different from that in 1997–1998, as it would likely be sparked by fiscal worries. To fund the large and rising fiscal deficits, the regional governments have run up large public sector debts. Many of them have a debt-to-GDP ratio above the 'comfort zone', defined by the International Monetary Fund (IMF) as between 25% and 50% of GDP. By looking at recent experiences in the emerging markets, the IMF reckons that the probability of a financial crisis erupting rises sharply as a country's public debt-to-GDP ratio rises above that range.

From a crisis point of view, the trouble with a large and rising fiscal deficit is that it erodes confidence in the government's ability to repay its debt. Overall, Asia has a very high public sector debt, driven by the regional governments' rising budget deficits. A fiscal deficit should not be a worry if it is cyclical in nature; that is if it goes away when the economy improves. But most of Asia's fiscal deficit is structural, which means that the deficit is entrenched in the system disregarding the economic ups and downs.

The last Asian crisis was unusual when compared with experience in other emerging markets. It was caused by prolonged asset bubble build-up and current account deficits, funded by short-term foreign borrowing with risk distorted/minimised by fixed exchange rates on the back of bad banking sectors. In the emerging markets in Eastern Europe and Latin America, economic crises were generally triggered by fiscal woes. Though fixed exchange rates and huge foreign borrowing aggravated these crises in many cases, worries about sovereign debt default were central to all crises outside Asia in the past decade. Costly debt defaults and distressed debt restructuring followed from these crises in Argentina, Ecuador, Russia and Ukraine.

So how bad is Asia's fiscal problem and how will it fare going forward? Gross non-financial public sector debt[1] in Asia, excluding Japan, averaged 60% of GDP in 2003, up sharply from 35% in 1995 (Figure 5:1). The most indebted governments were the Philippines (112%), Singapore[2] (102%), Indonesia (78%) and India (76%). Indonesia, Korea, Malaysia, the Philippines and Thailand have seen the biggest rise in public-sector debt since 1995, mainly because of the hefty outlays for recapitalising their banking sectors after the Asian crisis.

Behind this large debt build-up is rising fiscal deficits, especially between 2000 and 2003, except for Korea. On average, aggregate fiscal deficit in Asia rose from a roughly balanced position before the Asian crisis to about 3% of GDP in 2003. This may not sound too alarming yet because a deficit-to-GDP ratio of 3% is seen as sustainable. Beyond that 3% threshold, experience shows that economic dislocations will emerge. The problem with Asia is that its fiscal deficit dynamics seem to get worse going forward as most of the deficits are structural. This means

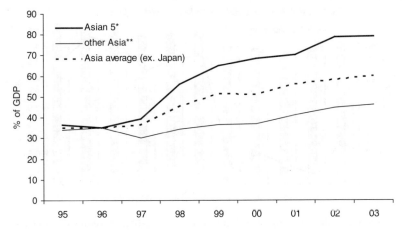

Figure 5:1 Asia's public debt
* Asian 5: Indonesia, Korea, Malaysia, Philippines, Thailand
** Other Asia: China, Hong Kong, India, Singapore, Taiwan
Source: CEIC

that even if Asian growth bounces back, the budget deficits will not go away. That raises the risk of the fiscal deficits eventually overshooting the 3% threshold.

Part of the problem stemmed from post-crisis banking sector recapitalisation, which was largely funded by borrowing. About one-third of the increase in Asia's fiscal deficit comes from interest payments to government debts. Another problem is Asia's low tax revenue relative to GDP. This has sharply reduced the regional governments' fiscal flexibility to deal with economic fluctuations in the face of both cyclical and structural headwinds. Hong Kong and Singapore went through the worst deterioration in their public finances since the 1997–1998 regional crisis, as their significant economic contraction weighed heavily on their fiscal budgets.

However, the crux of Asia's fiscal problem comes from rising public spending, which has persistently outgrown fiscal revenues since the late 1990s. Notably, the region's fiscal deficit jumped from less than 1% of GDP after the Asian crisis to over 3% (Figure 5:2), as a result of anti-recession public spending and hefty outlays on financial reconstruction programmes. Non-interest spending has risen strongly especially in China, Hong Kong, Malaysia and Singapore. Rising spending on social services has also been a key source of spending increase in all economies in recent years. This is non-discretionary spending and is thus difficult to cut.

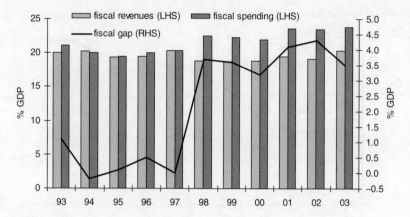

Figure 5:2 Asia's growing fiscal gap (fiscal spending–fiscal revenue as % of GDP)
Source: CEIC

There is also the question about the regional governments' will to control their fiscal spending. In China, the main concern is that if Beijing is willing to tolerate a rising budget deficit[3] when the economy is growing at an average of 8% a year, it is hardly likely to have the will to rein in spending during periods of slower growth. That raises the spectre of public spending spiralling out of control. Official data shows that China's fiscal spending amounted to RMB2.5 trillion in 2003 (or 21% of GDP), up from RMB793 billion (or 11.6% of GDP) in 1996. That was supposedly all in the name of salvaging the economy in the aftermath of the Asian crisis in 1997–1998 and the bursting of the global IT bubble in 2001. But no one knows for sure if that was the real reason or if bureaucrats were just caught up in the habit of runaway spending.

Even in the fiscally conservative Hong Kong, it seems that the government's attitude towards public spending has changed. The rise in the fiscal deficit after the 1997–1998 regional crisis reflects the government's unwillingness to tolerate economic pains on the back of deflation under the currency link regime.[4] Without high inflation in its post-bubble economic transformation, the days of rampant property price growth are gone for Hong Kong. Since land premiums and stamp duties from property transactions used to account for over a third of total fiscal revenue, the collapse of the property market since the Asian crisis has hurt fiscal revenue intake significantly. The shrinkage in the local property market as a source of fiscal revenue suggests that Hong Kong's budget deficit, at 4.7% of GDP in fiscal 2003/2004, has become structural under the currency link system.

If government spending is cut as revenues decline, the fiscal deficit can still be contained. But Hong Kong's public spending has risen persistently. Since 1997, fiscal spending has risen to 24% of GDP from 17%. Some have argued that this sharp rise in public spending was a clear sign of rising government intervention in the economy. Indeed, Hong Kong has the one of the highest public spending-to-GDP and fiscal deficit-to-GDP ratios in Asia. Large fiscal spending in Hong Kong looks likely to stay, as government thinking has shifted from a laissez-faire to a hands-on policy.

Overall, falling fiscal revenues have aggravated Asia's budget woes. Notably, the Philippines has seen her tax revenues as a share of GDP (at 12.4% in 2003) shrunk by 26% since 1997, bringing it to one of the lowest levels in Asia. Her fiscal deficit stood at almost 7% of GDP and the total public sector debt at 135% of GDP at the end of 2003. Experience shows that these are unsustainable if no corrective measures are made. A similar problem of tax erosion has also plagued Taiwan, with her tax-to-GDP ratio falling by about 20% in 2003 from 1997. Falling tax revenues and rising public spending are acting as a pair of pliers to erode Asia's fiscal flexibility to conduct counter-cyclical policies and to tackle any potential economic crises.

Destabilising outlook

Asia's fiscal outlook will be quite destabilising if nothing is done to contain the growth of the budget deficits and public debts. Private sector analysts estimate that Asia's average public debt-to-GDP ratio would zoom from 52% in 2002 to 150% by 2020, with some individual countries recording much higher debt ratios than the regional average. Notably, total public debt in India, the Philippines and Taiwan could overshoot 100% of GDP in just a few years. Admittedly, these debt projections are straight extrapolations of the current situation, and they could overestimate the situation, especially if the regional governments are able to implement fiscal reforms to contain their fiscal deficit.

However, these projections also do not include any contingent liabilities and potential exchange rate shocks, which are the primary drivers for Asia's worsening debt dynamics after the Asian crisis. These contingent liabilities stem mostly from the costs of bank recapitalisation, government's too-big-to-fail policy to guarantee state enterprises and unfunded pension and welfare/insurance systems. Realising these costs could have a devastating impact on public finances, as seen in Indonesia's dire economic adjustment when she was pushed to a debt restructuring after the Asian crisis. For financial sector contingent liabilities, which include bank restructuring and bailout costs, the estimated costs range between 10% and 50% of GDP in the region, with China seen as the system that incurs the highest cost.

The case of China is worth highlighting because it could happen to any economy with high contingent liabilities that tie the government to the corporate and banking sectors. Since Beijing implicitly guarantees the deposits that have funded the bank loans (which are, in turn, extended to those mostly bankrupt state companies), the hole in the bank balance sheets adds to the government liabilities, significantly lifting real government indebtedness (to over 100% of GDP, according to some estimates). This is less than in countries like Italy and Japan. But it is significantly more than the 55% debt ratio for Argentina before she defaulted in 2001.

China's contingent debt is highly unstable because growth in non-performing loans (NPLs) automatically inflates government debt, and each acts to reinforce the other through a vicious economic spiral. If a negative economic shock hurts corporate profits, boosts consumer defaults and forces borrowers to scramble for liquidity, that will lead to significant credit deterioration in bank loan portfolios. If the banks attempt to fight this by cutting lending, calling in loans and closes down unfinished projects, that will only worsen the economic shock. If the resultant credit contraction forces even healthy borrowers to stumble on their loan servicing, it can cause NPLs to soar. If investors/savers are alarmed by the impact of rising bad loans, they will cut spending sharply. Banks will, in turn, face tremendous pressure to hoard liquidity and drastically cut lending even further to all but the least risky borrowers.

The risk is that China falls into this vicious circle where rising bad debts undermine confidence in the government's credit, which causes a sharp contraction in investment, which leads to further loans going bad. If the jitters spread to Chinese savers, who begin to withdraw deposits to protect their savings, they could cause a systemic crisis manifested in bank runs.

Except for Hong Kong and Singapore, which have sounder banking systems than the rest of Asia, contingent liabilities stand out as a sore thumb in Asia's public finances and could cause substantial economic stress for years. Economies that are most vulnerable to a debt-deficit crisis include China, Malaysia, Thailand and the Philippines, with China and the Philippines being seen as the most vulnerable systems in Northeast and Southeast Asia, respectively. Market estimates put China's hidden contingent liabilities at over 100% of GDP, including bank recapitalisation costs of 30–50% of GDP, unfunded pension liabilities of another 50% of GDP and other contingent liabilities arising from education, medical health and other welfare needs. The World Bank and the ADB estimate that the Philippines' contingent liabilities amount to 70% of GDP, with unfunded pension liabilities of some 40% of GDP, deposit insurance of 10% of GDP plus other liabilities relating to government guarantees for build-operate-transfer contracts and various types of loans and tax credit certificates.

The point is that all these hidden liabilities will add to the existing fiscal deficit and debt loads anytime in the future, as no one knows when the contingent liabilities will be realised. Debt levels could easily exceed 100% of GDP in many Asian economies in the coming years. As and when the contingent liabilities explode, they could trigger a fiscal-induced economic crisis.

While many regional governments are not sitting on their hands to see their fiscal problems explode, the danger of a crisis remains significant if the fiscal consolidation efforts fail. Despite their efforts, the regional governments do not seem to have effective strategies to contain their fiscal deficits yet. Rising welfare and other non-discretionary spending will only worsen the fiscal deficits and add to public sector liabilities, eventually leading to a debt blow-out. The average public debt ratios in the region are already higher than the respective debt ratios in Argentina and Russia when they defaulted, and are close to the debt ratios of Ecuador and Turkey when their fiscal crises turned into sovereign debt crises. A loss in public (domestic and foreign) confidence in any of the regional government's ability to honour its debt obligation will lead to massive capital outflow, crushing the country's currency and creating a spiral of rising risk premia, higher interest rates and lower economic growth. The recent crisis experience from the emerging markets shows that it is extremely painful to break such a debt spiral.

Unfortunately, there is no sure way of predicting a debt-induced financial crisis. Research by the IMF[5] has refuted the conventional wisdom that the price of government bonds would reflect all relevant information of a debt default. Bond yields have often failed to signal impending crises timely enough for governments to avoid them. Credit ratings by international agencies, like Standard & Poor's and Moody's, are often reactive to crisis rather than predictive. This means that the international credit rating agencies often change their default risk rating for a country after the fact. Indeed, one cannot look for a single indicator that can act as an early warning signal for detecting a debt-deficit crisis because there is none. Rather, there is a bunch of indicators relevant to gauging the risk of a crisis. They include the ratios of public sector debt-to-fiscal-revenue, public sector deficit-to-GDP, public sector debt-to-GDP, short-term debt-to-total debt and foreign debt-to-total debt. Sustained high ratios in these measures usually spell trouble.

Vulnerability alone does not necessarily generate a crisis. A trigger is needed to break the markets' confidence in the government's debt repayment ability, thus sending interest rates higher and triggering a vicious debt spiral. The trigger could take any form, like a balance of payments crisis, an exogenous interest rate shock, the realisation of some large contingent liabilities, a political shock or even a natural disaster that causes significant economic damage that needs massive reconstruction with public funding. Experience shows that a crisis that starts in any one economy could enlarge into a regional, or even global crisis easily via contagion.

A trigger from balance of payments trouble is not likely for most Asian economies because they have mostly undervalued exchanged rates and balance of payments surpluses. Asia's cheap currencies are a result of the regional governments' deliberate policy to curb them from rising via massive intervention in the foreign exchange market in the face of current account surpluses. The purpose of doing so is to boost and protect their export competitiveness to generate export-led growth to make up for deficient domestic demand (see 'The inherent structural weakness' section below).

The combination of external surpluses and high domestic savings should also help make most of Asia relatively immune to global interest rate shocks. Why? A rise in global interest rates would put depreciating pressure on the regional currencies, as capital would flow from Asia to foreign markets for higher returns. To halt the slide in their currencies, the Asian authorities would have to raise rates too. But Asia's large external surpluses should offset some of the capital outflow pressures, thus avoiding the need for the local authorities to hike interest rates. High domestic savings mean ample liquidity in the local system, which would also help prevent a sharp rise in local interest rates in response to an external rate hike.

There are two exceptions, however. Indonesia and the Philippines have much weaker external balances and a markedly smaller pool of domestic savings than the rest of Asia. They are thus more vulnerable to a financial crisis triggered by external imbalances and external interest rate hikes. For the rest of Asia, the trigger for a crisis would probably come from a political shock or an unexpected realisation of contingent liabilities. Japan, with her large public sector debt, huge pension liabilities and a political environment surrounded by security issues from China to North Korea, should be a test case for the rest of Asia. If Japan cracks under these stresses, the rest of Asia would likely follow pretty fast.

Foreign reserves, angel or devil?

Asia's massive foreign exchange reserve build-up since the 1997–1998 regional crisis is often seen as a sign of economic strength, but it may not be. It could be a devil in disguise. This is because the reserve accumulation that at first reflected the prudent behaviour of policymakers appeared later to be fuelled by speculative market behaviour stemming from the rigidities in Asian exchange rates. Indeed, the ADB warned in its Asian Development Outlook 2004 report that Asia's massive foreign reserve accumulation might have become excessive and could lead to rampant domestic credit expansion and possibly create the conditions for a new Asian financial crisis.

Indeed, the most important monetary development in Asia since the regional crisis has been the staggering expansion of Asian central bank balance sheets, which mirrors their massive foreign reserve build-up. Total assets of the regional central banks doubled between 1999 and 2003. The regional authorities' policy to curb their currencies' strength via foreign exchange intervention in the face of an overall balance of payments (BoP) surplus caused this expansion. There are two drivers underlying the BoP surplus: the basic balance, which includes the current account balances and long-term capital flows such as long-term equity investment and borrowing, and portfolio balance. The latter is often seen as speculative hot money flows.

Most Asian economies that have recovered from the 1997–1998 regional crisis have stocked up on current account surpluses to build up huge reserves as firewalls against financial contagion, especially for fending off future currency attacks. But the reserve accumulation has become excessive since 2003, as there has been a sharp rise in the inflow of short-term, presumably speculative or hot, money.

For example, in 2003 and 2004, the growth rate of hot money inflow was over ten times faster than the rate of long-term (basic balance) money inflow (Figure 5:3), and the share of these portfolio funds jumped from an estimated 3.5% of total inflows in 2003 to 25% in early 2004. Indeed, the ratio of portfolio inflows to long-term inflows has risen sharply since 2003, reversing sharply the hot money outflows seen

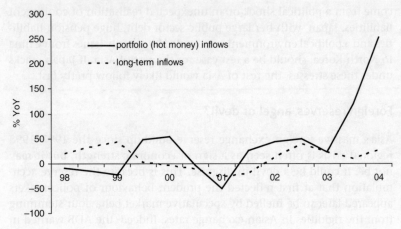

Figure 5:3 Asia's capital inflow growth rates
Source: CEIC

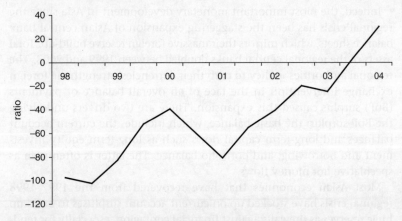

Figure 5:4 Ratio of hot money to long-term money inflows
Source: CEIC

in the years before (Figure 5:4). This sharp rise in hot money was prompted by global investors positioning aggressively for real exchange rate appreciation in Asia. In other words, many short-term investors, notably hedge funds, made bets on Asian central banks that they would sustain their undervalued exchange-rate policy to inflate GDP growth and boost investment returns and asset prices. An increase in hot money inflows can be seen as an inevitable result of keeping currencies undervalued.

The trouble with having too much short-term money inflow is that without capital controls it could reverse suddenly, sending negative signals about the economies affected, even though the economic fundamentals might not have changed. Excessive hot money inflow also deepens an economy's financial flaws, intensifying its financial stress and which could finally set off a financial crisis. This was clearly seen in the 1997–1998 Asian crisis. While much of the capital inflow to Asia in the 1980s was in the form of long-term foreign direct investment, the inflow composition shifted to short-term portfolio investment in the 1990s. In addition to funding Asia's widening current account deficits, this hot money also inflated the region's asset bubble in the first half of the 1990s. For example, much of Asia's excessive investment was focused on land and property before the regional crisis. When the crisis hit, asset prices crashed and most of those good old property loans turned bad, piling into the bad loans that defaulted under the downward economic spiral.

In the years before the last crisis, reliance on liquid hot money inflows had left Asia's domestic financial system susceptible to foreign interest hikes and/or domestic currency depreciation. There is a parallel this time in terms of capital flows. While long-term capital inflows was the driver of BoP surplus before 2003, the composition of capital inflow has changed to short-term money since 2003; just as what happened between the late 1980s and early 1990s. What is different this time is that Asia does not have current account deficits as it had in the years leading up to the 1997–1998 crisis.

But there is a catch. While the region's current account surpluses should act as a cushion to a potential crisis, they could reverse easily on the back of Asian central banks' cheap currency policy. When a central bank intervenes in the foreign exchange market to keep its exchange rate from rising in the face of heavy capital inflow, the intervention will lead to a surge in domestic liquidity. This is because in the course of keeping the exchange rate from rising, the central bank has to sell the local currency, thus buying foreign exchange and swelling its foreign reserves. This, in turn, increases domestic money supply.

The authorities could sell government bonds (thus taking in cash) to absorb the increase in money supply. This act is called 'sterilisation' and is commonly used by central banks to offset the impact of rising foreign reserves on domestic money growth under a fixed exchange rate system. And indeed, Asian central banks have built up quite a large sterilisation debt along the way.[6] But if they stop sterilising, the foreign exchange intervention could lead to a sharp rise in domestic credit, boosting consumption and investment to excessive levels and, thus, eroding the current account balances and creating the conditions for a new economic crisis.

China's experience in the aftermath of the global IT bubble-burst in 2001 could be a forerunner for the rest of Asia in the coming years. The central bank's intervention to keep the RMB from rising on the back of a large BoP surplus had caused domestic credit to rise sharply, boosting investment to excessive levels, especially in the steel, property, auto, cement and heavy chemicals sectors. The concern about an overheated economy prompted Beijing to tighten up its economic policies, mostly via administrative measures, in 2003 and 2004. Asian central banks' policy to curb their currency strength under BoP surplus is just what the Chinese central bank did in the early 2000s. The impact will filter through Asia's financial system so that its economic balance sheet expansion will play catch-up with the central bank balance sheet in the coming years.

This is another way of saying that Asian credit growth would accelerate to feed excessive domestic demand growth, which will eventually erode the regional current account surpluses. The relevant danger for Asia is that, unlike China, it has free flow of capital. A main reason for China being able to escape the 1997–1998 Asian crisis is her closed capital account, which restricts cross-border capital flows. But most of Asia's key economies have no capital controls. When some shocks trigger a loss of investor confidence, hot money withdrawal could easily create financial contagion, giving rise to another financial crisis.

The return of inflation, even though it may not necessarily be in a big way, would complicate the risk. The complication stems from the sterilisation debts that Asian central banks have built up. As inflation returns, nominal interest rates will rise, thus raising the cost of servicing these debts. Since sterilisation debts are sovereign debts, an increase in their servicing cost will add to the regional governments' fiscal deficits. If the rising fiscal burden prompts the authorities to stop sterilising, it will be more difficult for policymakers to deal with the 'unsterilised' capital inflow. This is because the resultant massive increase in domestic money supply will fuel domestic credit demand and thus be very inflationary. As private sector confidence improves when the business cycle turns up, risk appetite will rise exponentially. The monetary overhang resulted from the unsterilised capital inflow would end up boosting the financial imbalances in the economy, thus sowing the seed for the next financial crisis.

The inherent structural weakness

More subtly, Asia's 'cheap' currency policy acts to weaken the region's immune system to economic crisis. Remember the purpose of sustaining an undervalued currency is to boost exports as an economic growth engine. Structurally and from a current account perspective, this policy is like an export subsidy, which acts to crowd out domestic investment and consumption. A cheap currency policy thus distorts incentive for structural adjustment, which is needed for healthy long-term economic growth.

Arguably, the foreign reserves build-up under a cheap currency policy represents a nationalisation of private sector savings because the exporters' earnings are kept under the public coffers. This, in turn, allows the authorities to invest these assets on behalf of the private sector. But public sector investment allocation often distorts private sector decision to pursue any structural changes. As Asia realised in the early 1990s, undervalued fixed exchange rates also act to subsidise risk by eliminating foreign exchange risk. This reduces private sector incentive to hedge against uncertainty, distorts investment decision and, thus, capital allocation.

The region should have learned from the painful experience of the 1997–1998 crisis and pursue structural reforms to purge its banking and corporate woes. These reforms should not be limited to recapitalising the banks, but should also include uprooting cronyism, abandoning Asian banks' policy lending role, cutting bad debts, reducing moral hazard and increasing bank and corporate transparency, accountability and management. The corporates also need to de-leverage, improve transparency and shift their focus to long-term efficiency and profitability from short-term quick-profit trading practice. Asia as a whole needs to shift from the low-efficiency, manufacturing-based, export-oriented economic model to a high value-added, service-based, consumption-oriented model.

However, despite a good reform start right after the Asian crisis, the reform resolve faded by 2000. The strong economic recovery in the two years after the crisis had masked the urgency to reform. Many regional governments had not grasped the opportunity to pursue thorough structural changes. They instead opted for an easy way out of the post-crisis economic doldrums by pursuing an undervalued currency policy to boost exports. Anecdotal evidence for Asia's reform success does not add up to the macroeconomic trends. This suggests that despite some noticeable reform efforts, these piecemeal reforms are insufficient to heal the system relative to the amount of imbedded economic inefficiency.

Had the Asian economies bit the bullet and purged the economic excesses, the sharp economic rebound and fall in interest rates in the post-crisis years should have sustained corporate profit recovery. But macro data do not conform to anecdotal evidence of reform success. From a macro perspective, the gap between the consumer price index (CPI) and the producer price index (PPI) can be treated as a proxy for aggregate profits in the economy. This is because the former is the economy-wide sale price and the latter is the overall production cost. Evidence shows that Asia's profits have failed to sustain their strong recovery, despite the favourable economic conditions after the Asian crisis (Figure 5:5). The falling trend actually deepens, despite the reform improvement stories that the media have reported.

The declining profit trend suggests that there has been a steady erosion of pricing power, due to rising competition especially from low-cost China, insufficient domestic demand and excess supply. The lack of profit growth is also a symptom of economic inefficiency in Asia. As for the reform success stories, they are not necessarily the result of strong revenue growth under a dis-inflationary environment. Instead, they are

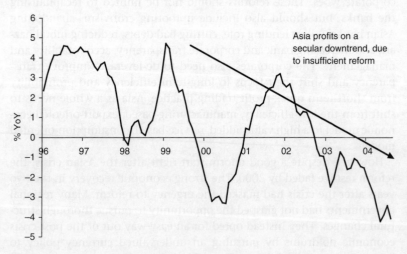

Figure 5:5 Asia's profit growth (approximated by the difference between CPI and PPI)
Source: CEIC

mostly the result of cost-cutting measures, like investment cut-backs, layoffs, plant closures and other spending cuts. But profits growth without pricing power is not sustainable. There is only so much a company can cut. Continued cost-cutting on the back of pricing power erosion will hurt confidence and eventually private spending. All this suggests that the legacy of the old structural woes still remains in Asia, constraining its ability to enhance value and raise prices. This structural burden has dragged on the region's internal growth ability, thus forcing it to rely on exports for growth momentum. In this structural context, Asia's current account surpluses should be seen as an economic weakness, instead of strength, because they are a result of domestic demand deficiency.

Asia's foreign exchange policy is another piece of evidence that it has not learned from the regional crisis. The reason why the regional currency regimes collapsed in 1997–1998 was simply because they were unhealthy. Most Asian currencies were plagued by bad economic fundamentals, like huge current account deficits, and rigged by the regional central banks. The regional authorities tried to sustain the bad fundamentals by doing three things at the same time: 1) to fix their currencies at rigid exchange rates against the US dollar, while 2) dictating domestic interest rates and 3) keeping their borders open to capital flows.

This is a self-defeating game. Under an open capital account (that is free cross-border flow of capital), a central bank can either fix its exchange rate and let local interest rates move according to market forces, or fix domestic interest rates and let the exchange rate float freely under market forces. But it cannot do both at the same time. If it wants to have full control of both the exchange rate and local interest rates, it must keep the capital account closed. China has chosen to close her borders to international capital flows so that she can fix both the exchange rate and domestic interest rates. Hong Kong has an open capital account and a currency link system that pegged the Hong Kong dollar against the US dollar, so it lets the market determine the level of domestic interest rates. Japan also has an open capital account and the central bank controls the level domestic interest rates. Hence, to a large extent, it lets the market determine the value of the Yen exchange rate.

That was why these three currencies did not suffer collapse in 1997–1998. The ones that collapsed were those that defied the rules of the game. But there is not much sign that these central banks have learned from the painful experience. After the currency collapse in 1997–1998, and despite their official rhetoric of shifting to flexible exchange rate regimes after the Asian crisis, the regional authorities have gone back to currency-fixing

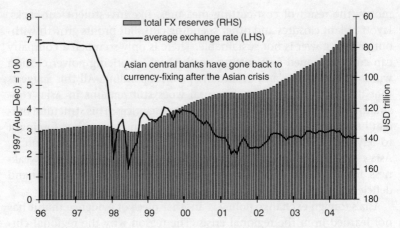

Figure 5:6 Asian exchange rate and FX reserves (excluding China, Japan, Hong Kong)
Source: CEIC

under open capital accounts, while at the same time trying to manipulate local interest rates according to domestic needs. To see this, witness the steady foreign exchange build-up on the back of flat exchange rate movement, especially since 2001 (Figure 5:6). To keep their exchange rates stable in the face of large BoP surpluses, Asian central banks have been selling local currencies, to keep them from appreciating, and buying US dollars, thus accumulating foreign reserves.

The bad apples fail to turn good

While there is evidence for structural changes in Asia in the years following the crisis,[7] the trouble is that the economic healing process has not been thorough enough, as the falling profit trend discussed above argues. This suggests that for every transformed bank and company in Asia, there are still many financial and business entities sticking to their old inefficient habits.

Take for example South Korea, dubbed by the IMF as a model reform pupil after the Asian crisis. Despite strengthening the law and prosecuting the worst cases of fraud, Korea Inc.'s old habits die hard. A notable case is SK Corp., whose chairman has managed to keep his job, without any regulators' objections, despite being convicted of a criminal offence for a 4.4 trillion won (US$4 billion) accounting fraud in 2003. For international investors, the failure of a bid by foreign shareholders to push for management changes at SK Corp. marks a major setback for corporate reform in Korea.

The bitter battle between SK Corp.'s largest foreign shareholder Sovereign Asset Management, a Monaco-based investment fund, and the company's family-controlled management came to a head at SK Corp.'s annual general meeting in Seoul in March 2004. A majority (52%) of the shareholders voted for keeping SK Corp.'s chairman and against management changes pushed by Sovereign, who got only 47% of the votes.

The annual general meeting was widely seen as a landmark test for whether shareholders, domestic and foreign, have the power to influence the internal affairs of traditionally closed corporate Korea. Foreign investors led by Sovereign wanted the company to hold executives accountable for mismanagement with zero tolerance. But domestic investors were more willing to give the company's chairman, Chey Tae Won who is also the nephew of the company founder, a second chance, despite Chey's criminal conviction of accounting fraud. Chey served only seven months of a three-year jail sentence and was out on bail appealing against his case at the time of writing.

Many domestic investors believe that SK Corp., along with other Korean companies, is making headway in structural improvement, but will do so in its own time. They also argue that when pushing for changes, investors have to consider what is important not only for SK Corp. but also for the country. But for many foreign investors, a vote for management's slate of directors and proposals flies in the face of the government's stated policy of improving corporate governance.

Foreigners also see the government's double-standard in attempting to preserve the old Korean Inc. A case in point is the government's treatment of Kookmin Bank, South Korea's largest bank. While no regulators ever objected SK Corp.'s chairman to retain office after his criminal fraud conviction, Kookmin's chief executive, Kim Jung Tae, was ousted in September 2004 by the Financial Supervisory Commission (FSC) on errors found in the bank's accounting for bad loan provisions. Mr Kim was also banned from executive posts in South Korean banks for three years. Yet, most foreign investors consider the errors to be honest mistakes rather than attempts to cheat. Foreigners own 78% of Kookmin Bank, a sign of their faith in the bank.

Mr Kim's punishment was disproportionately harsh when compared with the leniency that the government had shown to SK Corp. and other scandalous chaebol.[8] Koomin Bank's case might well be an example of reform inertia at the highest level. Mr Kim has been a vocal reformist who had crossed the bureaucracy many times. He protested strongly against Seoul's plans to bailout troubled firms, including SK Corp. He refused to extend any loans to SK Corp. and sold its SK loans at deep discount. He also complained bitterly about a state-arranged rescue of the credit-card affiliates of the LG and Samsung groups before his arm was twisted.

The FSC's move to oust Kim was seen as politically driven to silence an outspoken reform-minded executive. Even a member of the Bank of Korea's monetary policy board, quoted by the media as Mr Kim Tae Dong, criticised the FSC's decision as a move to divert public attention from the government's unwillingness to take responsibility for the credit-card crisis in 2003 and 2004 by finding a scapegoat in a bank chief who followed market principle.

Although crony capitalism was a deadly ingredient that brewed the Asian crisis, which started in Thailand in 1997, the Kingdom (which was dubbed by the IMF as another model reform pupil) shows little sign of eradicating the disease. Indeed, Prime Minister Thaksin Shinawatra has pursued economic policies that have blurred the line between big business and the government. In addition to an export-promotion policy, he has used expansionary policies to revive local business, pump up the stock market and set off a new asset market boom. This two-pronged approach that boosts both the domestic and external sectors is known by investors as 'Thaksinomics'.

The resulting surge in growth has put Thailand back on foreign investors' radar screens, helping the Thai stock market to soar since Thaksin came to office in 2001. The economic success has also earned Thaksin unprecedented political popularity. However, the way in which Thaksin appears to be using that strong mandate is worrying because the closer ties he has built and encouraged between big business and politics could easily create conflicts of interest. Thaksin's policies are keeping crony capitalism well and alive, which could sow the seed for another financial crisis.

The problem of conflicting interests stems right from the prime minister's office. Thailand's 1997 constitution included provisions to prevent conflicts of interest between elected officials and big business, including barring politicians from holding shares in companies. The provisions were seen as needed to avoid a repeat of the corruption in the previous governments that contributed to Thailand's 1997 financial collapse. But loopholes remain, including the fact that the constitution does not bar family members of elected officials from owning shares in companies that do business with government. Thaksin indeed made the best use of this loophole and transferred his shareholding in the Shin Group, one of Thailand's largest conglomerates, to his family members after becoming the prime minister.

There would not be a conflict of interest problem if Thaksin's economic policies were not relevant to his family business empire's interests. But this is obviously not the case. The Shin Group's businesses are focused on cell phone sales and services, property, media and consumer finance. Several of Thaksin's key policy platforms – cheap credit, a strong currency, stimulation of domestic consumption and stock market support – directly benefit Shin's businesses. Notably, both Thaksin's policies and Shin's business have a focus on consumption. Shin's cell phone arm, for example, has profited handsomely from the shopping spree under Thaksinomics. As one of Thailand's largest hand-phone importers, Shin also profits hugely from a strong Baht policy as it translates into cheaper cell phones and fatter margins. Meanwhile, Thaksin's low interest rate policy has benefited Shin's consumer-finance business.

Thaksin's stock market-boosting measures also benefit Shin more than other businesses. Though signs of overheating in the stock market emerged in 2004, Thaksin still blocked regulators' proposals in November to curb speculative activity. He has also given personal opinions about further strength in the Thai Baht and stock market performance. As one of Thailand's biggest consumers of equity finance, Shin certainly benefit from the bull market more than other firms. A strong equity market is also crucial to Shin's aggressive listing programme to exit or cash-in its investments.

Another showcase for crony ties between public and private interests came from the move in 2003 by SC Asset Co., a Thaksin family company controlled by his wife and son, into the residential property market. The problem is not only that this sector has benefited significantly from an array of government incentives for developers and buyers. The high profile investment by Thaksin's family has also acted as a distorted signal to the market that property investment would be underwritten by the government and thus would have minimal risk. This has resulted in massive investment inflow into property and risked the building of another asset bubble. Meanwhile, Shin Satellite, another Thaksin family-owned company, won an eight-year tax holiday in 2003 worth 16 billion Bhat (about US$402 million) from Thailand's Board of Investment for its new broadband satellite system. The tax break raised eyebrows because it was the first time the state agency, which is charged with attracting foreign investment to Thailand, had offered such incentives to a local company.

Thaksin's cabinet includes several former big business leaders. Like the prime minister, they divested all their shareholdings when they entered government. But their families have retained interest in everything from entertainment and media to finance and telecoms. These conflict of interest problems have not gone unnoticed. But the Thaksin government has vigorously suppressed criticism, pressuring opposition politicians and groups with the threat of libel suits. It has also resorted to money politics to divert criticism by offering the media huge advertising programmes from state enterprises and politically connected private companies. These moves have prompted critical comparison between Thaksin's administration and the governments in Malaysia and Singapore where the powers use democratic mandates to tame press, quash political opposition and guide economic development.

Onto Thailand's banking scene, despite the IMF's stringent reform requirements for Thai banks to restructure in return for its bailout funds, state controlled Krug Thai Bank's disclosure of US$1.1 billion in bad debts in late 2004 showed that serious structural woes still remain. The bank's 70% jump in bad debts in 2004 not only raised concerns about the banking system's financial health. They also stirred fears about the danger of crony capitalism being revived under Thaksinomics to create an asset bubble. There are hints that the bank's sharp deterioration in its balance sheet might be a result of possible irregularities. Between 2001 and 2003, Krung Thai's lending to the property sector surged 124%, when the country's top private banks cut their real estate exposure. Sources close to the central bank suggested that most of the bad loans were made to 14 property developers, with debt-troubled Natural Park and Krisda Mahanakorn getting the bulk of the credits.

Krung Thai's problems could be contagious, and they are strong evidence for the continuation of structural inefficiency in the Thai system. Krung Thai Bank was at the centre of Thailand's 1997 financial collapse. By 1999, the bank's bad loans had surged to 84% of its total loan portfolio. Many of those loans, as revealed by independent auditors in due course, were extended to well-connected borrowers by using political rather than prudential commercial criteria. Beginning in 2002, Thaksin gave Krung Thai aggressive lending targets to help spur economic growth. These include orders to lend to his favourite sectors like property development and retail. In 2003, Krung Thai accounted for over 70% of all new lending in the banking system, while many private sector banks had scaled back on the concern about rising credit risk and an overheated economy. Krung Thai's disclosure in 2004 of its bad loans looks like déjà vu all over again.

Even the reform resolve in Singapore, which is seen as a more progressive economy in Southeast Asia, is still uncertain. The island state is still stuck with its paternalistic capitalist model, despite the government's pledge to push through more structural changes and to become more transparent. Take a look at Temasek, the wholly government-owned conglomerate which hires 170,000 people and controls more than 20% of Singapore's stock market, including a big chunk of the country's industry and infrastructure. The company made public its annual report in August 2004 for the first time in its 30-year history because it needed to attract external capital to fund its expansion, including acquisitions overseas. And Temasek needs more transparency to attract foreign investors and get a credit rating from international credit-rating agencies like Standard & Poor's and Moody's. Greater transparency, in turn, means that Temasek's operations can be better scrutinised, and this is supposed to be good for structural changes.

No doubt Temasek has remarkable achievements in producing some of Singapore's notable successes. Singapore Airlines is one of the best-run and most profitable airlines in the world; PSA, Singapore's largest container-port operator, has an operating margin of 30%; and Keppel and SembCorp are global leaders in specialised oil rigs and tanker repair. Temasek has also boasted an average return of 18% to its shareholders over the past three decades.

What has gone mostly unreported is that there may be less to Temasek's success than meets the eye. A study by the private consultancy firm LEK, in early 2004 found that Temasek's 22 major listed companies had made an average return of only 1.7% a year since their respective listings. Moreover, some of Temasek's best-performing investments are either monopolies or operate in protected markets, helped by favourable regulations. For example, the government bears the capital costs of Singapore's subway system, allowing SMART, the operator, to undercut its private sector rival ComfortDelgro. Massive tax breaks have been given to Chartered Semiconductor to sustain its microchip production, despite doubts about its efficiency to compete in the international markets.

For those Temasek ventures that face serious competition, they have mostly flopped. Analysts have argued that DBS Bank overpaid its purchase price for Hong Kong's Dao Hang Bank, while SingTel's acquisition of Australian Telecom giant Optus and shipping giant Neptune Orient Lines purchase of American President Lines suffered more years of losses than expected before breaking even. Singapore Airlines' investment in Air New Zealand was a disaster and had to be written off after the latter went broke, as was SingTel's investment in C2C, an underwater cable operator. The biggest disaster has been Chartered Semiconductor whose inferior technology relative to its Taiwanese rivals has made it bleed money for years and it had to be bailed out by Temasek in 2002.

It is normal for companies to make mistakes so that investment losses result. But the concern about Singapore is the government's heavy involvement in the commercial decision making process. The potential distortion from the public sector's interference is larger in over-capitalised economies, like Singapore. There is just too much money pressuring the bureaucrats to invest/spend. While governments elsewhere have privatised their industries, Temasek has bought up companies mainly to eschew complaints from outside shareholders. But buying out other shareholders and delisting company shares fly in the face of the privatisation spirit, which is seen as an effective way to enhance economic efficiency. Arguably, despite Temasek's talk of being more open, at heart it is still a collection of government-owned assets that operate largely in protected markets with a trace of nepotism, characterised by the old habit of secrecy.

Meanwhile, the will to change has not grown any stronger, despite the ascent of Lee Hsien Loong from Deputy Prime Minister to Prime Minister in August 2004. The whole Lee dynasty in the Singaporean government has not changed much. Mr Lee is the son of former senior minister Lee Kuan Yew, Singapore's founding father. Lee senior, still sitting in government at the age of 80, was made Minister Mentor, a new position created just to rank above senior minister Goh Chok Tong (who was prime minister before stepping down) when Lee junior took office. And junior Lee's wife, Ching Ho, runs Temasek.

Lee Hsien Loong shares his father's measured, practical and technocratic approach to govern. He wants to keep this sort of dynastic arrangement. Despite his effort to push through some changes, such as relaxing restrictions on bungee-jumping and busking, making it easier to register a society, signalling a more liberal attitude to homosexuality, cutting some taxes, opening the banking sector to foreign investors and liberalising the pension system, he remains timid in pursuing revolutionary changes.

The government still refuses to discard its practice to hand-pick winners for industrial development. Nor has it followed through on talk of reducing government intervention in the economy, witness the continued expansion and dominance of Temasek and the Government of Singapore Investment Corporation (GSIC). The leadership under Lee junior seems to be sticking to Singapore's special blend of state control and free markets.

With these relatively more reform-progressive economies still stuck with many of their structural rigidities, one cannot hold too much hope for those weaker ones to purge their old woes. Indonesia is a case in point. This is not to deny her reform achievements, especially in the banking area. These include an increase in Indonesian banks' capital ratios to an average of 20% since 2000, an improvement in earnings and a reduction in bad debts to 8% of total assets. But many thorny, deep-rooted, problems remain and it seems that the government's will and power to eradicate them has been stretched.

The limited success of the Indonesian Bank Restructuring Agency (IBRA) in recovering debts from those bailed out by the government reflects how entrenched reform resistance and cronyism are in the system. The state-backed economic reconstruction agency, set up under the World Bank initiatives in 1998, wound up operations in early 2004 with trillions of rupiah in losses. This was because, despite its statutory power to reform the banks and recoup their bad debts, IBRA was not able to force debtors to return the lion's share of funds from banks it took over during the Asian crisis. Much of those funds were central bank loans to keep the troubled banks afloat in 1997 and 1998.

Blame it on politics. While President Suharto has long gone, the biggest players have shifted their allegiance to a succession of elites linked to his successors, B.J. Habibie, Abdurrahman Wahid and now Megawati. These allegiances have made it virtually impossible for IBRA to go after the big fish. Indeed, IBRA was stymied from the start. Those in the World Bank pushing for it to be an independent agency were over-ruled by government officials who have close ties with the state-owned companies, which had become in the Suharto years unregulated piggybanks for his cronies.

Hence, IBRA was hobbled by political interference from the start. In its six-year life, it had seven chairmen, with one only lasting for two months. The rapid turnover of leaders disrupted workflow and sapped morale. The agency was vulnerable to corruption and mismanagement right from the beginning. An audit of Bank Bali by accounting firm Price WaterhouseCoopers in August 1999 revealed extensive collusion between IBRA officials and the government, which was behind the US$50 million embezzlement, with much of the money going to individuals linked to the former ruling party Golkar. When IBRA was wound up in February 2004, only one of its debtors had settled most of its debts.

Meanwhile, despite five years of reform efforts, big concerns about the state banks, which account for almost half of all deposits in the system, still remain. The US$200 million fraud at Bank Negara Indonesia (BNI), the second largest bank in the country, between late 2002 and 2003 was an indication of the scale of unfinished reform business. The scandal erupted in October 2003, and flew in the face of the government's efforts to build corporate governance to win back confidence that the country could survive without the IMF loan programme, which ended at the end of 2003.

The loan scandal was about export credits being channelled to local companies without proper appraisals. BNI internal auditors discovered that some US$131.6 million and 56.1 million Euros (about US$64 million) were issued in 105 transactions without formal assessments conducted. Officials also found out that millions of Euro funds that were issued to finance commodity exports to Congo and Kenya were embezzled, as the exports never existed. The BNI scandal raises concerns about how widespread such abuses would be in the banking system. Debtors had tampered with documents and colluded with BNI officials to have the credits released. Most of the letters of credit and documents connected with the export credits had turned out to be faked.

Banking woes, déjà vu

Indeed, stubborn woes remain in Asia's banking system, despite some evidence showing that many regional banks have emerged from the ashes after the Asian crisis, building on government bailouts and economic recovery to create profit-making operations. The high prices paid by global groups like Citigroup and Standard Chartered for rivals in South Korea and Indonesia seem to underscore the recovery of Asia's banking sector. In 2004, Citigroup paid US$2.7 billion for Koram Bank, a price that valued Korea's sixth largest bank at a costly two times book value. Standard Chartered was even more aggressive. It paid US$3.3 billion for Korea First Bank in early 2005. The deal came only two months after it bought 51% of Indonesia's Bank Permata, one of Indonesia's leading lenders, with US$305 million, valuing the Indonesian concern at over 2.8 times book value.

But despite the post-crisis rebound, and despite some of these global financial groups' aggressive acquisitions, most Asian banks are not out of the woods. Their struggle for survival will intensify, making the regional system vulnerable to economic shocks, amid rising competition from larger foreign groups. The problem is that many regional banks have not bit the bullet to restructure sufficiently by leveraging on the favourable economic conditions at the turn of the millennium.

The main concern today, as it was before the Asian crisis, is that many Asian domestic banks do not have the systems and the expertise to assess credit risk, a problem that also affects their relationships with small and medium-sized enterprises. Many banking observers argue that, despite some years of profit recovery, most regional banks have still not invested in technology and training that would enable them to cut cost and minimise lending errors. To some extent, Asia's banking sector recovery has been driven by the sharp and swift post-crisis macroeconomic recovery. This has created complacency and eroded the government's reform resolve to uproot the banking woes. But close ties between the government and the banking sector also plays a crucial role in impeding changes.

A large number of Asian banks still lack efficient tools to centralise the analysis of credit and risk, leaving local branch managers in charge of critical lending decisions, a system that breeds frauds and mistakes. These problems are seen in the banks' financial performance. Despite a noticeable improvement since the regional crisis, the profitability of Asian banks is still lower than their counterparts in the major markets, according to estimates by management consultancy Bain & Company. The cost-to-income ratio, an indicator for operational efficiency of the regional banks averaged about 64% in 2004. That was much higher than the ratios in Australia, the US and the UK. Bain also estimated that Asian banks' shareholder returns, which measures share price changes and dividend paid, had under-performed their rivals in the rest of the world every year since the Asian crisis.

The key problems hampering Asian banks' performance have been the legal frameworks and institutional obstacles in the countries in which they operate. Only Hong Kong, Singapore and South Korea have a bankruptcy law, which allows partial recovery of the assets of bankrupt companies and individuals. Foreclosure legislation in many Asian economies to help banks taking over assets from defaulting borrowers is either non-existence or poorly enforced. But if crony capitalism is entrenched in the system, there is of course no incentive to rock the boat by purging the systemic faults.

In a nutshell, the post-crisis export-driven economic recovery has masked the urgency to uproot Asia's old bad habits. While some reform progress has been made, they are not enough to cleanse the system relative to the amount of inefficiency. However, it is likely that Asia will not be in a hurry to change its now defunct economic model. This is because the region's political and economic platform still favours the crony capitalists, who have indulged in political patronage and appropriated and shared huge economic benefits with the political elites who are the real masterminds of the economic excesses. As long as there are significant political vested interests in the economy, there is always a lack of political will to change. Crony capitalism is an inherent weakness that will continue to drag on Asia's reform, making it vulnerable to another financial crisis.

6
The External Stresses

Foreign capital inflows to Asia are normally seen as an external force to help strengthen the region's structural underpinning by bringing in market discipline and management technology. This should, in turn, help fortify Asia's immunity to future economic crises. However, one should distinguish between foreign direct investment inflows and foreign portfolio inflows. The latter has had a dark side in distorting Asia's structural reforms and, thus, contributing to its vulnerability to a future crisis.

In addition to China's economic stress and Asia's idiosyncratic flaws, there are many external factors that could trigger a financial crisis for the region, with the US being one big potential destabilising factor. America's bloated fiscal, and the related current account, deficit is no less dangerous than Asia's in terms of its potential damage on the global economy. This twin fiscal-current account deficit might even force a US dollar crisis as part of the adjustment to right America's economic imbalances. If it occurred, a dollar crash could trigger a terrible global slump.

The fiscal deadlock has reduced the US government's flexibility to deal with economic shocks and, partly because of this, prompted the Federal Reserve to keep monetary policy looser and longer than usual after the busting of the IT bubble in 2001. The impact of this ultra-loose US monetary policy has spilled over to Asia and created financial bubbles in the regional markets. This has, in turn, created a shaky economic backdrop for the regional economies and made Asia vulnerable to external shocks. These shocks may take any form, like a US fiscal blowout, US interest rate hikes, a US dollar crisis, an oil crisis or a sharp global economic slowdown. They would disrupt international capital flows, sending seismic waves of financial turmoil to Asia.

Subtly and in the longer-term, the rise of terrorism will aggravate the risk of a financial crisis for Asia. It may not be a direct cause, but it could act as a catalyst for a crisis by hitting the regional economies at the wrong time without the right reasons, as we shall explore below.

The dark side of capital inflows

While foreign direct investment (FDI) has mostly benefited Asia, foreign portfolio inflows are a different story. In theory, open and growing stock markets should help make Asian economies and capital markets more efficient. Foreign portfolio inflows, the logic goes, finances fast-growing capital-starved private firms in Asia. Armed with sophisticated and state-of-the-art earnings and valuation models, foreign fund managers should be able to allocate capital more efficiently than local punters chasing market rumours. Foreign investors will then push Asian managers to improve efficiency, corporate governance and transparency, while reaping for themselves higher returns than they could have got by investing in their home markets.

However, in practice, portfolio inflows have accomplished little for Asia. In many cases, foreign investment has merely sustained or replaced locally generated defects with foreign-sources flaws. The problems are two-fold – the way the fund management business operates and the integrated global capital markets, which imports the dominating influence of major markets, such as the US, to the regional markets.

Most funds are required by charter to mimic benchmark indices, forcing managers to hold index stocks. This in effect puts little emphasis on the need for the fund managers to pay attention to the companies' outlook. For those managers who venture outside the benchmarks to achieve higher returns, they often favour crony capitalist companies or the state-owned firms that professionals are supposed to shun. This is because these are the companies that could deliver above average-returns under the opaque market set-up. Sometimes, foreign managers introduce their own strain of irrational trading, as they did with the Internet bubble.

Then there is the IT revolution, which has brought the global capital markets closely together so that cross-border portfolio flows can be effected in seconds on a slight change in sentiment or news development in any markets. This means that the influence of major external markets, especially the US which is the largest in the world, often dominates movement in the small Asian markets. However, foreign capital inflows to the regional markets resulting from US market changes do not necessarily reflect better capital allocation to Asia.

Hence, instead of share prices reflecting expectations of local economic fundamentals and earnings growth, offshore fund flows often force Asian markets to follow trends in the US, irrespective of local developments. Indeed, foreign dominated markets like Hong Kong and Singapore display much higher statistical correlations with the US stock market than restricted markets like China, Malaysia, and India (Figure 6:1). Due to swift international fund flows, the Dow Jones's movement can often move the share prices of these open Asian markets more than changes in local economic fundamentals.

Meanwhile, the link with the Dow has increased Asian market volatility. For example, after Korea liberalised foreign trading in 1998, her stock market (as represented by the KOSPI 200 Composite) volatility rose by 27%, while capital controls in Malaysia in the same year cut stock market (KLSE Composite) volatility by a hefty 47% (Table 6:1). In other words, rather than transforming Asian markets from punters casinos to laboratories of scientific investment, foreign portfolio inflows have aggravated the local risks (as represented by higher market volatility) by adding a foreign element to them.

If foreign fund inflows were to benefit Asia's economies, they should have been funnelled into the vibrant and young companies, which need more external financing than the large mature and often state-owned companies. In practice, most foreign investors have focused on the biggest corporates because high transaction costs and opaque market

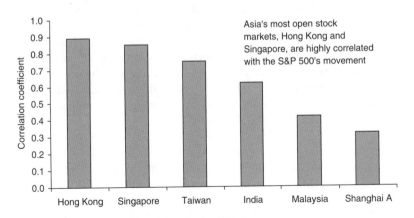

Figure 6:1 Asian markets' correlation with the US
Source: CEIC

Table 6:1 Stock market volatility*

	S. Korea	Malaysia
1990–1997	17.6	250.1
1998–2004	22.4	131.7
Change in volatility	27.3%	−47.3%

South Korea liberalised stock trading for foreigners in 1998
Malaysia imposed capital controls in 1998

* As measured by standard deviation from the mean stock index
Source: CEIC

conditions have prevented bulky foreign funds from buying young small Asian companies. This can be seen in Asia's new issue market. While small, fast-growing companies account for most new issues in the US, mega-stocks bought by foreigners dominate Asia's IPO markets. The region's entrepreneurial small firms remain largely starved of capital. As a result, Asia has seen limited gains from foreign pressure on improving its corporate governance. Only the few firms attracting foreign investment have been reformed. The numerous small companies remain unattractive to many investors. Without pushing for corporate sector reform, foreign portfolio inflows have failed to strengthen Asia's immunity against future financial crises.

In addition to de-regulating trading, Asian economies should encourage foreign investors to participate in local fund management. Development of onshore funds would enhance the influence of institutional investors without bringing in much of the erratic impact from foreign capital flows. As local funds grow, economic and companies' fundamentals would replace rumours as share-price drivers, and the importance of local events would rise to counteract Wall Street's influence on local market movement. More reliable market fundamentals would then encourage foreign investors to buy Asia's small cap companies and spread the benefit of market discipline.

But this is easier said than done. Financial liberalisation, like any kind of economic reform, threatens powerful vested interests. Like in the corporate sector, local financial institutions fear increased competition and resist changes. Unless foreign investors are committed to the Asian markets for the long-term (and many foreign investment banks still prefer the short-term trading profits when they invest in Asia to the uncertain return of long-term commitments), portfolio inflows could do more harm to the region than many have expected.

The US fiscal time bomb

Let us turn to the world's biggest potential problem, the US fiscal deficit. A fiscal calamity triggering a financial crisis is not an Asian monopoly. The US fiscal deficit has worsened fast under President George Bush junior, who won a second term office in November 2004. The ever-widening war on terrorism accounts for much of the soaring federal spending, which has outstripped fiscal revenues by a wide margin. According to the US-based think-tank the Cato Institute, US defence spending has jumped by 27% in real terms under Mr Bush, while non-military discretionary spending (i.e. spending that must be appropriated by Congress every year) has risen by 21% with the bulk of the increase coming from homeland security. Other major spending increases include farm subsidies and healthcare for the elderly. Sharp rise in public spending, tax cuts and slowing fiscal revenue growth due to a sharp economic slowdown after the bursting of the 2001 IT bubble have reversed America's fiscal surplus of 2.4% of GDP when Mr Bush ran for office in 2000 to a deficit of over 4% of GDP by 2004.

If the US falls into a fiscal crisis, it will certainly cause disruption to global capital flows and the international interest rate environment, sending shock waves to Asia. With inherent structural problems overhanging and worsening current account dynamics (see Chapter 5), Asia is susceptible to a financial crisis triggered by a large external shock, such as a US fiscal blowout. So the key question for Asia is how likely can the US fiscal deficit problem be contained?

The cyclical side of the American deficit is not so worrying. Part of the US fiscal deficit since 2001 has come from a slower economy, which has reduced fiscal revenues and raised public spending on unemployment and social benefits. The bursting of the IT bubble in 2001 cut into tax revenues further. Spending increases and tax cuts have both acted to enlarge the budget gap, but they have also helped boost the economy at the same time. Thus, the cyclical part of the fiscal gap should narrow as the economy turns up, fiscal revenues rise and public spending on welfare and unemployment benefits fall.

But the structural part of the fiscal deficit is quite worrying. The retirement of the baby-boomers, rising life expectancy and the resultant rise in medical costs are pushing up America's healthcare and other costs for its ageing population in the coming decades. The American Enterprise Institute estimates that public spending on social security and healthcare would soar from the current 7% of GDP to 11% in 2020 and 15% in 2040, giving rise to a budget gap of US$44 trillion, almost four times of today's GDP, just from the commitments to care for the greying population. Granted, this dire state may not necessarily happen, since America may be forced to cut entitlements and/or raise taxes to cope with its ageing society. There may also be policies to encourage more immigration of the people with the right skills and boost the fertility rate so that the working population may grow to fund the retirees. But the danger is there and not negligible, especially with Team Bush's lack of commitment to reform the social security and tax systems. This can be seen in the lavish spending behaviour of the Bush Administration compared with that of the Regan Administration.

The Regan administration cut discretionary non-defence spending by 14% in real terms and made an effort to overhaul social security entitlements by raising the retirement age as well as payroll taxes in 1983. But despite its Social Security reform rhetoric, all the Bush administration has done has been to expand public spending, in particular on entitlements. Mr Bush is also less keen on tax reform than Mr Regan, whose administration presided over the 1986 tax reform, which was the biggest tax reform in US modern history. The Regan reform broadened the tax base and cut tax rates without raising the overall tax burden.

President Bush's tax reform initiatives focus on consumption rather than income. But many US tax experts have argued that the Bush administration's tax reform via tax cuts would not produce a clean reform because many of the subsidies and loopholes of the current system will remain. That would likely result in a regressive tax system, which will shift the tax burden to the poor Americans, and a narrower tax base with distortions. Mr Regan was also not averse to raising taxes to curb a runaway fiscal deficit. Indeed, taxes were raised a few times and congressional rules on deficit reduction were introduced during Mr Regan's second term. But the Bush administration has not shown such flexibility.

Worst of all, Team Bush seems to be in denial of a fiscal mess. Indeed, the biggest worry about the potential of an American fiscal blowout is the administration's self-delusion. Both the Republicans and Democrats are equally keen on spending. They only differ on their priorities. The budget debate in recent years in Washington has been about where to direct public spending rather than how to cut or contain the fiscal deficit. At some point, Washington will have to face the reality and do something about the fiscal red ink. Back in the late 1980s and early 1990s, years of persistent fiscal deficits forced America to realise that it could not live beyond its means by borrowing money forever so that belt-tightening was needed. Budget rules were thus introduced and spending cuts and tax hikes were implemented by the Regan administration. It was politically painful for George Bush senior then because he lost the 1992 election, partly because of the negative economic impact of the belt-tightening measures. But the red ink was contained.

However, the reversal of the fiscal deficit this time will be much tougher because there is no 'peace dividend' from the end of the cold war to help out. In contrast, there is a new war against terrorism which will raise military spending in the years to come. There is also unlikely to be another stock market bubble to help rake in tax revenues. An ageing population will only put more pressure on social and healthcare spending. Thus, the road back to a sustainable fiscal policy will be very painful, even without any dramatic fiscal crisis.

The economic impact of all this is undeniably negative for America, and for Asia from a crisis-contagion point of view. Big fiscal deficits have reduced the US already low savings rate. As the spare economic capacity is being worked off, the US government's huge demand for funds will likely crowd out private investment and reduce long-term growth potential eventually. The US is already relying heavily on foreigners to fund her insatiable spending needs, as reflected by the bulging current account deficit[1] which soared to a historic high of 6% of GDP in early 2005.

Foreign confidence in America's economic management is thus crucial for attracting capital inflow to sustain its spendthrift habits. But budget deficits, by raising demand in the economy and hence sucking in more imports at any given level of exports, will worsen the external imbalances. Large current account deficits erode foreign confidence in the US ability to service her large foreign debt and, thus, raise the risk of financial volatility, including a dollar crisis (see 'The need for US dollar realignment' section below). In the next few years, that is perhaps the biggest risk that the US fiscal policy poses for the world economy. As and when economic adjustment unfolds, Asia will not be spared, especially if the US adjustment shock happens at the same time as the deterioration of the regional current account balances is underway (see Chapter 5).

Forcing the Fed's hand

Partly because of the US fiscal rigidity, which limits the government's ability to deal with economic ups and downs, the Fed has been shouldering the burden of keeping the US economy afloat after the 2001 IT bubble. But there are also other structural issues, both in the US and in Asia, that have forced the Fed into an ultra-expansionary mode and create bubble conditions for the global economy. The problem with this generous Fed policy stance is that it has created a shaky global backdrop on which Asia's growth depends. This, in turn raises the risk of a financial accident that could drag the regional economies into another black hole.

Arguably, the global central banks have moved together with the US Fed in creating a massive liquidity bubble, as the bursting of the IT bubble, the 9-11 terrorist attack and the Iraqi War prompted them to keep interest rates at record-low levels for an unprecedentedly long period. This liquidity bubble has turned into illusive demand growth for the global economy by encouraging speculation in asset markets, particular property. The resultant rise in asset prices has created a positive wealth effect and boosted consumption in the developed economies. The expansionary impact has spilled over to Asia, prompting an economic boom led by China.

Since the bursting of the IT bubble in 2001, the Fed seems intent on generating inflation and reflating another asset bubble, and Asia has played a crucial part in pushing the Fed into this unprecedented policy corner. First, the painful experience in post-bubble Japan has had a big impact on the Fed's policy approach to confront the US economic weakness after the bursting of the IT bubble. Like Japan, the US had a huge debt build-up before the bubble. Japan's experience shows that a post-bubble economy has a strong tendency of being trapped in a debt-deflation spiral. The Bank of Japan (BoJ), Japan's central bank, made the mistake of worrying too much about inflation in a post-bubble environment when debt-deflation was the true threat. It thus refused to reflate for the fear of reigniting inflation and the asset bubble. The resultant lack of monetary and fiscal stimuli eventually drove Japan into economic doldrums for more than a decade.

Second, China's emergence as the low-cost global manufacturer since the mid-1990s and the unleashing of massive excess capacity from Asia since the 1997–1998 Asian crisis have created a large deflationary drag on the global economy. Falling inflation has raised the real debt burden in the US, threatening to choke off consumer spending – the key growth driver for the US economy. A combination of excess capacity stemming from Asia and high debt burden in the US has been eroding pricing power, risking a deflationary trap in the US.

Third, the rest of the world has been either unwilling or unable to generate growth fast enough to pull the global economy out of the doldrums in recent years. Declining population, rigid factor markets, structural woes and inflexible policies are preventing Europe and Japan from acting as the world's growth engine. There are practically no alternatives to a US-centric global economy in the post 2001-bubble period, and Asia has remained as reliant as ever on the US as the buyer of last resort for exports to fuel its growth.

These Asian factors formed the platform for the Fed's monetary policy, which aimed at pre-empting deflation from taking hold. To do the job forcefully, policy easing needed to overshoot the normal magnitude to halt the deflationary tendency in a post-bubble economy. Though such a stance could lead to inflated asset prices, compared with the detrimental impact of debt-deflation, reflating the asset bubble seemed to be a price worth paying. From the Fed's perspective, it was extremely crucial to keep deflation from emerging because it could destabilise the US debt structure, which is the bedrock of the modern US and global economy in recent years.

For a heavily indebted economy such as the US, boosting asset prices should be a key part of an anti-deflation policy. This is because by inflating asset prices, the resultant positive wealth effect will help offset the wealth destruction impact of deflation on domestic spending. Falling interest rates between 2001 and 2003 indeed boosted the US real estate market, providing a cushion to the damage on the consumer's net worth that might have arisen from corrections in the stock market.

The Fed's aggressive reflation effort to insure against a potential economic crash in the US has created a super-stimulative environment for the asset markets. It is true that there are many structural problems plaguing the US long-term outlook. Notable is the massive debt accumulation in the post-war period, especially in the past 25 years. The booms and busts of the pre-war era, including banking crises, debt defaults, and recessions, constantly purged the US economy of financial excesses. The Great Depression was an example of forced debt liquidation. In the post-war era, however, the US economy tends to be more stable. But this economic stability has turned out to be a devil in disguise, as debt has grown steadily and there have been no robust cleansing forces to rectify the economic and financial imbalances. The emergence of deflationary pressures has also constrained the growth momentum of the highly-indebted US economy.

However, the Fed's generous policy has overwhelmed these structural negative forces. And by forcing the Fed to reflate aggressively, Asia is boosting its own growth by sustaining US demand for Asian exports. The trade benefits go to the US also, despite all the complaints from America about its trade deficit with Asia, notably China. The foreign reserves that the Asian economies have accumulated from their trade surpluses with the US are being recycled back to America. To curb their currencies' strength, Asian central banks have intervened in the foreign exchange market by buying US dollars. These dollar proceeds are, in turn, invested in US Treasury and mortgage securities. The huge demand from Asia for the US debts has allowed the Fed to keep interest rates low, underpinning the US economy and financial and housing markets. Low US interest rates, in turn, allow more room for monetary easing in Asia. The regional authorities are keen to avoid a large interest rate spread over the US, as that will boost Asian currencies and hurt exports.

The danger of the Fed's remedial monetary stimulus is that since it aims at averting a crisis by encouraging debtors to go deeper into debt, it will create a self-defeating process over the longer-term. The US authorities have gone to an extreme to inflate (by keeping interest rates low) in order to induce the public to take on more debt and to avoid deflation. This extreme policy stance will threaten to destabilise the world system. With Asia's heavy reliance on the US economy, it will not be able to escape from any US shocks as and when they emerge.

Meanwhile, Asian economies that try to fix their currencies against the US dollar have been forced to amplify the Fed's super-loose monetary policy. This is because Asian central banks have to print local currencies to buy dollars to keep their currencies from appreciating. This, in turn, boosts local money supply. But this gush of global liquidity has not pushed up goods price inflation, due to the entrenchment of deflationary pressures. Instead, it has boosted asset prices, inflating a series of asset bubbles across the global system and making it vulnerable to financial accidents.

Asia's irrational exuberance

There were also structural problems in the US economy that forced the Fed to pursue a super-loose policy stance after the IT bubble burst. The trouble was that the Fed's aggressive reflation stance had also created euphoria in the global financial markets that had priced in a bullish outlook based on the expectations of sustained US growth on the back of prolonged low inflation and low interest rates. Asian markets even experienced another equity mania between 2002 and 2004, with massive foreign portfolio capital flowing into the region and initial public offerings (IPOs) experiencing dotcom-like surges in their first day of trading.

The negative impact of all these distortions on Asia may unfold in the coming years as a trigger for further financial turmoil. Behind all the euphoria, the regional markets have underestimated the risk of the sustainability of a US economic recovery and, hence, overestimated its benefits to Asia. That risk could bring global growth to an abrupt end anytime. The root problem is in America's post-2001-bubble economic recovery, which saw falling unemployment insurance claims, rising industrial output, improved managers and consumer sentiment and a gradual rise in employment. The ugly truth is that it was a jobless economic recovery. Despite better profits, US firms are not creating the needed jobs that will solidify this economic recovery.

The bulk of the jobs created in the US after the IT bubble was in temporary staffing, healthcare and education. These were jobs were shielded from foreign competition. Jobs in manufacturing, finance, retail and information services have continued to shrink. Over three years into the post-bubble economic recovery, overall private-sector jobs in 2004 just climbed back up to levels seen at the trough of the recession in November 2001. So what made the post-2001 recovery jobless, and prompted the US Fed to recreate bubble conditions again?

Intensifying international division of labour, driven by globalisation, has been the powerful force curbing job growth in America. Such force has manifested itself in cross-border outsourcing, facilitated by Internet connectivity. With pricing power being eroded, profit-driven US corporates are under high pressure to raise productivity and cut costs to keep their margins. And cross-border outsourcing imports productivity and lowers costs.

This is notably seen in the IT services industry, where the knowledge-based output of remote foreign white-collar workers can easily be input to the production platforms in the developed markets at a fraction of the cost of the local US staffers. Hence, over three years after the post-2001-bubble economic recovery, the IT and information services jobs in the US were still contracting. In contrast, IT-related employment rose by almost 4% within two years in the US economic recovery of the early 1990s. Meanwhile, computer professionals in India's IT sector had risen to over 600,000 by 2004 from about 50,000 in the early 1990s, underscoring the US outsourcing process. This trend is spreading to many other areas, including legal, accounting, engineering, marketing and design, back-office settlement and even financial analyses.

This revolutionary labour-arbitrage process has turned the traditional non-tradable services into tradables. The resultant job leakage from the US has impaired the conventional multiplier effect of economic policy stimuli. Normally, policy stimuli generate income, employment, private spending and investment. The process will snowball into a self-sustaining cycle of spending, hiring and income growth. But this internal dynamics of the US business cycle is not working this time due to the structural change in the labour market and corporate strategy.

Without self-sustaining income growth dynamics, spendthrift American consumers need other sources of spending support. These have come in the form of massive tax cuts before the 2004 presidential election, low interest rates, excessive borrowing and extraction of cash from property via equity financing. But this foundation for the US economy is shaky because it has encouraged profligate habits and depleted national savings further, leading to a record current account deficit and a huge debt build-up. The jobless economic recovery will only aggravate these imbalances, and thus cast doubt on the sustainability of the economic upturn. The US authorities are happy to provide fiscal and monetary stimuli to keep the economy afloat for as long as they could. But with low interest rates and a rising fiscal deficit, they are running out of options to save the economy if it cracks under the weight of the economic imbalances. The upturn of the American interest cycle since late 2004 only complicates the US policy dilemma. The conundrum is that the US authorities also cannot remove these life-support measures for the economy.

The profligate US consumer is supporting millions of jobs in Asia. And because of their large American trade exposure, Asian economies are vulnerable to the US predicament. The US net trade with the region accounts for almost half of her trade deficit. This means that any unwinding of the US current account imbalance, which will involve a fall in US net intake of Asian exports, will have a large and painful impact on Asia. If and when the US structural stress forces a major US exchange rate realignment against the global currencies as part of the economic adjustment process, the potential US dollar crisis would disrupt international capital flows to the emerging markets, force up international interest rates and wreak havoc on the global markets, thus initiating an external trigger for a financial crisis in Asia.

The need for US dollar realignment

In a nutshell, the heart of these global concerns lies in the US current account deficit, which mirrors America's excessive consumption over savings. America's current account deficit is running in excess of US$650 billion a year, or over 5% of US GDP and well over 1% of world GDP. To fund this deficit, the US is absorbing massive capital inflow amounting to almost two-thirds of the aggregate current account surpluses of all the world's surplus countries. This current account deficit is not only unprecedented in American history. It is also the largest deficit of any countries relative to the global economy.

The trouble with the US current account deficit does not only lie in its huge size, but also in its nature. It is true that US economic growth has greatly exceeded the growth rate of her major trading partners in recent years so that she imports significantly more from them than she exports to them. The US current account deficit can thus be cured by slower US economic growth, right?

Not so simple. The trouble lies in the spendthrift habits of the Americans. The problem is seen in the US import elasticity with respect to domestic economic growth. This elasticity is a ratio of the percentage change in imports to the percentage change in economic growth. In other words, it tells how much imports have risen/fallen when income growth has risen/fallen by one percentage point. For a long time, America has had an import elasticity that is far higher than the other economies. This means that the US has been importing a larger amount of goods and services for every percentage point of US growth than her trading partners' growth sucking in US exports. In other words, the US has been selling less export to foreign countries for every percentage point of their growth than they have been selling to the US.

When economists first discovered this empirical evidence in the late 1960s, they could not explain the Americans' spendthrift behaviour and had thus written it off as some sort of a glitch that would disappear after some years. But over the 30 years since this 'anomaly' has been discovered, it has not gone away. The entrenchment of this import elasticity differential means that even if US growth were to slow to the same rates as her trading partners, America's current account deficit would still worsen. Thus, it is very difficult, if not impossible, to cut the US current account deficit by slowing down US economic growth solely; or the growth slowdown in the US would have to be very drastic – such as a prolonged recession.

A current account deficit is by definition the difference between net national savings[2] (which is the sum of personal, corporate and government savings) and net national investments (removing the effects of depreciation). Since 2003, the US net national savings rate has ranged between 1 and 2% of GDP. This represents a sharp deterioration from the late 1990s and is the lowest net national savings rate in American history; and perhaps the lowest among any major nations. But net investment in the US has dropped since the turn of the millennium. This suggests that all of the deterioration in the US current account deficit has come from reduced saving funding consumption rather investment. A consumption-induced current account deficit is bad because, unlike an investment-driven deficit, it does not create future growth potential and hence produces no income stream to pay for the deficit.

This is not only bad for the US, but also bad for Asia because the spendthrift US consumers have made Asia's growth dependent on them (even though China has increasingly become a driver for Asian export growth) so that the shock of a correction in the US current account deficit will be transmitted to the region swiftly. In other words, America's current account deficit has trapped Asian economies in over-reliance on US growth thus making them vulnerable to the US shock.

Foreign, mainly Asian, central banks have been funding the US current account deficit via foreign exchange intervention, as many of them are keeping a fixed or quasi-fixed exchange rate against the US dollar to boost export performance. In this intervention process, they have recycled back a large amount of their foreign exchange reserves to the US by investing in US, mainly Treasury, securities. But the US reliance on foreign governments for short-term financing cannot go on forever. Optimists argue that foreigners would keep funding the US deficit as American assets offer high returns and a haven from risk.

However, the situation is changing. Many foreign investors are turning away from the dollar assets, as exchange-rate adjusted returns on US investments have fallen below those in Europe and even Japan since 2002. A sharp drop in the US dollar would cause significant valuation losses on central bank reserves and private investment portfolios, eroding the safe haven status of the US assets. Meanwhile, Asian central banks' 'cheap-currency' policy will do more harm than good to their respective economies in due course, making it sub-optimal for them to keep intervening in the currency market and recycling their foreign reserves back to the US. Just look at Japan. Much of her speculative bubble in the late 1980s that had a catastrophic long-run impact on the Japanese economy was driven by liquidity created by a desire to sustain an undervalue currency to boost exports. Hence, Asia is unlikely to pursue foreign exchange intervention to support the US dollar forever.

All these are eroding foreign confidence in the US dollar and the incentive to continue funding the US current account deficit. This thus brings us to the potential of major US dollar exchange rate realignment, or a dollar crisis as some like to call it. There are only two ways to correct a current account deficit: either via a fall in import demand (through slower economic growth) in the deficit country, or by changing the relative import/export prices. The latter means a fall in the exchange rate of the deficit country so that exports can be made cheaper and imports can be cut by making import prices dearer, all in one stroke.

Given the huge size of the US current account deficit and the reliance of global, especially Asian, economic growth on the US, any attempt to correct the US external deficit by solely slowing American growth would inflict huge damages in both the US and global demand. That would risk a global economic implosion, and thus will not be an acceptable solution to anyone. Further, the import elasticity differential between the US and her trading partners means that if the US current account deficit were to be cut by slowing US growth only, the US would have to go through a sharp and prolonged recession. That would risk a global economic implosion, and thus will not be an acceptable solution to anyone. Thus, an appropriate adjustment must also involve a change in the relative prices between the US and the rest of the world; that is a fall in the US dollar exchange rate in this case. But the complexity and large amount of structural and financial imbalances in the global system suggest that the currency adjustment may cause significant financial volatility, such as a US dollar crisis, along the way.

In fact, this 'dollar problem' has been inherent in the global system for a long time, but its potential damage to Asian economies has risen sharply recently. After World War II, Europe and Japan did not have the money to import the needed food and machinery for economic reconstruction. The US came to help with foreign aid and policies encouraging US multinationals to invest abroad. These policies provided dollars to lubricate the world economy. Due to the significant export of US capital and consumption goods for post-war reconstruction, America was running a big trade surplus with the rest of the world.

The problem now is similar in nature but different in essence. Like in the post-WWII period, there is a massive outflow of US dollars to stimulate the world economy. But unlike the 1950s, the US has been running a chronic current account deficit with the rest of the world since the 1990s (Figure 6:2). That current account deficit was only US$70 billion, or 1.4% of US GDP, in 1990. But it ballooned to US$665 billion, or 5.6% of GDP, in 2004. It was a result of both a high dollar in the 1990s that hurt US exports and excessive US demand growth that sucked in massive imports. The rising US current account deficit has been financed by foreign capital inflows to the US, with Asian central banks and private investors buying massive amount of US Treasury bonds and other securities. As of 2004, foreigners owned about 13% of US stocks, a quarter of corporate bonds and 43% of US Treasury securities.

Up to a point, this arrangement is good for everyone. Asian economies get a boost in growth by exporting to the huge American market; US consumers get cheap imports from Asia; the world's savers (from Asia in

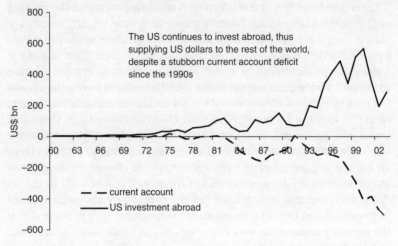

Figure 6:2 US external balances
Source: CEIC

particular) get an investment outlet for their funds in the US capital markets; and American spenders get the finance for their profligacy from the world savers. But this global equilibrium is unstable. The global economy may now have passed the point that balances the world's savers and dis-savers so that hazards may outweigh benefits. In other words, the world may be getting more US dollars than it wants, as the appetite for US dollar investment is waning. A sell-off of the dollar could spill over to the capital markets and cause a deep global economic slump. Here is how a dollar-crisis contagion would unfold.

When players sell dollars in the foreign exchange market, the US exchange rate would plunge against the Euro and the Yen and other currencies, leading to sharp decline in the value of the foreigners' investment in US assets when measured in terms of their currencies. Hefty exchange losses would deter foreign appetite for US investment, prompting foreigners to sell their US holdings. The US stock market would fall sharply, hurting American consumer confidence and spending. If foreigners also flee US bonds, bond yields would surge, sending long-term interest rates higher and hurting American domestic demand, including that for imports. Meanwhile, stronger currencies would hurt European and Japanese (and other Asian) exports, eventually hurting their domestic industries. Economic recessions in Europe, Japan and the US would, in turn, drag Asia and other emerging markets that export to them into a global recession.

No one knows when a dollar crisis will unfold. The massive US current account deficit has gone on for years. It could go on for a while longer, as long as foreigners are willing to invest in US stock and bonds. But if foreign confidence in the US fades, the consequence will be bad for everyone and Asia will not be spared.

Back in Asia, although growth is reviving across the region, the headline economic reports mask a lack of domestic demand in the region. Insufficient structural reforms and bad banks have curbed Asia's internal growth dynamics, forcing the regional economies to rely on exports to generate growth momentum (see Chapter 5). From this perspective, China's economic ascent as a market for Asian exports is cold comfort for the region.

It is true that after the US, China has been the second growth driver for the world economy in recent years by being a big importer, especially of Asian goods. Her imports reached $561 bn in 2004, up 300% from 1998 when the Asian crisis ended, while the trade surplus was down almost 30% to $32 bn in the same period. Over 80% of the rise in China's imports was in raw materials and machinery. The surge in Chinese demand for these products have pushed up many commodity prices, with nickel prices leading the pack by rising over 100% between 2003 and 2004. Copper, tin and lead prices had also risen by over 50%. The surge in China's demand for equipment imports was the most crucial factor for boosting Korean and Japanese exports between 2002 and 2005 when the US market slowed down. Europe also benefited by exporting machinery equipment to feed China's hunger for growth and industrial upgrading.

However, China still cannot replace the US as the lead growth engine for the world. In terms of absolute market size, China is still small, compared with the US. Further, the Chinese authorities are trying to slow economic growth from over 9% a year in recent years to a more sustainable, i.e. slower, pace. The point to note is that despite all these years of reform, government control still plays a significant role in determining the direction of the Chinese economy. When Beijing wants to halt the growth rate, it can still do so effectively. As a result, China's GDP growth can be expected to slow down in the medium-term, thus weakening its impact on sustaining Asia's export growth.

In a nutshell, Asia's reliance on US-centric growth makes it susceptible to US shocks, be it in the form of a failed US recovery, a US fiscal blowout or sharp US rate hikes due to excessive US dollar weakness in the process of the current account adjustment. The Fed has been using an ultra-loose monetary policy to revive the US economy without much structural adjustment to cure the financial excesses, witness America's stubborn current account deficit and excessive debt load. The spillover effect from this policy has also created asset bubbles in the Asian markets, increasing the risk of a financial accident and hence the odds for a future crisis.

Terrorism – a subtle catalyst

Subtly, the rise of terrorism will aggravate the danger of a financial crisis for Asia. With all the internal and external stress points scattering over time and across borders, a terrorist shock could act as a catalyst for an economic crisis by hitting the regional economies at the wrong time for non-economic reasons. To understand the potential economic damage of this factor, we need to examine the root concern for terrorism. Even if Osama bin Laden, the alleged master-mind behind the 9-11 attack in New York, were caught eventually, terrorism, and its disruption to the world's economic well-being, is unlikely to go away. It could even get worse in the future, due to some disturbing demographic and geopolitical trends.

The destabilising population trends reflect three simultaneous problems. First, the working-age populations in most developed economies will decline sharply in the next 25 years and beyond. Second, the size of the ageing population will grow significantly throughout the developed world. Third, the growth of the young population in the developing world, notably in the Islamic countries, will soar. These demographic forces will likely intensify the clash between an assertive US power and a growing Islamic population in the unstable parts of the world. Hence, global instability will linger on. Emerging economies, including many in Southeast Asia, that are exposed to Islamic fundamentalism will be more vulnerable to being a catalyst for setting off shocks that could lead to another regional crisis.

Determined to fight terrorism, the US has grown more assertive both militarily and economically. Population growth dynamics will only make America a more dominant global power in the coming decades. This is because the US is the only major developed economy that has favourable population dynamics supporting her economic development. Ageing population and declining labour force will become a big problem for most developed economies in 25 years' time. Immigration aside, keeping a population stable requires, on average, every female to give birth to 2.1 children – the extra 0.1 takes into account the infant mortality rate and the trend that less females have been born than males. The population grows if the replacement rate is higher than 2.1, and shrinks if the replacement rate is lower than 2.1.

Table 6:2 Fertility rates (1995–2000)

US	2.05	Yemen	7.30
UK	1.70	Turkey	2.70
Spain	1.19	Saudi Arabia	5.09
Japan	1.39	Pakistan	5.48
Italy	1.21	Nigeria	5.92
Germany	1.34	Iraq	5.25
France	1.76	Iran	2.53
Canada	1.56	India	3.45

Source: UN World Population Prospects, 2002

Table 6:3 Working population (15–64 years old) forecast % change

	2000–2025	2025–2050
US	16.9	9.7
UK	−0.6	−11.8
Spain	−10.4	−34.8
Japan	−15.7	−23.6
Italy	−14.8	−31.8
Germany	−10.7	−19.5
France	−0.5	−7.9

Source: UN World Population Prospects, 2002

In almost every developed country, the fertility rate has fallen significantly below 2.1 (Table 6:2), except the US. On the other hand, the fertility rate in many developing countries, notably those Islamic states, has remained high. According to the United Nations' (UN) projections, the low fertility rates in the developed world will create an ageing population and a shrinking work-force (those aged 15–64) in the next 25 years onwards (Table 6:3).

The falling demographic trends in Europe and Japan contrast with growth in the US, which benefits from a fertility rate close to the replacement rate and high level of immigration. Meanwhile, Europe's net immigration is not enough to offset its low birth rate and Japan has no net immigration. The major economies in Asia are facing a similar trend, as economic liberalisation, rapid development, better education and changing values are prompting late marriage and couples to have fewer children. Hence, birth rates fall, workforces shrink and the share of the greying population rises. The region's four biggest economies – Australia, China, South Korea and Japan – are all afflicted by the ageing phenomenon.

One-third of Japan's population is expected to be aged 65 or older by 2050. In China, nearly 300 million people, or over 20% of the population will be over 60 by 2025.

Potential economic growth is based on the growth of the labour force, or more precisely employment, and productivity. If productivity growth is constant, these population trends suggest that the US will grow faster than Europe and Japan in the coming decades. Europe and Japan can only close the growth gap by having faster productivity growth than the US. But their ageing population is not conducive to innovation, dynamism and hence faster productivity growth.

This means that Europe and Japan's economic importance will fall steadily relative to the US. Even their military significance will diminish, as they will have to cut military spending to tackle high fiscal deficits and growing demands for ageing population welfare. On the other hand, the US demographic trends have allowed her more economic flexibility and strengthened her role in global economics and geopolitics.

The US decision to attack Iraq in early 2003 could partly be attributed to the strategic implications of these demographic trends. The high fertility rates in the Islamic states suggest that their young populations will rise sharply. Facing poor economic prospects, they will likely create more instability in the already volatile parts of the world. By overthrowing Saddam Hussein and helping Iraq to rebuild a more liberal regime, the US hopes to use the influence of democracy to pre-empt terrorism from disrupting global stability.

But long-term trouble remains, as tension between the US and the Islamic population will intensify. The UN projects that the world's population will grow by 47% between 2000 and 2050. Within that total, the population of the developed countries will rise by 2%, while that of the developing world will rise by 58%. Within the developing world, population growth is expected to be especially rapid in the major Islamic countries. The population of the ten major Islamic countries (Afghanistan, Algeria, Indonesia, Iran, Iraq, Pakistan, Saudi Arabia, Sudan, Somalia and Yemen) was less than half of the developed world (576 million versus 1,194 million) in 2000. Their high fertility rates suggest that their population will almost match that of the industrialised world in 50 years' time.

Thus, many countries in the volatile part of the world will see a large rise in the size of the young population in the years ahead. This is a double-edged sword. On one hand, the young population could be a catalyst for positive changes if they move away from fundamentalism and push for a liberal regime. There are signs that many young Iranians are doing that. On the other hand, it is a huge challenge for the developed nations to turn those authoritarian states that have no history of democracy into liberal regimes, and a dynamic population could aggravate political instability. This is especially true when the global economy is struggling as poor demographics are undermining growth in the developed world, which is the source of export demand and economic aid for the developing world. Population trends tend to move at a glacial pace, and cyclical forces tend to overwhelm many of the economic, geopolitical and social implications from secular forces like demographic changes. The impact of the demographic shift is thus not necessarily obvious in the next few years. After all, population projections are also subject to errors.

Nevertheless, the threat of terrorism will linger on in the foreseeable future. This has profound implications for creating economic frictions in the global economy. This demographic outlook will force structural changes in different economic sectors and in different countries. For example, the expected sharp decline in the working population in the developed world, notably Europe and Japan, will drag on their domestic demand growth. This, in turn, will bode ill for consumer goods and real estate in these markets in the long-term. Meanwhile, the developed world's demand for ageing-related goods and services will rise. But that may not be enough to outweigh the growth drag from the falling demand in the shrinking work-age group. Overall aggregate demand growth will be constrained, curbing pricing power so that disinflation, with periodic deflation, will be a characteristic in the developed world in the coming decades. Thus, industrial structure will have to change and resources will have to be re-allocated. Economic stress will arise during the structural transition, raising the risk of economic dislocation.

Ageing population will also weigh on government finances as the pension liability continues to build up. The risk of a fiscal blowout due to the pension burden is especially acute in Japan and Europe, as they have fast ageing populations but do not have fully-funded pension systems. Their PAYE (pay-as-you-earn) pension systems, which rely on their shrinking workforce to pay taxes to support the ageing, are the root of the pension-induced fiscal problem. This means the threat of a fiscal time bomb is becoming a global problem, creating potential disruption to global capital flows and the international interest rate environment that would send negative shocks to Asia.

The bottom line is that Asia is facing many external risks that could tip it into another economic crisis. By adding to the region's economic stress, China is only one of those risks. The region also has itself to blame for self-inflicting crisis potentials by failing to purge its economic excesses after the 1997/1998 regional crisis. Arguably, the US is the biggest threat to the global economy in the coming years, as her huge twin (fiscal and current account) deficit is threatening to cause a US dollar crisis that would have disruptive global effects. Another risk is rising oil prices, which could hit US$60–$70 a barrel, according to some industry experts, even without a major political and terrorist disruption.

Most of these risks reinforce each other. An oil price shock, a dollar collapse and a soaring US budget deficit would all generate higher inflation and interest rates. This will risk the emergence of stagflation – stagnant economic growth and rising inflation – if global demand failed to sustain growth under the weight of excess capacity and structural rigidities. A US dollar crisis would raise the likelihood of further oil price increases. Larger budget deficit would boost the US current account deficit further, and thus create more US dollar volatility. Further weakness in the US external balances will also encourage more protectionism, which is a more imminent threat to Asia (and the global economy) than a financial crisis (see next chapter).

Fears of a hard-landing for the US dollar and the world economy are not new. The situation is more serious today because of the record US current account deficit and international debt, and the high odds of further and swift increases in both. The rapid rise in oil prices since 2002 increases Asia's vulnerability to another economic crisis because of its heavy dependence on oil imports. Industry experts estimate that every sustained rise of US$10 per barrel in the world oil prices would cut about 0.5 percentage points, or US$300 billion, off annual global GDP growth for a few years. US Fed Chairman Greenspan also notes frequently that all three major post-war recessions were triggered by a sharp rise in oil prices. Oil prices could climb more if political or terrorist events erupted to unsettle output in the Middle East, the former Soviet Union and elsewhere.

Even worse scenarios can be envisaged: a terrorist attack with far worse economic impact than the 9-11 attack in New York or a sharp fall in American productivity growth, as occurred after the oil shocks of the 1970s, that would further damage the outlook for both the US economic growth and the dollar. There is a high probability that one or more of these risks to global prosperity and stability would play out. The impact on Asia of several of them reinforcing each other is potentially disastrous. However, this does not mean that another economic crisis is unavoidable. Rather, a more imminent risk for Asia is growing protectionism, as we shall discuss in the next chapter.

7
The Real Danger Isn't Another Crisis

Despite Asia's inherent systemic flaws, the external shocks and China's economic threat aggravating these problems, another regional financial crisis is avoidable. Notably, today's Asia has had some economic buffers that will help mitigate the macro instability. They include large external surpluses and foreign reserves accumulation, high domestic liquidity, undervalued currencies and lower exposure to global interest rate volatility.

Timely policy actions can also reduce the risks of another financial crisis. For Asia, this requires the regional governments to sustain their reform efforts and make thorough structural changes. China is showing progress in both macroeconomic management and structural changes. That should help lessen her perceived economic threat to other economies. More crucially, the US needs a credible programme, including both spending cuts and revenue increases, to cut her fiscal and current account deficits in the coming years and to sustain the improvement thereafter.

Instead of another financial crisis, the real danger facing Asia is rising protectionism. The biggest source of it comes from the US, where her large current account deficit is generating strong protectionist pressure. You see it in political debates over trade; you see it in the furore over outsourcing. Despite the expiry of the Multi-fibre Arrangement on Textiles (MFAT) in January 2005, the US Commerce Department has set new quotas on imports of clothing from China to protect America's sunset textile industry. Geopolitical strains due to the weakening power of Japan and Europe (see Chapter 6 section 'Terrorism – a subtle catalyst') could also foster increased protectionism, which will become an entrenched risk for Asia, and the global economy, in the coming decades.

The crisis cushions

Despite its economic faults, Asia today is economically safer than it was in the years leading up to the 1997–1998 regional crisis. While the crisis potentials are there, the region has several buffers to cushion them. Unlike in the years leading up to the Asian crisis when cheap credit alone drove economic growth to excessive levels, economic fundamentals (like aggregate demand growth and external surpluses) have supported growth in the post-crisis Asia. The problem with the pre-crisis growth was that it was entirely money driven. Hence, when the economic excesses amassed to a breaking point in 1997, investors lost confidence in Asia and the party ended. The subsequent withdrawal of foreign creditors from the region sent the markets into a tailspin, taking the regional economies along with them.

This time around, the crisis trigger (current account deficits) is absent. In the early to mid-1990s, some Asian economies (notably Thailand, which set off the regional debacle) were running huge current account deficits amounting to over 5% of GDP. These deficits were financed by significant short-term capital inflow. So fickle hot money inflow supported Asia's excessive spending. But since 1998, the regional current account deficits have been reversed to large surpluses, averaging almost 10% of GDP now. Greater China – China, Hong Kong and Taiwan – accounts for the bulk of the surplus accumulation. The turnaround in the deficit was the most dramatic in the three crisis-hit economies of Korea, Thailand and Indonesia (Figure 7:1), where their external balances zoomed from an average deficit of over 5% of GDP in 1996 to a surplus of 10% of GDP in 1998. Their average surplus has since been sustained at about 4% of GDP.

What all this means is that Asian economies today are not held hostage by the funds provided by short-term creditors and speculators. It is true that Asia has again seen rising portfolio (short-term money) inflows since 2004, but these inflows are accompanied by large current account surpluses (long-term money inflows). This has allowed Asia to accumulate large foreign exchange reserves, which will act as a buffer against hot money outflow.

Foreign exchange reserves are a war chest for the authorities to defend their currencies against speculative attacks. Hence, bigger reserves give a country stronger ability to ride out external volatility. Indeed, foreign reserves accumulation underscores an even starker difference between Asia today and before 1997 (Figure 7:2). In the years prior to the Asian crisis, Asian (excluding China and Japan) foreign

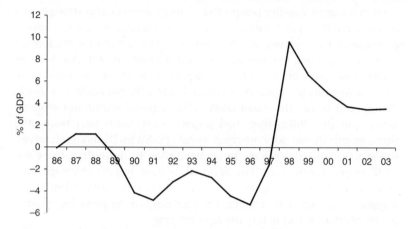

Figure 7:1 Asia's current account turns around (average of current account balances of the crisis-hit economies: Korea, Indonesia and Thailand)
Source: CEIC

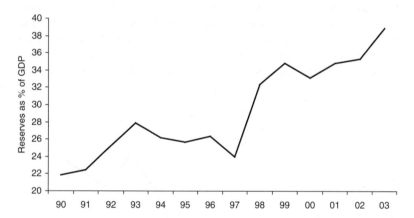

Figure 7:2 Asia's FX reserves have soared
Source: CEIC

reserves averaged 25% of GDP, with a growth rate of less than 2% of GDP a year. But since 1999, foreign reserves have averaged 35% of GDP, and the growth rate has accelerated to over 9% of GDP a year. In 2003, Asia's average foreign reserves amounted to almost 40% of GDP. This sharp improvement should allay fears of disappearing foreign reserves triggering another financial crisis.

From a macro stability perspective, foreign reserves also strengthen a nation's ability to pay for its imports. So it is crucial to look at the import coverage of the reserves. A safety rule is that if an economy's foreign reserves are enough to cover more than three months of import bills, its external balances are sound. Any import coverage of less than three months suggests the country is vulnerable to external payments shock. During and before the Asian crisis, some regional economies, notably Korea and the Philippines, had import cover ratios well below the three-month threshold. Post-crisis, as Asia builds up its foreign reserves, the average import coverage ratios have risen to more than twice the 1997 levels (Figure 7:3). The regional average import coverage now amounts to 8.4 months compared with only four months in 1997. This suggests that Asia is in a much stronger position to meet its external payments than it was before the regional crisis.

Remember one of the systemic flaws underlying the Asian crisis was fixed exchange rates barring adjustments to the economic woes in the regional economies. But after the crisis, most regional currencies (except the Chinese renminbi, Hong Kong dollar and the Malaysian ringgit) have gone floating. And flexible exchange rates will help absorb financial shocks and, hence, lower the risk of another financial crisis. In practice, Asia may still act as a quasi US dollar bloc after the crisis, as the regional authorities have not discarded their habit of fixing their exchange rates to the US dollar. But Asia's post-crisis exchange rate

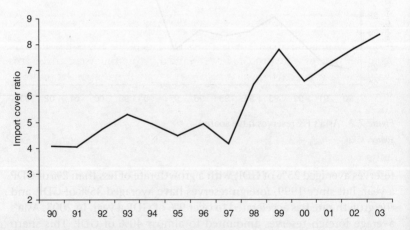

Figure 7:3   Asia's import cover has risen sharply
Source: CEIC

Table 7:1 Asian foreign exchange rate volatility*

	Jan 1990–July 1997	Aug 1997–Dec 2004	% change in volatility
Indonesian rupiah	182.52	1,773.05	871.4
Thai bhat	0.60	3.08	412.3
Philippine peso	1.45	7.08	389.9
Korean won	46.37	123.94	167.3
New Taiwan dollar	0.82	1.50	83.0

* Approximated by standard deviation from the mean exchange rate in the sample period
Source: CEIC

policy is still quite different from the outright fixed exchange rate system in the pre-crisis period. Despite being controlled, most Asian exchange rates have fluctuated more than they did before 1997 (Table 7:1).[1] Notably, the volatility (as measured by the standard deviation of the exchange rate from its mean in the sample period) of the Indonesian rupiah has jumped by over 870% after the Asian crisis. Even the fluctuation of the tightly controlled New Taiwan dollar has increased by 83% after the regional debacle.

Flexible exchange rates may also lower speculative motives, which are often a catalyst for triggering a financial crisis or a force aggravating a crisis. A fixed exchange rate tends to create unrealistic expectations of guaranteed returns by eliminating foreign exchange risk. Such expectations encourage excessive investment and currency speculation. But a flexible exchange rate incurs volatility that tends to limit speculation incentive.

Further, judging from their underlying current account balances, Asian currencies were probably over-valued before the Asian crisis. This was because Asian exchange rates should have fallen due to the underlying current account deficits, but the fixed exchange rate regimes barred them from adjusting before 1997. After the Asian crisis, the region's current accounts have turned into surpluses, arguing for appreciation for its currencies. But the extent of appreciation allowed by the regional authorities has been less than the market forces warranted. Thus, Asian currencies are likely to be under-valued since the regional crisis.

The relative currency valuation matters because it was the expectations of massive devaluation of Asia's over-valued currencies that fuelled capital outflows and set off the regional crisis in 1997. The under-valued currencies today should reduce such expectations and, thus, the odds of large capital outflow triggering another financial crisis.

A detrimental force that pulled the rug from under the Asian economies and contributed to the regional debacle was excessive, especially foreign, borrowing. Over-reliance on foreign borrowing puts an economy at the mercy of foreign creditors' sentiment, which could often change without reference to local fundamental developments. Asian banks and firms made precisely this mistake in the pre-crisis years by borrowing heavily from abroad to fund economic activity at home. Not only that. They borrowed mostly short-term foreign loans to fund local long-term projects. This created a serious balance-sheet mismatch problem that aggravated the financial vulnerability of the banking system. There were two mismatching problems. One is currency mismatching and the other is loan-maturity mismatching.

Currency mismatching exposed the banks to foreign exchange risk – as and when the local currency dropped sharply, the debt burden of the foreign currency loan soared. This is because more local currency was needed to exchange a given amount of foreign currency to repay the loan. Loan-maturity mismatching exposed the banks to interest rate risk – as and when interest rates surged, the banks' funding cost also surged as they borrowed short-term and thus needed to renew the loans frequently at the prevailing (rising) interest rates. But their return from the long-term investment was fixed. Thus, soaring funding cost under fixed income pushed the banks into financial difficulties.

The regional banks also did not hedge their foreign exchange exposure, despite the availability of various financial vehicles for them to do so, on the belief that their governments would sustain the fixed exchange rate regimes forever. Thus, the resultant build-up of external liabilities was in the form of un-hedged debts, giving rise to significant currency risk in the banking systems. The naive belief that Asian governments would keep their fixed exchange rate systems had also eliminated any perceivable currency risk for foreign creditors. Together with higher Asian interest rates relative to foreign countries, the fixed exchange rate regimes thus enticed massive foreign lending, often imprudently, to Asia.

Indicating the region's over-leveraging behaviour are its loan-to-deposit and foreign debt-to-GDP ratios, which rose to over 100% by 1997. Obviously, Asia needed to cut debt to correct this problem after the fixed exchange rate regimes collapsed in 1998. Led by the IMF bailout packages, the regional governments did just that. As a result both domestic and foreign loans have fallen sharply since the end of the crisis (Figure 7:4). Asia's de-leveraging process has combined with its balance of payments surpluses and foreign exchange intervention to create ample liquidity in the system, giving it stronger immunity to the outbreak of another financial crisis.

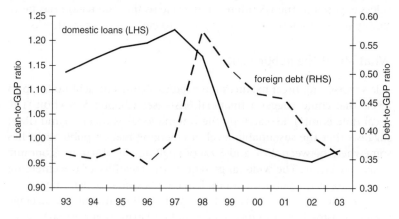

Figure 7:4 Asia de-leveraging
Source: CEIC

Last but not least, running a managed float exchange rate against the US dollar, as Asia has been doing since the Asian crisis, is not the same as keeping a fixed exchange rate regime, as it did before 1997. This is because the managed float system allows more exchange rate flexibility to absorb economic shocks. More crucially, the under-valuation of the Asian currencies post-crisis allows more monetary policy flexibility for the regional authorities. In principle, when Asia is intervening to keep its currencies relatively stable against the US dollar, it has to import US interest rate policy. This also means that Asia loses its monetary policy control. Asian and US interest rate gap must be kept stable so as not to create currency arbitrage opportunities. Hence, Asian and US rates have to move in tandem to prevent capital flows disrupting the managed exchange rate.

The interest rate parity condition states the difference between any pair of countries' interest rates is approximately equal to the expected change in the exchange rate. So if Asian (treated as one aggregate region) interest rate is lower than the US interest rate, the market must expect Asian exchange rate to rise, and vice versa, in order to remain in equilibrium. With most Asian currencies under-valued since the regional crisis, this argues for lower Asian interest rates relative to the US rate. Indeed, lower Asian rates have been manifested in the regional central banks' foreign exchange interventions to curb their currencies from appreciating. Such intervention allows the Asian authorities to deviate domestic interest rates from US rate movement; in particular to cut them below US levels to boost domestic growth. Hence, post-crisis Asia is less exposed to the US interest rate cycle so that the region has more leeway to use domestic monetary policy to cushion external shocks.

What about the public debt?

Asia's worsening fiscal balances have led to significant debt build-up to levels that could trigger a financial crisis (see Chapter 5, section 'The fiscal time bomb'). Research by the International Monetary Fund (IMF) suggests that the sustainable level of emerging market public debt lies somewhere between 25% and 50% of GDP, above which an economic crisis may ensue. The wide range reflects the volatility of the emerging economies, as the public debt problem could explode depending on the fickle economic conditions and investor sentiment. But the average public debt-to-GDP ratio for Asia (excluding Japan) is almost 60%, with Malaysia, India, Indonesia, Singapore[2] and the Philippines recording significantly higher ratios. This puts Asia in the crisis danger zone as defined by the IMF (Figure 7:5). Worse still, these debts do not include contingent liabilities, such as unfunded pension liabilities and the financial cost of cleaning up the banking systems. These contingent costs could easily add another 35% of GDP to Asia's public debt.

However, Asia's debt woes may not necessarily push it into another crisis, thanks largely to the financial cushions the region has accumulated. Japan is an example for those cushions helping to avert an

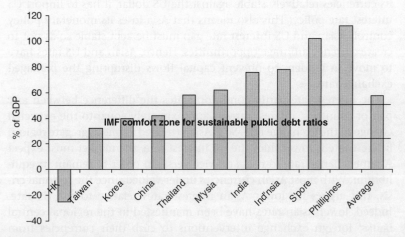

Figure 7:5 Asia's public debt
Source: CEIC

economic crisis, despite serious economic woes. Japan has a public debt-to-GDP ratio of 160% of GDP (excluding contingent liabilities) and a budget deficit of more than 6% of GDP since 1998. A mountain of bad debts has crippled her banking system and the economy has barely grown. All this would have pushed most countries into an economic crisis, but Japan has managed to escape the deadly consequences so far.

One big advantage that Japan has is that, Japan's huge public debt is entirely domestically owned. Only a tiny fraction is held by overseas investors. This means that Japan's financial system is not held hostage by foreign creditors, and is thus not vulnerable to the risk of sudden foreign capital withdrawal. Crucially, private savings in Japan are very high, and many domestic institutions are required to invest a large share of their assets in domestic bonds. Japan's interest rates are among the lowest in the world, with zero overnight rate and long-term (ten-year) bond yield of less than 2% for many years. Real interest rates are a little higher due to mild domestic deflation. This low interest-rate environment has not only helped ease Japan's economic pains in her post-bubble economic transformation, it has also kept her debt-servicing burden low and thus reducing the risk of a debt crisis.

Japan's flexible exchange rate (despite periodic official intervention) and the constant appreciation pressure on the Japanese yen have also helped contain the crisis risk by keeping investors from moving out of Japanese assets. Arguably, the potential foreign exchange gains from the persistent yen appreciation pressure (due to a persistent current account surplus) has kept investors glued to Japanese assets, even though the high liquidity overhang has kept interest rates (and hence short-term returns) low in Japan.

The relevance of the Japan story to Asia is that the region sees the same combination of these cushion factors. Asia has been de-leveraging since the regional crisis, and thus reducing its exposure to foreign creditors. Like Japan, it also has very high savings, a low interest rate environment and under-valued exchange rates that are under appreciation pressure. Hence, Asia is less prone to another financial crisis than before, despite its large debt build-up.

However, these favourable factors will not last forever, and they already vary greatly among individual economies in Asia. Without a return of the economic conditions to the mid-1990s boom years, Asia's budget deficits are unlikely to go away anytime soon and its public debt will likely continue to grow. The economies that are of greatest concern (with the largest public debt-to-GDP ratios) are Japan, India, the Philippines and Indonesia. If we add contingent liabilities to the future deficit dynamics, China (which is currently seen as low risk) could move up the risk league due to her large pension and bank rehabilitation liabilities. The risk of other economies like Taiwan and Malaysia, which currently have low public debt ratios, could rise if they fail to solve the structural problems behind their current deficits.

Unfortunately, no one knows what exactly could trigger the next crisis. Looking at the emerging markets over the past two decades, some of the most risky economies managed to escape the worst, even as trouble erupted in other less risky economies. In Asia, which has the cushions to absorb global interest rates and balance of payments shocks, a crisis trigger could come from an external shock, such as an exogenous political event, terrorist attack or a sudden recognition of large liabilities.

On a positive note, the regional governments are not sitting on their hands to let a crisis emerge. Among the ten major Asian economies,[3] eight have plans to cut their budget deficits or balance their budgets in the next few years; and three of these eight have made consistent progress. Only Korea and Taiwan do not have any fiscal reform plans yet, as of end-2004. While China has not announced any formal deficit reduction plans, she has been phasing in fiscal reform plans to raise tax revenues and scale back public investment and spending. Indonesia and Thailand have set targets to balance their fiscal budgets by 2006 and have consistently met or done better than their reduction targets since 2001. Singapore has aimed at continuing to run budget surpluses over the course of the business cycle. She has raised taxes and cut spending in recent years to ensure achievement of the fiscal surplus goal. Hong Kong has plans to balance the budget by 2009. It has raised income and corporate taxes and is considering introducing a goods-and-services sales tax to strengthen its tax base.[4] India and Malaysia have announced plans to cut or balance their fiscal budget, but their success will depend on their resolve to raise taxes and cut spending. The bad apple is the Philippines, which has consistently missed her budget reduction targets since 2002, despite Manila's intention to balance its budget by 2009. The Filipino government lacks a coherent and credible fiscal reform strategy.

And the China trigger?

What about the risk of the Chinese economic woes pulling Asia into another financial crisis? This risk is four-fold: policy mistakes aggravating the country's boom-bust cycle, a broken domestic financial system, a fiscal time bomb and a huge pension liability. However, there are good reasons to believe that these risks are well contained.

Since 1996, Beijing has made progress on improving policy management that avoids boom-bust economic cycles. It has made anti-inflation its monetary policy goal. The policy has been successful, as seen in the death of high inflation since 2000. Financial liberalisation is an integral part of Beijing's better economic management strategy. The current foreign exchange controls have distorted China's capital allocation. They have locked up massive domestic savings, forcing local capital to invest at home disregarding return performance. Worse still, much of this investment has gone to the inefficient state-owned enterprises (SOEs). Meanwhile, the impaired banking system cannot fully utilise the funds, leading to a deposit surplus over lending. This surplus amounts to financial suppression. It not only misallocates capital and deprives local savers of better returns but also creates highly volatile boom-bust cycles, with the surplus savings propelling unsustainable investment booms only to be busted by harsh policy measures later.

In a move to solve the capital misallocation and boom-bust cyclical problems, Beijing is granting more investment freedom to local funds to go abroad so that they can seek better returns. The authorities are not opening the floodgate all at once though. They only allow local financial institutions to invest in overseas markets gradually. This measure will help ease speculative pressure on local asset prices and strengthen the Chinese banks' balance sheets by allowing them to buy better quality assets. The proposed Qualified Domestic Institutional Investors (QDII) scheme is a step towards this goal. The next step will be to allow Mainland institutional and retail investors to buy increasing amounts of hard currency to make foreign investments, with an eventual goal of achieving full capital account convertibility.

There is evidence showing that China has pursued a better reform-growth policy mix than many of her Asian peers since the Asian crisis. Thus the risk of boom-bust economic volatility is much lower going forward. While keeping a steady macroeconomic growth environment, Beijing has engineered massive creative destruction in the economy; witness the significant decline in SOE employment and the rise in private sector jobs (Figure 7:6). The rapid shrinkage of the state sector is a result of the government destroying old and inefficient industries and replacing them with new and more efficient ones. Since the Asian crisis, the number of SOEs has fallen steadily from 40% of total enterprises in the economy to 15%. Meanwhile, the SOEs' aggregate asset value has fallen from 70% of the total corporate asset value to 50% during the same period. In terms of production, the SOEs now account for less than 20% of total industrial output, compared to over 80% in the early 1980s.

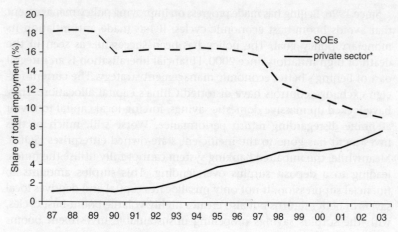

Figure 7:6 Creative job destruction
* Including private, foreign firms and self-employed entrepreneurs
Source: CEIC

The trend of the shrinking SOEs is expected to continue, given Beijing's economic restructuring and privatisation programmes.

There are also signs for the growing role of market forces and increased competition driving China's economic restructuring. Notably, average Chinese tariffs have fallen from 43% in 1997 to about 10% now, and they will keep falling in the coming years under the WTO requirements. Lower tariffs have increased competition and raised Chinese productivity. Output per Chinese worker has been rising by an average of 5% a year since 1999, compared to less than 1% before that. Western technology, machinery and management brought in by foreign firms have prompted more competition in the domestic economy.

More competition has allowed greater choice for Chinese consumers, lessening the demand–supply mismatch problem in the economy. Chinese firms used to focus on producing for the official quotas but not on market demand under the old system. Hence, wasteful production flooded the market with goods that no one wanted. But economic liberalisation and increased profit incentives have changed the production structure to market focused. Overall growth quality has thus improved. Meanwhile, unemployment has soared as the closure of the SOEs releases millions of surplus workers a year. Employment in the SOEs fell by over 40 million, over a third of the total, between 1993 and 2004. Rising bankruptcies and unemployment are clear signs of China's willingness to pay a high cost of adjusting to increasing competition in the domestic market. Many SOEs have been privatised and the non-state sector has been creating new jobs to help absorb the surplus labour from economic restructuring.

The biggest concern of a China-induced Asian crisis is the collapse of the Chinese banking system, which is still dominated by the Big Four state banks – Agricultural Bank of China, Bank of China, China Construction Bank and Industrial and Commercial Bank of China. Their huge bad debt problems, with non-performing loans (NPLs) estimated by most independent experts at over 40% of total banking assets, have led many pessimists predict a financial collapse in China. Nevertheless, a banking crisis has never happened, and there are reasons to believe that it will not happen in the near future.

First, the conventional wisdom for banking crisis does not apply to China. Second, China's half-baked market economy has turned out to be a blessing in disguise for keeping the system from falling apart. Third, the overall banking environment in China has improved, reducing the risk of a systemic meltdown. Fourth, Chinese banks have made some progress on improving their operations and system controls. Last, but not least, the central bank is phasing in, albeit slowly, market-determined interest rates, thus improving market discipline for controlling system risk.

Normally, a bank goes under when it is insolvent,[5] and the banking system collapses when most, if not all, of its banks are insolvent. But in China's context, the key is not whether Chinese banks are solvent but whether they have positive cash flow.[6] From a systemic view, there is a confidence issue. A bank will not go bankrupt simply because it is insolvent, unless there is a loss of public confidence that prompts all depositors to withdraw their money all at once. This will cause a run on the bank, draining its liquidity and forcing it to fail. But Beijing's 'too-big-to-fail' policy basically underwrites all the local banks, so the system is unlikely to go belly up. The implicit government guarantee of the banking system has kept public confidence high so that the probability of bank run is low.

Technically, a bank becomes non-viable when it lacks money from its interest income to pay its depositors; that is when its cash flow turns negative. A bank's cash flow is determined by the spread that it charges, i.e. the difference between the lending and the deposit rates. Given that depositors will not withdraw money from the bank all at once, as long as the interest charged on the performing assets covers the interest paid to the depositors, the bank will not go bust. Thanks to official interest rate control policies that have kept China's lending rate consistently and significantly above the deposit rate since 1995, Chinese banks are always cash-flow positive, despite all the bad debt problems.

The absence of a banking crisis so far in China can also be attributable to her half-transition from a planned economy to a market system. This mixed system has allowed the authorities to perform an economic balancing act between growth and reform. First, the combination of a closed capital account and a small foreign debt has shielded China from the risk of withdrawal by the foreign creditors.[7] In other words, unlike those Asian crisis economies, China's banking system is not held hostage by the foreign creditors. Second, the combination of China's high savings, averaging 40% of income over the past decade, and robust income growth have generated a huge amount of liquidity. Without a developed capital market to offer alternative savings products, the bulk of household savings goes into the state bank deposits. China also limits the operating scale of non-state commercial banks and foreign banks through licensing requirements and restrictions on funding sources. All this has acted to direct household savings to the state banks, keeping them liquid.

China's overall banking environment has improved. The progress, though slow, should help contain the risk of a banking crisis going forward. Since 1998, not only has the state sector downsized, but overall internal governance and transparency at Chinese banks have improved. The shrinkage of the state sector suggests that the role of state-directed lending has declined. With the closure of many SOEs, there is simply a smaller need to lend to the state sector.

This is not to say that state banks are not generating new bad loans. Indeed, they will continue to add NPLs as reform continues because many SOEs loans will turn bad as they are restructured or closed down. However, the pace of bad loan growth has slowed. The official revelation of a high bad loan ratio also suggests improvement in transparency, though the problem is not resolved completely.

Chinese banks are also making progress on reforming their operations, reducing the risk of failure. On the audit side, banks have adopted new accounting standards and the international five-tier system for classifying NPLs. They have broadly computerised and centralised credit databases, though audits are still done by internal auditors (this still raises doubt about the independence of the audit results). Banks have also gone through significant risk management training. In a controlled interest rate environment, there is little scope for serious implementation. But even this is changing slowly.

Since late 1999, all Chinese banks have been putting in efforts to improve credit-risk management, especially in the under-writing of new loans. Most of them have used the credit-check process that is familiar to western bankers. Not surprisingly, many SOEs – the banks' traditional borrowers – cannot meet the new lending criteria. Hence, lending to the SOEs has dropped while loans to government projects and to individuals buying houses and durable goods have risen. The banks have also been investing funds in government bonds to improve asset quality in their balance sheets. From a portfolio-risk and cash-flow angle, this is an improvement, though the change is still slow. Meanwhile, major Chinese banks have vastly raised their bad-debt provisions, and cut NPLs by increasing write-offs.

The People's Bank of China (PBoC), the central bank, is allowing more interest rate flexibility under market forces. In early 2003, it approved an unprecedented experiment with banking overhaul in the eastern city of Wenzhou, which allows market forces to set interest rates for bank deposits and loans. It has also lifted the ban on the city's private-sector investment in local commercial banks, and set up a small-loan system targeted at private businesses. These measures go a long way to correct the distortion of interest rate controls and capital misallocation that starve the private sector of credit.

Also in early 2003, the Ministry of Finance announced it would allow hedging in the Chinese bond market. The new rules allow investors to use risk-hedging tools, such as forward contracts and short-selling,[8] in the domestic Treasury bond market. The purpose is to encourage Chinese banks, which are the main investors in government bonds, to hedge exposure to the government's ballooning debt. Without hedging instruments, Chinese banks have been lacking the tools to protect themselves against price volatility in the Treasury market as interest rates fluctuate. It is thus obvious that by allowing interest-rate-risk hedging, Beijing is prepared to liberalise interest rates further, allowing them to fluctuate under market forces.

Further liberalisation did follow, when the PBoC pushed interest rate liberalisation to the national level in October 2004 by abolishing the interest rate cap on bank lending and allowing banks to set deposit rates according to market forces. Though this was only partial liberalisation on credit pricing, it marked the transition from administrative measures to market-driven policy.

Finally, Beijing has been skilful in finding its way through the banks' bad debt problem, and it still enjoys considerable scope for manoeuvre.

In the 1998 recapitalisation effort, a big portion of the Big Four's NPLs was transferred to the four asset management companies. That allowed the government to contain the immediate impact of the bad-loan losses and spread it over a long period of time. In the recent recapitalisation effort since 2003, Beijing has enlisted help from investors, including foreign players. The government wants to list the main banks, including the Big Four, on the stock exchanges both in China and overseas to attract capital for recapitalisation. In the coming years, every one of the 16 major Chinese banks, perhaps with a few exceptions, will have a significant share of its equity owned by foreign investors. The game plan is to engage the foreign investors' interest so that they will transfer modern technology and management techniques to help strengthen China's banking system. If successful, this strategy will go a long way to help solve China's bad debt problem and, hence, reduce the risk of a Chinese financial crisis spreading to Asia.

Some have fretted that the huge sum of money needed for fixing China's financial system amounts to a potential fiscal time bomb. The fears are exaggerated. There are ample funds available in the form of household savings sitting idle in the banking system. They amount to over US$1 trillion and will continue to grow as long as there is a lack of alternative investments. The bad-debt-burdened state banks are under pressure to repair their balance sheets. So they are wary of using the deposits to make fresh loans. This means that Beijing could easily tap into this big pool of private savings by issuing treasury bonds to the public and the banks, and use the proceeds to boost economic growth and recapitalise the banking system. Given the low level of public debt (at less than 10% of GDP), it can easily finance spending through borrowing for some years.

If the potential revenues from privatising the Big Four state banks are counted, Beijing's finances look even better. A 50% reduction in its stakes in the state banks after they are recapitalised could yield as much as US$40 billion (or 4% of GDP), according to some private estimates. Beyond the banking system, state-owned shares of listed companies are valued at roughly 30% of GDP. Selling these state-owned shares will raise tens of billions of RMB for sustaining the fiscal book. However, these potential revenues from privatising the state banks and companies could prove to be illusive if structural reforms fail.

While the pessimists may have painted an overly bleak fiscal picture for China, it is a valid concern that the Middle Kingdom is facing a rising risk of fiscal bust in the medium-term, though this outcome is avoidable. A clear resolve to tackle the country's fiscal woes is the only way for China to preclude suffering a fiscal crisis. Beijing must pursue a two-pronged approach to both raise fiscal revenues and cut wasteful spending. Fiscal reform is part of the structural reform programme for dispelling any misunderstanding about the government's policy direction and keeping investor confidence.

Another related problem for China's financial system is her huge pension liability. Only 10% of China's population today is over 60 years old. But this share will double in ten years, and it will reach 26% by 2050, according to the United Nations' projection. An ageing population may not be a problem if there are enough young workers to replace the retiring ones. But China does not seem to have the needed working population to the support the ageing. The current pension system is severely under-funded, with the size of the shortfall estimated at between RMB4 and RMB7 trillion (US$480–850 billion), or 45–75% of GDP.[9] Adding this pension shortfall to the estimated RMB2.5 trillion needed for bank recapitalisation, China's total contingent liabilities to keep the financial system afloat easily surpass 100% of GDP. That is why pessimists who see China walking with a fiscal time bomb, irreparable SOEs and a pension puzzle cannot help but predict an inevitable financial implosion, with the far reaching effect of pulling other regional economies with it.

In principle, the government can fund the pension debt through raising taxes (including the pension contribution rate), or borrowing, or asset sales, or a combination of the three. But the first two options are not practical and not fair. Funding the current pension payments out of taxation and public borrowing will effectively put the financing burden on the shoulders of the current and future workers. They will have to save for their retirement as well as paying higher taxes for repaying today's government borrowing in the future. The current pension contribution rate of over 20% from employers has already caused complaints and resistance from the business community. Further increase in the burden would only undermine business confidence. This means that the only feasible way to fix the pension problem is through asset sales.

Surely, not all state assets are saleable, especially those bad SOEs with high debt burden and low profitability or even losses. But Beijing does own some assets with good market value. They include telecommunications, oil, power, transport and media agencies. Further, about 30% of the manufacturing businesses are still under state ownership, even after Beijing ordered the People's Liberation Army to get out of the business sector a few years ago. There are no official records for the total value of the government's assets, but the following gives some clues.

The total market capitalisation of the listed SOEs was RMB4 trillion as of the end of 2003. The government's 65% stake was worth about RMB2.6 trillion. Meanwhile, the government owns about 80% of the country's services sector, which accounts for about 30% of GDP (or RMB2.5 trillion). This means the government's stake is worth about RMB2 trillion. The manufacturing sector accounts for about 54% of GDP, or RMB4.5 trillion. Thus, the 30% government ownership is equivalent to about RMB1.3 trillion. Meanwhile, Beijing has huge foreign exchange reserves amounting to over RMB5.1 trillion and overseas assets worth more than RMB2 trillion. The government also owns all the country's land and natural resources that potentially have great value. Finally, if privatised, the market value of the services industries will likely command a premium over their face value suggested by the GDP estimates, due to keen foreign investor interests in them.

The point is that while the situation in China's pension system is not ideal, it not likely to crush the financial system anytime soon. The Chinese government owns a lot of assets, with growing value. Rising reform momentum under the WTO membership, combined with the need to cover the pension debt, means that the government will sell state assets on a large scale in the coming years. This, in turn, supports the urgent need for capital market reform because the pension funds will need assets to invest in to generate a decent return over time to meet their future liabilities.

In a nutshell, China's financial system is not in a danger of collapse, and hence it is not threatening to cause another Asian crisis. After all, China's seemingly large pension debt, estimated at between 45% and 75% of GDP, is not that large by international standards. The US has an estimated pension debt of around 110% of GDP, Italy 240% and Brazil 190%. China's cash- and asset-rich government still has room to fix its financial problems through continuous reforms, with capital market reform being the centerpiece of the whole programme. Privatisation is the only way out of the financial mess facing China today. The government needs to allow more market discipline to guide the system. It is not an overnight job, but there is no reason to conclude a financial implosion in China just because tough reforms take longer time.

The real danger

Thus, the danger facing Asia in the medium-term is not really a financial crisis or China's economic threat. Rather, it is the rise of protectionism. Rising protectionism will not only hurt rich countries who have benefited from cheap imports of finished goods and raw materials, it will also slow global trade and create a lose–lose outcome for both rich and poor economies. Notably, the rich countries' reintroduction of new textile quotas after the end of the 1973 Multi-Fibre Agreement (MFAT) in January 2005 (see below for more discussion) under the excuse of counterbalancing China's production clout will hit the developing world hard. The poor economies will be denied the opportunity to use the textile industry as the first step on the path to industrialisation.

Unfortunately, protectionism is likely to intensify as the structural changes in global manufacturing continue. The shift in manufacturing production from the rich economies to Asia will not end anytime soon. Due to rising labour costs in the industrialised world, the developed economies will move further into service-oriented and high value-added activities. Sluggish demand growth, due to worsening population dynamics in these economies will also leave little room for their high-cost manufacturing to grow. Hence, outsourcing to Asia will continue. While this should be a natural process of international division of labour, the resultant cross-border structural changes in the product and labour markets will inflict economic pains in the rich countries due to their structural rigidities. This will, in turn, strengthen the anti-globalisation and anti-free-trade forces. Protectionism will likely to be a contentious issue in the coming decades.

The theory that underpins the free trade argument is the 'law of comparative advantage'. It has the vision that all countries can raise their living standards through production specialisation and trade. Even if one country can make everything cheaper in absolute terms than others, it still gains from focusing on making and exporting the goods in which its relative (but not absolute) advantage is the greatest – i.e. in which it has a comparative advantage – and importing the rest. But the problem with this idea is that the process inflicts short-term pains before delivering long-term gains.

Suppose a developing country, spurred by technical progress, improves productivity in making export goods that sell to a developed country. Think of China's advances in semiconductors or India's in software engineering and their exports to the US. Trade can turn entirely to the poor country's advantage in the short-term. This is because improvement in the poor country's productivity can put significant downward pressure on export prices. While this will help the poor country's exports, it will hurt the high-cost developed country by cutting into its export margin, despite the increased availability of cheaper goods for the rich country.

Many in the developed economies are not willing to bear the short-term pains, or they are too myopic to see the long-term gains. In the short-term, it may not be just that some Americans lose, but that the whole country is worse off. As the production of goods, and increasingly services, is outsourced to developing economies, many people in the developed world worry that new development in international commerce will do them more harm than good. The protectionists want to fight China's economic threat. When the global system of textile quotas – the MFAT[10] – ended in January 2005, the US Commerce Department responded by enacting new unilateral quotas on imports of clothing from China.

Such action is myopic and wrong, especially when China has become the world second most important economic growth driver after the US. China has become especially important for Asia. Both Korea and Taiwan's exports to the US have fallen steadily and they now export more to Mainland China than to the US (Figure 7:7). Even Japan and Germany have seen their exports to China surge by 40% since 2003, when exports to America have fallen (Figure 7:8). China is now Europe and Japan's second largest trading partner after the US. If Hong Kong is included, Greater China will soon overtake the US as the largest export destination for Japan.

China's economic integration into the world market is the best hope for more balanced growth that relies less on the US. But American and

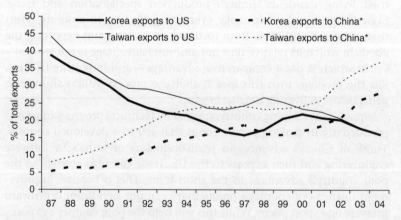

Figure 7:7 Korea and Taiwan exports to the US and China
* Mainland China plus Hong Kong
Source: CEIC

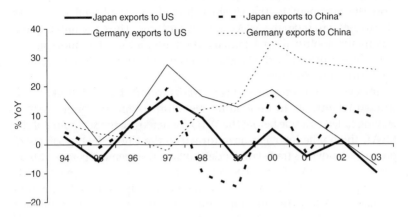

Figure 7:8 Japan and Germany exports to the US and China
* Mainland China plus Hong Kong
Source: CEIC

many developed economies' manufacturers view China as threat. If trade protectionism caused China to retaliate, that would even be a bigger danger for the global economy. Unfortunately, protectionism is likely to intensify. If the developed world is making so much fuss about China when her manufacturing capacity is only 7% of the world's capacity, the protectionist's voice is going to get louder as and when the Middle Kingdom's manufacturing capacity climbs further, especially when it starts to compete with even more advanced production lines in Asia, Europe and America.

The danger of protectionism is imminent. The US has gone back on free trade after years of efforts on promoting globalisation. Given its powerful leadership role in the global economy, America's protectionist attitude could set a bad example for the rest of the world to follow. The textile lobbies show that America's protectionist forces are set to grow. These forces, if left unchecked, could endanger the global economic prosperity over the longer-term. The textile protectionists all started with the 1973-MFAT, which was an institutionalisation of the small-scale effort in the 1950s by the UK and US to restrict imports from Japan, Hong Kong, India and Pakistan. The MFAT imposed import quotas on all developing economies, an unfair measure that had distorted allocation of resources, misguided production, forced rich countries' importers and retailers into sub-optimal supply arrangements, and indirectly taxed consumers. After years of negotiations, the developing economies won the argument in the Uruguay Round of multilateral trade talks (1986–1994) to scrap the MFAT in ten years time. Thus, the unfair quota was finally abolished on 1 January 2005 after a four-step quota phase-out. It was replaced by the World Trade Organisation (WTO) Agreement on Textile and Clothing.

However, the US textile industry wants to put the clock back. It has worked relentlessly to undermine the effort to end the quota system. Having failed to argue before the WTO for deferring the scrapping of the MFAT, the textile lobbyists have turned to the China Textile Safeguard provision under US trade law. Under a bilateral agreement before China's accession to the WTO, the US can re-impose quotas on Chinese textile and apparel goods (by limiting the maximum import growth rate from China to 7.5% of the previous year's volume) if a surge in imports disrupts the US domestic textile market.

Before the 2004 November presidential election, the US administration gave in to the lobbyists' pressure (presumably as a *quid pro quo* for votes for President Bush) and decided that quotas could be re-imposed even without a surge in imports. Simply the threat of market disruption would be enough to trigger US action. The textile industry swiftly responded by filing nine threat-based petitions calling for quotas on Chinese apparel like underwear, trousers and shirts. Having won the November 2004 presidential election by a significant margin in the textile states, President Bush is under pressure to grant the textile industry's wishes to re-impose import quotas.

The US government is in a catch-22. It would be damned (by free-trade advocates) if it gives in to the textile lobbyists and damned (by the protectionists) if it rejects their demand. Granting the lobbyists' wishes would likely prompt the Chinese to challenge the US quotas in WTO courts, on the grounds that the accession agreement does not allow threat-based sanctions. The dispute would weaken the US credibility to influence China to honour her WTO commitments. If a WTO settlement panel found the US guilty of breaking the agreement, the loss of US credibility as major economic player would be significant. The damage to the global system will be even bigger. The broken US credibility will not only erode the political capital that the US has accumulated for pushing China to keep and improve her implementation of WTO commitments, it will also embolden other American protectionists, like the steel industry, sugar producers and agricultural interests, to step up their distortion to the global trade system.

On the other hand, rejecting the petitions could also backfire on America's trade liberalisation efforts. If the textile industry failed to get what they wanted after pledging support for President Bush in his 2004 election, it could retaliate by fighting against the US–Central American Free Trade Agreement (CAFTA), which needs US Congress endorsement. The textile lobbies carry significant weight because in the last trade vote in the Congress in 2001, their last-second support gave President Bush a one-vote margin of victory for securing the 'trade promotion authority' to negotiate trade deals with other governments. The textile-state votes came only when the president agreed to change certain textile trade laws that protected the industry. This blackmail precedent makes it likely that the US administration will be held hostage again by the textile lobbies, who want to push through threat-based petitions against China in exchange for their support for CAFTA.

However, this blackmail tactic is completely wrong-headed, and reveals the myopia of the protectionists. This is because CAFTA will help the US address the Sino-American trade deficit by allowing the Americans to compete more effectively with China. So it should be used as a tool to compete, but not as a threat to force the US Administration into protectionism. In the clothing business, for example, CAFTA will provide specific incentive to use US yarn, fabric, thread and elastics in making clothes in the American part of the world. After CAFTA, over 90% of all apparel made in Central America or the Dominion Republic will be sewn from fabric and yarn produced by US workers. If the US fails to solidify her trade relationship with this region through CAFTA, these factories are likely to move to Asia, where US inputs account for less than 1% of the clothes made there.

Forcing a China threat

In a nutshell, Asia (and the world) is facing an imminent danger of rising protectionism, led by the US whose effort on trade liberalisation has been thrown out. Catering to the myopic interests of the sunset textile industry will undermine the economic interest of both the US and the rest of the world. While economic logic suggests that the US should reject these threat-based quotas, geopolitical and sociological developments in the developed world suggest that the force of protectionism is going to rise.

The protectionists have used China as an excuse to advance their distortion to global trade, despite the empty content of their arguments. Consider their claim that China's cheap wages are the most imminent threat on the global scene. Such claim is meaningless. Cheap Chinese wages will hurt those manufacturers who compete directly with Chinese goods. However, Chinese export workers make textile, toys, sporting goods and light electronics. These are industries that the developed world mostly gave up a long time ago. It is the left-over groups of sunset manufacturers in the rich countries, like the textile and steel lobbies, pushing for their self-interest because they are resisting adaptation to the world's structural changes.

Further, the threat posed by China's economic innovation is overblown. For example, the number of graduates likely to take over white-collar jobs from the rich economies is nowhere near the 300 million that are often talked about. As skills in China improve, trade with her will become more like that with any other developed markets, from which the rich countries have historically benefited. Outsourcing abroad is also too small to matter much. One of the commonly cited estimates, by US firm Forrester Research, is that 3.4 million jobs in the US would be outsourced by 2015. That may sound a lot, but it implies an annual outflow of only 0.5% of the jobs in the affected industries in the US. In an average year, the US economy destroys some 30 million jobs and creates slightly more, dwarfing the impact of cross-border outsourcing.

But the protectionists' myopic actions could backfire and force the emergence of a China threat. Protectionist efforts against China's rising economic progression may lead to a backlash in China against the foreigners who control ever-greater swathes of the Chinese economy. Foreign firms control a large (55% and rising) share of China's export facilities, and are even more dominant in hi-tech areas. Foreign investors are likely to be major buyers of Chinese manufacturing facilities when the industry is consolidated under rising production costs in China in the next decade or so. At some point, the charge that the government is selling out the country to foreigners could become a mobilising force among the armies of Chinese who are disgruntled by rising income inequality and unemployment due to continued structural changes. The outcome could be Chinese xenophobia and a hostile global trading environment.

8
What China Threat?

There will be no more important strategic issue for policymakers and investors to manage over the coming years than the continuing rise of China's economic power. But this is no reason to see the Middle Kingdom as a major economic threat to the world. Fears about her threat have been exaggerated. Distorted views about her development have been blindly followed. China's economic ascent is in fact not different from the experience of the other Asian economies. Low production costs will not enable China to take over the world economy, as some have naively asserted. In fact, cheap costs – the most feared competitive edge of China – will not get China ahead in the long run. It could even hinder her development. Further, China's economic reform has produced lower efficiency than has been hyped so that production cost is not really that cheap as many have feared.

An economically assertive China is a fact. The world will have to live with that as it lives with the other major economic powers. To treat China as a strategic threat would likely at some point make her one. Instead, engaging China and integrating her into the global system fully should produce a far better outcome than resisting her. China's entry to the World Trade Organisation (WTO) is a crucial step towards making a better world economy. And it has worked. The WTO system has not broken as some predicted, and membership has helped pushed necessary reform in China. Managing China's economic progress is the central issue for the international community in the coming decades, in the new economic paradigm where rising competition and prolonged economic restructuring will constrain pricing power and profitability. There is much potential for miscalculation, and blindly seeing China as a threat will not help lower that risk.

The Chinese reform hype

If you ask the CEOs of the listed companies in America what is the single factor that is going to change the world, most of them will say China's economic clout. And indeed, having grown by an average of 9% a year in the past 25 years, China's economy seems to be on the way to one day overtake the size of the US economy which has been growing at an average of 3% a year in real terms in the past quarter century. Some analysts are predicting that China would overtake the US economy in the next 30 years or so. All these predictions have been based on the view that China's economic reforms have made her a super-efficient economy. This has, in turn, created the much feared China economic threat. But are China's reforms that effective?

There is no doubt that China has made significant progress in structural reforms. But relative to the huge amount of inefficiency in the system, China's structural changes have moved much slower than perceived. One needs to separate hype from real progress so as to clear the distortions in reading China's economic reforms. Despite some of the overly optimistic views that China has created a bourgeoning private sector that is now driving the economy, there is still significant reform inertia dragging on structural changes.[1] To create a functional private sector that has full legal protection, China still has a long way to go in reforming the underlying economic and institutional frameworks. This includes implementing legal reform, improving contract and bankruptcy laws, allocating capital more efficiently to the vibrant but still vulnerable private sector and, most crucially, eliminating bad incentives of local officials that hurt private businesses and capital allocation.

China's private sector has indeed grown rapidly. A lot of creative destruction – destroying the old inefficient industries and replacing them by sunrise industries – has been going on. The most obvious evidence for this is the sharp decline in the state sector (Figures 8:1 and 8:2), whose shares in the nation's fixed-asset investment and gross industrial output had fallen from 80% in the 1980s to 40% in the case of investment and to 13% in the case of output in recent years. Many have also claimed that over half of the industrial output in China is now produced by the non-state sector. But this does not necessarily mean a robust private sector. Despite its rapid growth, China's private sector remains fragile, fragmented and constrained, as the nation is toiling through a bumpy economic transition. Then, how does this square with the decline in the state sector?

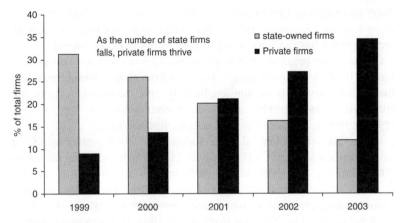

Figure 8:1 China's creative destruction
Source: CEIC

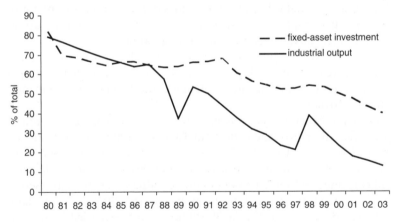

Figure 8:2 State sector output and investment
Source: CEIC

Indications for China's private sector growth, and hence the depth of her reform, are distorted by data reporting. Beijing reports two sets of industrial output numbers, gross industrial output and industrial value-added, each with a different output breakdown by sources. The gross industrial output data has breakdowns for the state-owned enterprises (SOEs) and the private enterprises. They show that the SOEs' output share had fallen to 13% in 2003, while the private firms' share had risen three-fold to 15% since 1999. This evidence shows that the private sector growth has not been as significant as many have claimed.

Crucially, the breakdowns also show that 19% of the output came from limited liability companies and 13% came from shareholding firms. It is likely that most of these limited liability and shareholding firms are still state-controlled. This means state companies still control 45% (13% + 19% + 13%) of industrial output, but not 13%.

Meanwhile, the industrial value-added data, which enters into GDP calculations, shows that SOEs accounted for 45% of industrial output in 2003. Granted, this share was down from 54% in 1994, but it was not down as dramatically as some have claimed. This data set also includes 'shareholding companies', which accounted for an estimated 17% of total value-added in 2004, up from 6% in 1994. It is wrong to assume, as many have done, that these are all non-state firms because the state remains the majority shareholder in many of them. This means that the state still controls over 60% (17% + 45%) of industrial value-added. Since the industrial value-added data does not have a private enterprise category, it is impossible to determine from it the share of industrial output by the private sector in the national output.

The point is that although there is undeniable progress in China's structural reform, its depth and speed have been exaggerated by people lumping those limited liability companies and shareholding companies into the private sector.

Even in the high profile banking reform, progress is much slower than perceived. After two failed efforts in 1998 and 1999, Beijing launched another bailout in late 2003 for the Big Four state banks, which control over 60% of all banking assets. The bailout dealt with the banks individually and used some US$45 billion of China's huge foreign reserves to boost their capital. Arguably, the move came too little too soon. Many experts estimate that about US$300 billion would be needed for sustaining the banking system. But even the small US$45 billion capital injection might have come too early. This was because the banks should have proven their commercial viability before getting further government funds, but they had not.

Despite the progress in banking reform and two recapitalisation programmes, the efforts have yet to uproot the way the state banks do business, which is still politically driven and plagued by corruption. For example, new lending took off in 2001, as Beijing tried to boost growth in the face of a world economic slowdown. Then, the authorities tried to clamp down on lending in late 2003, especially on property loans,

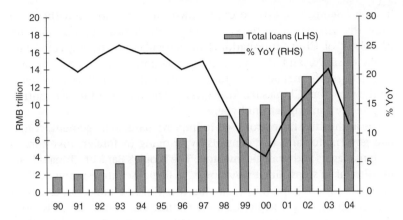

Figure 8:3 Chinese banks total loans
Source: CEIC

to avoid overheating (Figure 8:3). What this shows is that Beijing has once again directed the recent lending cycle, which means the Chinese banks are still taking orders instead of lending on a commercial basis.

This long-term policy-lending guidance has resulted in a politically-driven banking monopoly system. Since bank credit is allocated by administrative guidance but not based on risk assessment under commercial terms, Chinese banks have lost their function as financial intermediaries. With rising household savings and the lack of alternative investment outlets for these savings, banks are flooded with excess funds. But because bank officials hold the ultimate power of lending, the system has thus become the hotbed for corruption and fund embezzlement.

Aren't the banking reforms supposed to right all this? Unfortunately, old habits still die hard; the banking reform progress has been exaggerated. Evidence of thick banking woes can be seen in the escalating scandals recently. Just in 2004, there were big fund embezzlement and bribing/kick-back scandals from the Bank of China, the China Construction Bank and the Agricultural Bank of China. In May 2005, Gou Shu-qing, chairman of the China Construction Bank,[2] and Xie Ping, who runs the Central Huijin Investment,[3] complained publicly in China's vocal *Caijin* financial magazine about party influence. They were quoted as saying a party committee within the Bank even made decisions on small loans and largely controlled personnel decisions. Some argue that the exposure of these scandals is a positive sign because it shows Beijing's resolve to crack down on corruption. But they also show that the problems have spread from the banks' overseas affiliates (the Bank of China International in particular) to the Big Four state banks onshore, and the bank officials committing the crimes have spread to senior management from junior staffers. All this casts doubts on the view that China's banking mess has been brought under control, despite the banking reform hype.

The authorities have promised to improve bank management, corporate governance and risk controls by bringing in foreign investors as both managers and strategic investors. The People's Bank of China (PBoC) has also taken steps, albeit very slowly, to liberalise interest rates. It abolished the lending cap on interest rates that Chinese banks can charge in October 2004. In principle, Chinese commercial banks can now price credit according to the borrowers' credit risks, though there is still an interest rate floor to restrict the lower limit of interest rates that banks can charge.

However, such changes are slow to filter through the system, which is still dominated by a Marxist mindset (see below). The domestic capital markets are dysfunctional, which makes it impossible for China's asset management companies to price bad assets properly and sell them off successfully. The government still owns two-thirds of China's 1,300 listed firms. The stock market is also constantly rigged by the immature securities industry. Most of the 130 brokers are corrupted; they are staying afloat by amassing and keeping investment funds by guaranteeing investor returns that they fail to honour. The company listing process is politically driven, with all but a handful of the listed companies being SOEs.

Hence, the stock market is still largely a tool for subsidising Beijing's industrial policy instead of allocating capital effectively to private companies. Banking and capital market reforms should go hand in hand. But Beijing is still seeing the two disjoint events, which is strategically wrong for reform. Last but not least, China's non-performing loans (NPLs) are a moving target, as restructuring the SOEs will produce more bad loans in the short-term. No one knows how many new NPLs have been created, including those by the lending spree since 2001. Until this is sorted out, it will be difficult to attract long-term foreign strategic partners in Chinese banks.

The biggest drag on reform is the communist mindset. On paper, the constitutional amendment to elevate the status of private property in March 2004 gave private property the same legal status as state-owned property. In fact, Karl Marx's legacy still dominates, as seen in the subtle difference between the treatment of the state and private firms.

For example, the constitution clearly states state property as 'sacred and inviolable'. The amendment has failed to apply the word 'sacred' to private property. Further, the amendment states that only 'lawful' private property is protected, but all (lawful or not) state property is protected by the constitution. While the constitution is not supposed to protect unlawful property, the amendment's stress on lawful private property suggests the leadership remains suspicious of private businesses.

It is no use just to amend the constitutional status of the private sector without changing the legal system underpinning it. Chinese courts are not used to hearing and judging cases that challenge the constitution. Finally, other constitutional rights, in particular freedom of speech and religion, are often ignored. Hence, there is still lots to be done in reforming the legal, institutional and financial frameworks.

The competitiveness myth

Hence, much of the perceived threat of China being transformed into a super-competitive economy crowding out the others has been exaggerated. After all, being cheap is not everything, and that alone should not make China a formidable competitor. In fact, low wages are a two-edged sword for China. While it helps Chinese manufacturers to compete, it also locks the economy in low-end production depriving it of the ability to climb the value chain. The trouble with the low-wage trap can be seen in the move by Chinese computer maker Lenovo to buy IBM's personal computer business in late 2004. Lenovo's bet was that if it could turnaround the ailing IBM PC business, it would have found a niche to survive in a cut-throat low-margin business. Lenovo's move was desperate since it had failed in efforts to diversify its product portfolio and to establish its own brand in the foreign markets. If it did not want to wind up its business or put itself up for sale, why not take a punt and see if it could leverage on IBM's brand and network to help work its way out?

Prior to Lenovo's deal, China's TCL Multimedia Technology Holdings also made a move to buy a majority, 67%, stake in Thomason of France in August 2004 to become the world's largest television maker. TCL was hoping to fight cut-throat competition in the TV market and turnaround its dire money-losing situation by increasing scale through acquisition. Like the PC business, the TV market has been facing stiff competitive pressure from Europe and the US, which has depressed prices for flat panel and cathode ray tube (CRT) televisions. Thomson's TV business was already in the red before the TCL deal. It lost 185 million euros (or US$1.9 billion) in 2003, amid a bruising pricing war in the CRT

TV segment and from slowing demand. But only six months after the acquisition, TCL announced that its expected profitability (if it ever materialises) would be delayed by another year, due to unforeseen operational difficulties overseas.

TCL and Lenovo are cases reflecting the dark side of cheap pricing faced by Chinese consumer goods companies. They won market shares by undercutting their foreign rivals with ever-lower prices. But now they find themselves trapped in hypercompetitive, low-margin businesses at home. Their razor-thin margins make it almost impossible to accumulate funds to invest in research and development that would enable them to move up the value-added ladder to higher-profit businesses. That inability also makes it tough for the Chinese firms to make inroads in developed markets, where price is less crucial than quality, design and brand. Some Chinese companies, like white goods maker Haier, have responded by diversifying into a bewildering array of products. But this has only trapped them in dozens of cut-throat, low-margin businesses, instead of one or two.

Fears about China's low wages should not be exaggerated because wages alone do not decide an economy's competitiveness. Hence, low wages will not give China the economic power to gobble up the world economy. If the simple logic of low wages equalling high competitiveness were true, Bangladesh and Somalia, which have wages even lower than China, should be very competitive and manufacturers in the developed world should fear them more. Similarly, if cheap wages were of paramount importance, foreigners should be focusing on investing in China's inland regions where wages are far cheaper than the coastal regions. But they have not. This is because when considering a country's competitiveness, it is vital to look at labour productivity also instead of just absolute wages. In countries where wages are cheap and labour productivity is high, its competitiveness should be strong. But if productivity is very poor, then even with cheap wages its overall competitiveness is still weak.

A better way to gauge an economy's relative competitiveness is to look at wage and labour productivity together. More precisely, one can look at the ratio of their wage rate differential to their productivity differential. This ratio is indeed a proxy to unit labour cost differential between two economies. Why? Consider the simple ratio of wage rate to productivity. The wage rate is dollar per man hour input ($/hr, where hr is man hour), while labour productivity is output per man hour (Y/hr, where Y is output). Dividing the wage rate by productivity gives dollar per output ($/Y), which is just labour cost per output, or unit labour cost.

Hence, if country A's wage rate is 27% that of country B's, but its productivity is 44% that of B's, then country A's unit labour cost is 61.4% (= 27/44) that of country B's. In other words, A's wage cost is 38.6% (= 100% − 61.4%) cheaper than B's, but not 73% (= 100% − 27%) cheaper as the headline wage rate differential shows. On the other hand, if country C's wage rate is 43% that of country A's, but its productivity is only 24% of A's, then C's unit labour cost is 179.2% (= 43/24) that of B's. Hence, C's unit labour cost is 79.2% (= 179.2% − 100%) dearer than A's, despite its lower headline wage rate. These are in fact real-world examples. Country A is South Korea, B is the US and C is Taiwan. These calculations show that Taiwan's unit labour cost is much dearer than for the US, while South Korea's cost is cheaper.

Labour cost in China is not really that cheap under this perspective. The point to note is that the world is not static. While China has experienced productivity growth, other economies (notably the US) have also recorded productivity growth so that the productivity gap between China and other economies has remained wide. For example, although the average wage rate in China is only 2.1% that of the US, productivity is also relatively low at only 2.7% that of the US, according to the Research Institute of Economy, Trade and Industry of Japan (RIETI). Hence, unit labour cost in China is 77.8% (= 2.1/2.7) that of the US. This is still lower than the US, but it is significantly higher than the headline wage rate shows. In this sense, China's labour cost is even higher than South Korea's. If other costs such as China's high capital costs, poor infrastructure and weak legal system are taken into account, her cost advantage is further diluted.

Exchange rate movement also affects a country's unit labour cost. For example, if China devalues the renminbi (RMB) in an attempt to expand exports, her unit labour cost in US dollar terms would fall, thus improving export competitiveness. However, this improvement would be temporary, since domestic prices and wages would rise over time thus offsetting any competitive gains from a cheap currency policy. Over the long-run, wage levels basically move in line with labour productivity. Based on estimated unit labour cost comparison, China's labour cost is not super-cheap as many have feared. Mexico, Korea and Indonesia are cheaper than China, just to name a few. Indeed, empirical studies have shown that there is a strong positive correlation between productivity and wages. In developed economies, high productivity corresponds directly to both strong competitiveness and high wage levels. The large productivity gap between China and the developed world means that when China integrates in the global markets, she will naturally do so by focusing on labour-intensive products in accordance to her comparative advantage based on low wages.

Hence, there is really nothing special about China's low wages. So long as China depends on low wages to compete in international markets, she can at best be the world's factory rather than a true industrial power that would rule over such high value-added areas as product standards, design, brand names and core technologies. Since the optimal strategy for most Chinese companies is still to expand labour input rather than improve productivity, low wages could actually be a factor retarding industrial advancement, and should thus be seen as a sign of China's industrial weakness rather than strength in the long-term.

Further, wages are only one of the business cost components. There are other operational and regulatory costs and externalities in China that cut into her competitive edge. But these are often overlooked or ignored, especially by interest groups and politicians trying to score points against China. These other costs have even affected China's special economic zones, in spite of their lower taxes and less onerous regulations. The problem is reflected in the skinny profitability in China's beer market. China overtook the US as the world's largest beer market in 2004. But the largest Chinese breweries, which account for a total 35% of the market, made a combined profit of only US$100 million that year. That was only one-seventh of Heineken's profits and 5% of Anheuser-Busch's in 2004.

In general, for most manufacturers, costs of imported energy and raw materials – on which China is relying ever more heavily – far outweigh those for land and labour. In fact, Chinese manufacturers often have to pay more for energy and raw materials than their foreign counterparts, not only because of higher shipping costs but also because of import tariffs and the value added tax. While input costs are rising, excess capacity and falling entry barriers will continue to squeeze profit margins. Then, there are regulatory costs, which mainly stem from uncertainty about government policies, and amount to a serious burden for Chinese companies. For example, Beijing has kept the world guessing on when it would grant 3G telephone licences, even though demand and technology for such phones are ready. Many Chinese corporate executives also complain about endless government meetings and perpetual random inspections.

Finally, there is externality which stifles profits and product development. For example, a budding entrepreneur may think she has a new fashion design to offer, but only to find a dozen other stores selling the same design the next day. Thus, weak enforcement of intellectual property rights raises business costs in a subtle way. Scarce resources do not get channelled into product innovation, but instead wreak havoc on existing well-run businesses. The small copy-cat operators may be inefficient, but their ability to sabotage pricing power is huge.

In a nutshell, there is really no point to focus on fretting about China's cheap labour cost. It is not really that cheap after all, when relative productivity is taken into account. The big advantage of cheap wages is limited to some simple exporting processing sectors.

As far as the exchange rate issue is concerned, China has come under criticism from the international community since 2003 that she has kept the renminbi (RMB) artificially low by pegging it against the falling US dollar so as to boost Chinese exports at the expense of the others. Developed world manufacturers also exploit this issue to accuse China of posing an imminent threat to the world economy. Such a claim is hypocritical. Chinese export workers make textiles, toys, sporting goods and light electronics. These are the industries the rich world mostly gave up a long time ago, due to the erosion of their comparative advantage in these areas. This is evident in the change in the global trade structure.

Chinese exports have been penetrating European, Japanese and US markets at an average growth rate of 35% a year recently, but other Asian exports have not. This is not because China is gaining at the expense of her Asian neighbours. Rather, many Asian economies have simply moved low-end processing and assembly functions to China as a final stop on the production chain before shipping off to Wal-Mart, Carrefour or Tesco.

China has a comparative advantage on labour intensive production, and she benefits from the migration of low-wage assembly functions from other economies. But this is not an evidence for the Chinese authorities manipulating the RMB to maximise the country's competitive edge against the others. If they were, they would not have kept the RMB from weakening in the post-Asian crisis years when all other regional currencies, except the Hong Kong dollar, fell sharply. That decision to keep the RMB fixed in fact stopped Chinese wages from getting cheaper, thus avoided hurting other economies, at the time when the rest of Asia was going through a painful post-crisis transition. The RMB has only come under appreciating pressure since 2003.

The growth threat – debunked

Most analysts agree that China's economy could grow by an average of 8% a year for the next two decades. This looks staggering. Based on this trajectory, China will have taken over as the world's biggest trading power and the largest economy in 20 years' time. While average Chinese farm income will remain relatively low, the emerging urban middle class could have grown to 400 million people (larger than the US total population today). To some, China's economic ascent will cause painful dislocations for the global economy: declining living standards, significant loss of manufacturing jobs and failing industries. But is this threat really the case? No. Japan, South Korea, Taiwan and other Asian economies recorded similar growth rates over long periods of time. In this sense, China is just another 'Asian Tiger' economy, but not a global economic threat and not something that the world has not seen before.

China's expected 8% long-term growth rate looks high by any standards. But not when one looks at Asia's growth experience (Figure 8:4). The Japanese economy grew by an average of 8.5% a year in its high-growth period between 1955 and 1975; and so did Korea and Taiwan in their high-growth years between 1965 and 1995. A similar pattern can be seen in per capita GDP growth at purchasing power parity.[4] China's per capita GDP rose by 370% between 1978 and 2004, implying a trend rate of 6.1% a year. Yet between 1955 and 1975, Japan's GDP per head rose by 460%, with a trend rate of 8.2%. Between 1965 and 1995, South Korea's per capita GDP jumped by 680%, a trend rate of 7.6%, while Taiwan's GDP per head soared by 600%, a trend rate of 7.1%. China's growth is far from spectacular by Asian standards.

But China's huge size, with 1.3 billion people, will have a much bigger impact on the global economy than the earlier Asian growth leaders,

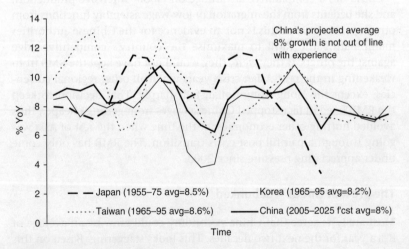

Figure 8:4 Real GDP growth
Source: CEIC

right? Not really. China is bigger, but so is the world economy. From only 4% of global output today, the 8% annual growth trajectory for China (and 4% growth assumption for the world economy) suggests that the Middle Kingdom would account for 11% of world GDP by 2025. That looks impressive. But it is no different from other Asian economies' experience. In 1965, Japan, the Asian Tigers[5] and ASEAN[6] also accounted for 4% of global GDP. But the share had risen to 13% in 1985 and 16% in 1990. On the foreign trade front, China is also projected to rise fourfold from 4% of global trade today to 16% in 20 years' time. But this looks no different from the experience of her East Asian neighbours, whose trade share rose from 6% of the world total in 1960 to 15% in 1990.

What about China's rapid industrialisation? China's gross fixed investment, at over 40% of GDP, is higher than that of the other Asian Tiger economies when they were at a similar development stage. The Middle Kingdom's unprecedented record of industrial concentration and fast growth at such low current income levels is creating fears that it would soon displace the global manufacturers. One can gauge such fears by looking at China's huge import appetite for raw materials and commodities, which reflects the dramatic pace of her manufacturing growth in recent years. Take steel for example. With a per capita GDP of just over US$1,000 a year, China's current per capita steel consumption has already reached a level first seen in Korea when her per capita GDP was at US$4,000, and in Japan when her per capital income was at US$7,000. It is the rapid speed of China's manufacturing growth that makes many worry about her causing economic dislocations in other countries.

However, comparing China's experience with the others based on per capita income is misleading due to differences in their economic development, income distribution and effects of exchange rate valuation. So it is better to compare their steel demand, in terms of per capita steel consumption, during their high-growth years with China's demand at this high-growth development stage. In this perspective, China's industrialisation process is not much different from the other Asian economies in their high-growth years. In Japan, for example, steel consumption went from less than 0.1 tons per head in 1952 to 0.3 tons in 1962, and to 0.6 tons in 1972. The Korean experience was similar, with per capita steel consumption reaching 0.5 tons in 1990 from 0.03 tons in 1970. China is no different in this perspective. Since 1990, her steel consumption growth has followed a growth path similar to that of Japan and Korea. In particular, China's per capita steel demand was about 0.05 tons in 1990, and it is now a little less than 0.2 tons. Further, the

Japanese and Korean experiences both show that steel demand growth accelerated at a faster rate in the latter part of their high-growth periods than in the earlier years. There is no reason for expecting China's growth trend to differ dramatically from Japan and Korea's in the coming years.

Many also worry that China is rocking the world economy by pushing investment and growth rates at the expense of profitability and investment return. These concerns are not unfounded. But they are exactly the same fears that some exploited a few decades ago to sound the alarm on Japan and the Asian Tigers that their economic ascent would kill the European and the US economies. But life goes on without the damages that the pessimists had predicted.

The point is that the world has seen the economic ascent of other Asian economies before, and China's impressive economic growth in recent years is nothing new. Whether it is economic growth or international trade or industrialisation, China has just been following in the footsteps of the other Asian economies. However, despite rapid development China has not yet succeeded in matching the economic dynamism of Japan and the other Asian Tiger economies when they were in their heydays. The world indeed faces challenges, not threats, from China's rising economic clout, but these are challenges that the world has already seen.

The investment threat – debunked

Robust Chinese economic growth has also raised the fear that China will soon buy up most of the world's assets. Remember the late 1980s, when it seemed like Japanese, Korean and Taiwanese investors were buying up ever-increasing amounts of US property assets, equities and bonds. Now it looks like it is China's turn. Since 2004, China has been the third-largest foreign holder of US treasury bonds, after Japan and the UK. The Chinese will soon be buying other corporate and property assets through her government agencies if not private corporates, the fear goes.

However, for this fear to be realised, China's buying of foreign assets must have a significant impact on the global asset pool. This is simply not true. According to country balance of payments (BoP) data, Asian countries bought US$2.3 trillion in foreign portfolio assets between 1994 and 2004, bringing their total outstanding holdings to US$3.7 trillion. Among these, China accounted for about US$800 billion, only about 20% of the total. Further, while the US$3.7 trillion is a huge nominal sum, it is less than 1% of global GDP, with China's purchases accounting for a little over 0.1%.

Nevertheless, fear still stems from China's rapid accumulation of foreign reserves that they would enable China to buy up global assets sooner rather than later. Indeed, China's foreign reserves jumped by 286% to US$640 billion in early 2005 from US$166 billion in 2000. However, the rapid rise in foreign reserves in China does not necessarily mean that she is amassing a vast amount of foreign assets.

First, the foreign exchange reserves are public money, and governments do not usually use foreign reserves to buy private foreign assets. A lot of the money that the Japanese, Taiwanese and Koreans spent on buying US assets was private funds buying both private and public US financial and non-financial assets. Beijing has only been buying US Treasury and government agency bonds. It is not likely to use the foreign reserves to buy foreign, especially non-financial, assets in the private sector.

Second, Chinese buyers have been financing a large part of their foreign asset purchases with either foreign portfolio sales or foreign borrowing. This means that on a net basis, China is not accumulating a huge amount of foreign assets as many have feared. China's BoP data gives a clue to this. The Middle Kingdom's basic balance (defined as current account balance plus long-term capital inflows, such as long-term foreign direct investment, or FDI, and long-term loans) has been relative stable since the 1990s, averaging 6.3% of GDP. But other capital inflows, including hot money and illegal capital inflows, have swung sharply from large outflows (negative balance) to a large inflows in recent years (Figure 8:5).

Most of these other capital inflows have come from Chinese firms reversing their capital flight in the late 1980s and early 1990s, when the economic environment was bad, or from Chinese banks borrowing from abroad. In other words, China's foreign reserve build-up is a result of large and steady long-term capital inflows and, in recent years, the reversal of capital flight. This returned capital flows into the foreign reserves too. This also means that a large part of the purchase in recent years by China's central bank of foreign portfolio assets is financed by the returned Chinese capital via foreign asset sales. Hence, the buying does not represent a huge net accumulation of Chinese assets abroad.

This is underscored by the diverging trends of rising official foreign reserves, which is mostly a result of long-term capital and FDI inflows, and falling foreign portfolio holdings, which reflects Chinese sales of foreign assets (Figure 8:6). When there is net asset accumulation, like the US$73 billion in 2004, it is far less than the foreign reserve accumulation (US$610 billion in 2004). Even on FDI accumulation, China's net

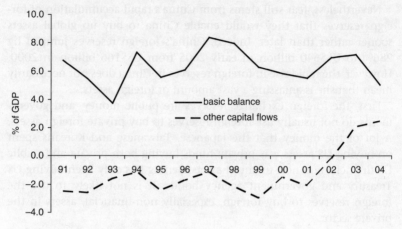

Figure 8:5 China's balance of payments
Source: CEIC

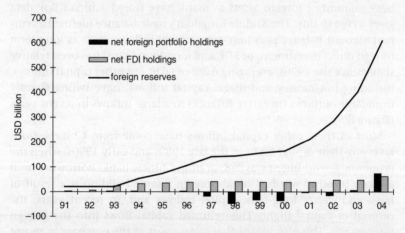

Figure 8:6 China's net asset holding & FX reserves
Source: CEIC

accumulation is far less than the growth of foreign reserves (Figure 8:6). This is because foreign investors are also accumulating significant FDI claims on China at a rapid rate. All this suggests that China has not been buying up foreign assets with her huge foreign reserves.

Some also claim that China was advancing her economic hegemony by suppressing imports and boosting exports to maximise foreign

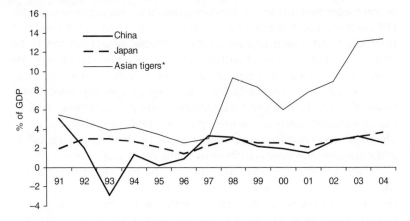

Figure 8:7 Current account balances
* Korea, Hong Kong, Singapore, Taiwan
Source: CEIC

reserve accumulation for purchase of world assets later. This claim has no economic grounds. If China were running such policies, she must have accumulated a chronic and growing current account surplus. However, China's current account balance has been stable through the years, and it is not excessive by Asian standards, especially when compared with Japan and the Asian Tiger economies (Figure 8:7). The latter have been running current account surpluses averaging 3.5 times larger than China's.

Hence, there is no reason to expect China would buy up the world's assets and crowd out investment opportunities for other economies. If China is not throwing her investment weight around, there is also no reason to expect the RMB to replace the US dollar and the Euro in the global markets anytime soon. Fundamentally, the Chinese RMB lacks the conditions to become a global currency. There are two prerequisites for a global currency – full convertibility and deep domestic capital markets. China has neither at present, and she will not be able to acquire them in a short period of time.

Full convertibility requires the currency to be convertible on both the current and capital accounts. But the RMB is still not convertible on the capital account. It can only be exchanged for trade-related transactions and to a limited extent for FDI purposes. Almost all portfolio capital transactions are still prohibited. China's economic reform policies have not focused on capital account liberalisation so far. Current plans point to some relaxation of export revenues repatriation requirements, greater FDI outflows and some portfolio outflows (via the so-called Qualified Domestic Institutional Investors (QDII) scheme, which has yet to be implemented at the time of writing), but not much acceleration in the years ahead. Indeed, the Chinese authorities have no incentive to push for faster full RMB convertibility until they successfully reform and recapitalise the banking system. Otherwise, they run the risk of widespread financial instability, witness the 1997–1998 Asian financial crisis. The crisis-hit economies were characterised by bad banks, poor regulation and open capital accounts (fully convertible currencies).

The other precondition for becoming a global currency is the depth of the domestic derivative market and the availability of hedging products. However, China's rapid economic growth has not been accompanied by corresponding financial market development. Chinese firms can only buy and sell RMB forwards with maturities up to one year on-shore. Longer maturities, currency swaps and RMB futures are not yet available. Further, the forwards market can only handle a tiny portion of the potentially huge hedging demand arising from China's annual US$1.2 trillion (and growing) international trade. Almost all private financial assets are held in banks and China's combined tradable equity and bond markets, estimated at about US$600 billion, are a very small fraction of the financial markets in the developed economies, like the US, Europe and Japan. China's financial markets will grow over time, but they will not be able to close the gap with the developed world in the next decade or so.

The manufacturing threat – debunked

The reasons why China is not a threat to the world's manufacturers are two-fold: First, she will not produce everything, even though she can make almost everything cheaper than the developed world. This is simply because countries produce and trade according to relative, but not absolute, advantage.[7] Second, while China sells consumer goods to the world market, she also buys a significant amount of machinery and inputs from her trading partners. In other words, China supports high-end manufacturing jobs in the rest of the world.

When a developing and labour-intensive economy, like China enters the global trade system and begins to trade with capital-intensive research-rich nations, each trading partner should specialise in production where its comparative advantage lies. In other words, a country should specialise in goods that are made with factors of production that it is better endowed with. Naturally, China should focus on making labour-intensive manufacturing goods and export them in exchange for higher-end goods and primary resources. This gains-from-trade process produces a win–win outcome for the global economy. China gains from relatively cheaper access to capital goods and resources, the rest of the world gains from cheaper consumer goods. Chinese producers gain access to overseas markets, and producers abroad gain from increased demand from China. Letting each trading partner play to its strength raises income for everyone.

However, a low-wage country will not make and sell everything because absolute cost advantage does not drive international trade. It is relative cost that drives production for cross-border trade. In a world of scarce resources, nations must choose to specialise in selling goods that they make relatively cheaply for goods that are relatively dear at home. This is exactly what happens in China's trade and production relationships with the world. In gross terms, it looks as if China is taking over even high-tech exports, like electronics and IT equipment. But on a net trade basis, China is a net importer of these items and heavy machinery, equipment and raw materials. She has become a net exporter of light manufacturing goods, like toys, textiles, sporting goods and appliances in recent years (Figure 8:8). Despite the strong growth in electronics shipments, China is not a significant net exporter of IT goods. This is because most of China's electronics trade is re-exports, involving labour-intensive processing and assembly.

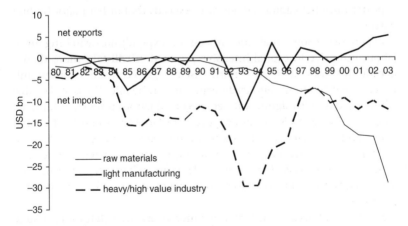

Figure 8:8 China's net exports
Source: CEIC

Meanwhile, the US production mix is predominately capital-intensive, with high shares of machinery and equipment, chemicals and metals and high-value electronics and tech products. Low-end goods like textiles and light manufacturing are an insignificant share of the total. The structure of US imports from the rest of the world, excluding China, is quite similar to her domestic production. It reflects the fact that much of the US trade is with other high-income countries like Japan, Canada and Europe. This is a result of the so-called intra-industry trade, which is driven by economies of scale.

Economies of similar income levels and industrial structure, like the US, Europe and Japan, trade with each other because intra-industry trade also creates gains from trade. While the increase in market size leads to lower costs through the effect of scale economies, competition between firms forces them to pass their lower costs on to consumers in the form of lower prices. But US imports from China are quite different. They are almost entirely concentrated on low-end manufacturing. This, in turn, reflects specialisation based on comparative advantage, with China serving as the key, if not the sole, trading partner for low value-added consumer goods.

Will this change fairly quickly because of inflow of foreign investment and technology, and China's own investment resources are increasingly flowing into higher-end sectors like autos, semiconductors, IT and biotech? Not likely. This is because it will take quite sometime for a country, especially a huge one like China, to shift its comparative advantage to other production. China will not become a capital-intensive exporter until her capital–labour ratio exceeds that of her major trading partners.

Experience shows that the process of expenditure-switching from labour-intensive to capital-intensive production will take more than a decade. Just look at the two north Asian Tiger economies Taiwan and Korea. Their economic and trade structures in the mid-1970s looked like China's today, with significant net exports of labour-intensive manufactures and low-end electronics exports and large net imports of capital goods and raw materials. It took them ten years to move noticeably up the value chain, shifting out of low-end exports into high-value electronics. Then it took them another 15 years, when per capita income surpassed US$10,000 a year, to become net exporters of heavy industrial products.

Some would argue that China is different as she is letting in a large amount of foreign capital and technology, which supposedly will speed up her structural changes. Indeed, even as net investment flows to the rest of emerging Asia fell to almost zero after the bursting of the IT bubble in 2001, net FDI inflows to China were still growing at an annual amount of US$60 billion a year. Would this significant gain in foreign capital not allow China to speed up development and flood the world with cheap products of all sorts, displacing other manufacturers? A detailed examination of China's FDI inflow shows that foreign capital will not necessarily speed up her industrialisation. The latest data shows that about 28% of FDI has gone into export-oriented sectors like light manufacturing and low-end electronics. The rest has gone to domestic-oriented manufacturing and sectors like property and services (Figure 8:9).

This means that 72% of FDI is aimed at China's domestic market, producing goods and services for local consumption. This is consistent with market-level surveys of foreign businesses in China, which show that factors such as domestic market size, proximity to suppliers, physical infrastructure support and a favourable policy environment top the list of foreign investor priorities. Labour cost often appears much further down the list. What attracts FDI is the large rapidly growing Chinese economy.

Thus, rising FDI into China does not threaten other exporting economies. It is also not true that China and her Asian neighbours are competing for a fixed pool of investment resources. Rather than taking

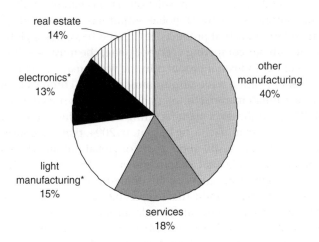

Figure 8:9 China's FDI inflow by sector (2003)
* Export-oriented
Source: CEIC

markets away from other economies, foreign investment in China is a vehicle for expanding the size of the Chinese market to which other exporting economies can sell. This also means that while other Asian economies have to improve their competitiveness to face China's challenge, pursuing a cheap currency policy and erecting trade barriers are not the ways to go. China's experience with FDI shows that Asia needs to integrate their markets to maximise economies of scale and offer a large, unified, stable and viable domestic environment for foreign investment.

Other arguments for China posing an economic threat to the rest of the world include an undervalued currency and state-subsidised capital costs in China, promoting high-tech and capital-intensive industries. These are certainly issues that China has to address. They were also burning issues for the north Asian Tiger economies in the last two decades. But the tiger economies graduated from their developing status without inflicting damages in the other economies. In other words, currency and industrial policies are not the reason to expect China to move any faster than her neighbours and threaten global economic stability.

What about China's rapidly rising industrial might? It seems to underscore her threat to world manufacturing by taking away industrial market share and stealing jobs from her developed and developing neighbours. For example, the Middle Kingdom's industrial output share in the world total has risen to over 7% now from 2.5% in 1990. These numbers should not be seen in isolation. This is because while China's industrial output as a share of global output has almost trebled, so has her demand for industrial products. If China is becoming a global manufacturing hub out-competing everybody else, she must be selling more and more of her industrial products in the world market than she takes in. Her manufacturing trade surplus must be rising chronically. But this is not true. China's manufacturing trade balance has not changed much since 1997, when she ran a manufacturing trade surplus of US$50 billion, or 0.3% of global manufacturing output. In 2004, that trade surplus had risen to US$60 billion, still about 0.3% of global output. The reason is that China's fast industrial output growth in recent years has been matched by significant increase in domestic demand for industrial goods so that the rise in industrial exports has been matched by a rise in industrial imports, leaving a small trade surplus.

There is also no evidence of China's cheap manufacturing goods displacing the rest of Asia's. Excluding China, the rest of Asia's exports to the US have risen to over one-third of total US imports from 25% in 1990. Crucially, this rising share has come on the back of a growing pie, with total US imports from Asia rising from US$490 billion a year to

US$1.5 trillion over the same period. Merely looking at US market share gives an incomplete picture of the overall trade trends. If Chinese manufacturers had displaced others and gained export market share at the expense of other Asian economies, their export growth trends should diverge; China's export growth should be rising while the rest of Asia's should be falling.

However, evidence shows that trade growth in Asia and China moved in tandem for most of the last two decades, with the exception in 1997–1998 and 2001–2002 when Chinese exports out-performed the rest of Asia significantly (Figure 8:10). These periods were the Asian crisis and the global IT downturn. This means that China performed better than the rest of Asia simply by not collapsing during these economic shock periods. This should not be surprising because China was insulated from the Asian crisis by her relatively closed capital account, and the bursting of the IT bubble mainly hurt investment goods, and especially electronics equipment, which China does not specialise in.

The whole point about this trade argument is that although China is a competitive stress to the global system, she is also supporting high-end manufacturing jobs in the rest of the world and export growth in her

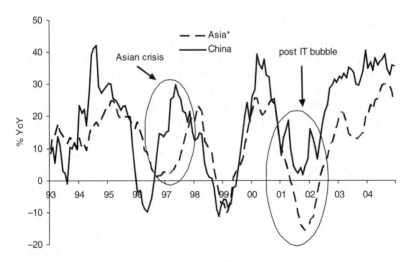

Figure 8:10 China and Asia export growth (3-month moving averages)
* HK, Indonesia, Korea, Malaysia, S'Pore, Taiwan, Thailand
Source: CEIC

low- and middle-income neighbours by being a demand source. Although the Middle Kingdom runs a consistent trade surplus with the developed world, she runs a large trade deficit with the non-Japan Asia, to the tune of 2% of the region's GDP. China buys from the rest of Asia agricultural and mining products, electronics, machinery and equipment, chemicals, plastics and metals. About 50% of China's total imports are for domestic consumption, including a large share of machinery and basic materials.

A China model for development?

In a nutshell, China's challenge to the global economy has often been exaggerated to an economic threat, while her potential opportunities for international trade and business expansion are often ignored. As China continues to grow, her demand for raw materials and capital-intensive products from the rest of the world will rise. Her need for natural resources will likely be even larger than the needs of Europe and Japan for post-World War II reconstruction. Exhaustible resources could be persistently dear for decades. This will shift the global terms of trade in the favour of those resource-rich, and often developing, economies. The production patterns in these economies will also change, with their primary outputs from agriculture and mining rising while that from manufacturing output falling.

In this sense, ASEAN economies would gain, due to their better endowment in natural resources and hence comparative advantages in the exports of rice, oil, mineral, wood and paper and petrochemical products. Oil-rich economies will also see a notable benefit from China's huge demand for energy. As millions of Chinese join the motoring class, oil prices could trend higher for years. To some extent, the growing Chinese demand would slow the pace of industrialisation in these economies by increasing the relative attractiveness of the primary sector. The changes in the terms of trade will also favour the developed economies that have significant comparative advantages in making land- and capital-intensive goods. Commodity and capital-goods suppliers like Australia, Canada, Japan, the EU and the US should gain from increasing exports to China. Some analysts estimate that, in terms of auto exports, Japan, the EU and the US would capture over 85% of the expected gains from increased exports to China. Even the consumer product sector will gain. Prestigious global brands could appreciate in value with China's growth as more Chinese become able to afford higher priced, branded products.

Those who allege that China is running a mercantilist policy by suppressing imports and keeping her doors shut to foreign competition should note that, political issues aside, and despite China's overall relatively poor economic status and socialist background, she is one of the most rapidly liberalising economies in the world. After a disastrous era of promoting collective organisation, in which almost 30 million people died of starvation, China pulled her way out of the economic disaster she had created by implementing the Household Responsibility System, which improved farm incentive and productivity. This system in turn led to the township-village enterprises and sequential commercial development built on their momentum.

In a space of just two decades since 1978, China has pushed through significant creative destruction to shed the onerous trappings of the socialist planning system, witness the dramatic shrinkage of the state sector giving way for the emergence of the private sector (Figure 8:1). The Middle Kingdom has thrown open the doors to foreign companies and generated the world's fastest growing import bill. It is also putting ever-increasing amounts of state assets on the auction block, or shutting them down completely. Between 1996 and 2003, layoffs from the urban state companies alone were more than South Korea's 48 million-strong population.

This is not to say the Chinese have got a correct development model. Indeed, it is still unclear what the long-term outcome for China (and the world) will be. But the Chinese experience should force the world to rethink some of the fundamental tenets of development economics. Two key issues stand out. First, while the institutions China employed are different from the developed nations, the incentive implications are similar. Second, China has been facing new problems, but she has also been pragmatically attempting new solutions. This is also not to say that China is problem-free. Far from it, as we all know. There are still daunting problems with transparency, corporate governance, legal infrastructure and in the banking and corporate sectors. But recognisable improvements have been made in these areas, albeit slowly. Meanwhile, private capital is gaining significance in the economy. It is not unthinkable that in another 20 years, China could have more billionaires than any other economies, though the issue of unequal income distribution could remain a thorny one.

Though China has made little progress on liberalising the political system, she is a vibrant supporter of economic globalistion. She is an active participant in regional and multilateral institutions, such as APEC, the IMF and the World Bank. Her entry to the WTO is one of the defining moments in history of that organisation as well as China's economic reforms. The significance of China's achievements lies more in the margin and momentum of change than in the quantity of the changes. Going forward, China could be a role model for economic liberalisation in the developing world. India is already borrowing a lot from China as a guide for her own reforms. Even countries in Latin America and Eastern Europe are examining the factors behind China's rapid economic ascent on to the global stage.

9
Hollowing-out, Revisited

The perception of the China economic threat is especially acute in Southeast Asia, because many economies there have structural frameworks similar to China. The 'hollowing-out' fear has been in existence for quite sometime. However, the process of production migration to China has accelerated since the Asian crisis. The final outcome of this process for the region is far from certain. It could be pessimistic, benign or optimistic. In the short-term, many of Asia's regional economies will likely see a decline in their living standards. What happens to their economic well-being in the longer-term depends on how willing and how fast they can adapt to the new economic paradigm dominated by China's manufacturing clout. One thing that is certain is that the surviving strategy for China's Asian neighbours boils down to a focus on core competence. The rise of China's economic might is not the end of the world for Southeast Asia; it is not the end of the world for the global economy; and China does not have to be a catalyst for the next Asian crisis as some fear.

Southeast Asia's fate

The hollowing-out thesis – that China's competitive manufacturing power will crowd out its competitors by drawing investment and production resources from other countries and hence hollowing-out their economies – has stirred fears among China's neighbours for some years. When we look at the issue systematically, there are three possible outcomes for Southeast Asia facing the China challenge. The worst case is a complete hollowing-out of Southeast Asian manufacturing, as the regional governments are too slow to respond to China's economic ascent. Under this case, China's inroads to into global manufacturing would be unstoppable, with the Chinese manufacturing industry stretching across the whole value-chain, out-competing the rest of the world. China's rise would hit Southeast Asia the hardest as the latter was the preferred manufacturing outsourcing and production region for global multinational corporations (MNCs). The decline of Southeast Asia in this scenario would be rapid, as the other sectors would not have grown significantly or fast enough to offset the destruction of its manufacturing industry. In this pessimistic 'destructive destruction' case, China would thrive at the expense of the rest of Asia.

At the other extreme is the scenario that proactive reforms and successful shifts in development strategies by the regional governments would offset China's hollowing-out impact on Southeast Asia. Attracted by Southeast Asia's successful reform responses, global MNCs would diversify into the region to avoid over-dependence on China. Meanwhile, Chinese labour costs would rise as production capacity was pushed towards the limit. Rising competition would also force Southeast Asia to be more efficient. All this will raise Southeast Asia's competitiveness and limit the hollowing-out impact. The region will lose some, but not the bulk, of its manufacturing. The governments' focus on developing alternative growth areas, such as services and natural resources, would allow the region to rejuvenate its economic livelihood and make good or better the losses in manufacturing. This would result in a win–win situation for China and Southeast Asia to prosper together.

In between these two extreme cases is a scenario where massive manufacturing hollowing-out from Southeast Asia would be met by some degree of economic reform and some change in development strategies by the regional authorities to counter the China challenge. The structural relationship between China and Southeast Asia would shift from one of manufacturing competition to a service and natural resource complement. Southeast Asia's ability to grow its complementary role as a supplier to China's need for services and resources would be crucial for its economic well-being. This case suggests an ambiguous outcome for Southeast Asia, whose outlook would depend on whether its policy responses and structural changes would bear enough fruit to make up for the losses stemming from the hollowing-out of its manufacturing sector.

Sceptics believe that China is destined to become the world's factory and Southeast Asia's decline will be severe and prolonged. This is an extreme view. On the other hand, Asian policymakers appear to be subscribing to the benign view of successful development of a complementary relationship with China. Indeed, the region is already responding or planning responses to the rise of China's economic clout. Hence, the pessimistic case is unlikely to play out. However, simply responding is one thing, succeeding in that response is another. The region's inherent structural weakness and reform inertia (see Chapter 5) suggest that many Asian policymakers are still complacent. If this complacent attitude goes on, Southeast Asia as a whole would not be able to change fast enough to create high value-added alternatives to manufacturing.

Being a low-value service provider and generic resource supplier to China and the rest of the world would not prevent a fall in living standard for Southeast Asia. Since profits from such activities are razor thin, the region's corporate sector would not have the financial resources to support the training and research and redevelopment programmes that are needed to climb the value chain. The outcome could lie somewhere between the worst-case scenario and the benign case. In other words, the rise of China will inevitably raise the economic stress in the region in the medium-term.

Breaking up Asia Inc.

But all is not lost. Asia needs to uproot some of its old habits to face China's economic ascent and to avert another economic crisis. Even before getting to the tough part of breaking the cosy politics–business relationship, there is one crucial thing Asia can do to kick-start deeper fundamental changes – break up the old conglomerate model and focus on core competence. Despite their restructuring efforts after the Asian crisis, many regional governments are still stuck with the 'bigger-is-better' strategy. For example, China is building her own Chinese Fortune-500 companies; Japan (after breaking up the *keiretsu* in the 1990s) is amalgamating her banks again to create the largest financial institution in the world; Singapore is expanding her government agencies, such as Tamasek and the PSA (Port of Singapore Authority), albeit with a different focus for these companies on amassing overseas instead of local assets; Thailand's politicians are enlarging their business empires with their political powers.

Those economies, notably Korea, which have abandoned the bigger-is-better mindset serve as examples for why breaking up the conglomerates and focusing on core competence is a better way to strengthen an economy's structural immunity to a financial crisis than the old model. The Americans had already rejected the bigger-is-better model after their experience in the 1970s, when companies like International Telephone and Telegraph ran a multitude of businesses that embraced everything from hotels to copper mining. By the 1980s, these US conglomerates began to unwind, as the theory that diversification offered the best protection against different business cycles in specific industries was discredited by the development of capital markets.

Without the capital markets, investors had no choice but to invest in the conglomerates (and hence encourage their growth), letting the companies hedge risks by investing in different business lines. But the development of capital markets offered investors a more efficient way to diversify risk, by investing in market leaders in different industries rather than a single conglomerate. The buzz phrase in American boardrooms and MBA classrooms in the 1980s was 'core competence' – break up the giant and focus on what the business can do the best.

Ironically, when European and American companies were focusing on their core competencies, they were losing, but not gaining, global market shares to large and diversified groups in Korea and Japan. Korean *chaebol* and Japanese *keiretsu* built business empires with units in completely different and unrelated businesses, making everything one could imagine and providing a full range of services from operating travel agencies and hotels to banking. But their goods days did not last for too long. The Japanese *keiretsu* began to fall apart as the asset bubble began to deflate in the late 1980s. The long-term stock market decline destroyed the *keiretsu* system that was built on cross shareholdings. Banks were hit by a mountain of bad debts and a severe erosion of their capital base, which was built on shareholdings. The same thing happened in Korea, although at a later date when the Asian crisis hit in 1997.

Both the Korean and Japanese conglomerate systems were a classic case of government policies creating competitive advantages for their industries, even though they did not have comparative advantages support. In business terms, the competitive edge that the Korean and Japanese conglomerates enjoyed had nothing to do with core competencies, and everything to do with subsidised (and distorted) capital allocation. In Japan, the capital came from banks within the *keiretsu* themselves. In Korea, although the *chaebol* did not control the banks, the government ordered the banks to lend to the business giants to enable relentless expansion both in Korea and overseas without reference to fundamentals like cash flows and profits. While Japan had a long protracted decline (as she was rich enough to afford to get by, languishing without flourishing), Korea's fall was abrupt and swift. The ensuing capital flight and the failing of the Korean banking system eliminated the *chaebol*'s competitive edge at once by cutting off all cheap funding sources.

That crisis led to significant changes. The Korean government forced the *chaebol* to cut debt, which had zoomed to over 500% of equity among the 30 largest firms before the Asian crisis. At that time, the average debt of American companies was 70% of equity. Then after bailing out the banks to the tune of US$130 billion – or one third of Korea's GDP – the government tightened banking regulations and refrained from policy lending. Robbed of the edge of subsidised capital, Korean businesses were forced to focus on core competence like their American and European counterparts. One after another, the *chaebol* were broken up and restructured so that individual units could focus on their main business without worrying about the performance of siblings. Though more work needs to be done (see Chapter 5, section 'The bad apples fail to turn good'), the change was in the right direction and had helped make the Korean economy more flexible and efficient than it was before the crisis.

As long as Asian conglomerates compete for capital not on the basis of inherent advantages, but on political favours or government guided lending, there will be growing inefficiencies. In the end, it is a company's core competence that can reliably sustain its global competitive power in both good and bad times. Experience shows that companies will only be forced to develop such competencies if banks have restructured and developed a true commercial culture. Thus, breaking up Asia's political connections to business and crony capitalism is the key to strengthen its ability to compete with China as well as avoiding another financial crisis.

Doing it the wrong way

To form an amalgamated market in Asia, some have floated the idea of creating an Asian Monetary Union (AMU), modelled after the European Monetary Union (EMU) as a way to counter-balance China's rising economic weight. The idea is to create an enlarged and unified market by adopting a single currency. An AMU would also foster regional economic stability by promoting trade and investment growth via closer economic cooperation and integration of the diverse regional markets. If Europe can do it, Asia should also be able to do it, the thinking goes.

Unfortunately, the idea will not work for Asia, and it is definitely not a quid pro quo for painful structural reforms. Worse still, a monetary union would even cause some disastrous effects on the region. The trouble lies in Asia's vast development diversity. By merging economies with different income levels, an AMU would inflict significant deflation in high-income economies in the long-term. The low-income economies would gain at the expense of the rich ones. This will create regional inequalities among AMU members making the union arrangement unsustainable.

Imagine merging advanced Asian economies like Singapore, Hong Kong or Taiwan, which have income levels at or close to the developed world, with their developing neighbours like China and India, where average nominal wages and domestic prices are only a fraction of those in the developed world. All the AMU members should gain from greater integration, currency stability and lower transaction costs in the short-term. However, in the long-term, the poorer members would see substantial inflation while the richer members would suffer from protracted deflation. This is because the developing economies will dominate the tradable goods sector. Significant expansion of external demand (from both within AMU and outside) for the developing economies' manufacturing exports will raise aggregate demand, putting upward pressure on their exchange rates. But with nominal exchange rates fixed within the AMU, their real (inflation-adjusted) exchange rate would have to rise to adjust for the demand pressure. And the only way to do that is for domestic inflation to rise within these developing members.

The opposite would occur in the developed member economies, whose higher cost of production would price them out of manufacturing exports. Their aggregate demand would fall, putting downward pressure on their exchange rates. But with fixed nominal exchange rates inside the AMU, their real exchange rate would fall, meaning domestic deflation. This process would not be noticeable in the short-term, but it will emerge over the longer-term like a decade or more, as empirical evidence from economic development shows.

It is true that developing members, like China, would gain from trade expansion and higher inflation. These would, in turn, push up their asset prices and fuel economic growth. But the richer developed members would suffer from prolonged deflation, with potentially negative impact on domestic asset prices and growth. All this is not to deny the benefits from trade and the monetary union, it is just that the idea is not workable with wide income disparity and development gaps in Asia. The crux of the problem lies in forcing economies at vastly different stages of economic development into a single exchange rate policy. The lack of exchange rate flexibility as an adjusting factor for absorbing economic shocks will force domestic prices to adjust. And domestic price adjustments could be quite painful for some members. What makes the EMU work is precisely that income levels among EMU members are very close to each other so that there is no significant deflationary pressure coming from relative income gaps.

It's not the end of life

The glass is half empty if one chooses to see China as an economic threat with damaging impact on the global economy. But the glass can well be half full if one sees China as an opportunity for bettering the global economic well-being. According to the World Trade Organisation (WTO), China is now the largest merchandise trader in Asia and the third largest in the world (after Germany and the US) for both exports and imports. This makes her an important driver for world trade growth. The 'China will take over the world' rhetoric is an unfortunate but unavoidable by-product of China's rapid rise in importance in the world economy. It is true that China is growing and her growth will temporarily dislocate markets for manufacturing goods and commodities. But this does not spell economic doom for the regional economies and developed countries. Experience tells us so. The rise of America as the world's industrial powerhouse in the late nineteenth and early twentieth centuries did not impoverish Europe. Japan's economic ascent in the 1980s did not impoverish America either.

China's rise this time should not be different, despite her huge size (see Chapter 8, section 'The growth threat – debunked'). The fears that the Middle Kingdom's hunger for food and raw materials would starve, bankrupt and deplete the Earth and hollow-out other economies are exaggerations. They also reflect an unrealistically static view of the global economy. For example, there is an increasing concern that China looking to the same sources for oil that the US has long tapped would increase competition for the limited supply and lead to the next round of geopolitical strife. But is this really the case?

The US Department of Energy estimated in 2004 that the US consumption of oil would rise by 60% to 32 million barrels a day in 2025 from 20 million barrels in 2000. During the same period, China's demand for oil was estimated to rise by 133% to 14 million barrels a day. In percentage terms, China's increase would be huge, but in absolute terms America's is still far greater. So, whose insatiable demand should the world worry about more? A similar observation can be made on the environment. Between 1992 and 2001, China's air pollution, as measured by her emission of carbon dioxide, rose 63% to 175 million tons. America's pollution rose only 14% in the same period. But in absolute terms, America emitted 668 million tons, almost four times more than China's amount. So whose pollution should the world worry about more?

All this is not to demonise the US, but to point out that rhetoric is often exaggerated to paint a China threat. The world is not static.

As global oil demand and prices rise, pressure will also rise in the developed world to look for alternative sources of energy, be they renewable or nuclear- or hydro-based. The rich countries will invest heavily in these new technologies. The higher the oil price, the more cost-efficient they will endeavour to become. Technological advancement and transfer to the developing economies, like China, will eventually make these new forms of energy affordable to them.

We have also argued that China could well be an opportunity for growth and investment by being a source of demand so that the much feared hollowing-out process would end, or be reversed, in the longer-term. More subtly, the integration of China (and India for the same matter) into the world economy, along with her vast supply of cheap labour, could raise the return on capital in a lasting way. This is because the addition of China's vast labour supply to the global pool would raise the global ratio of labour to capital. The law of diminishing returns states that given the capital stock, the return on labour would fall, as labour quantity rises, while return on capital would rise, as the amount of capital per unit of labour falls.

This higher labour–capital ratio (as a result of China's integration into the world economy), in turn, has a far reaching implication on labour earnings. Outsourcing may not have destroyed many jobs in the developed world, but the threat that firms could produce offshore would help keep a lid on wages worldwide. As a result, the share of profits in national income could stay relatively high for a long period of time. Labour's share would remain low, though workers may still be better off if the cake itself is growing bigger in terms of higher purchasing power. For example, cheaper consumer products from China have helped raise the real purchasing power of the developed world so that their workers are better off.

Economic development is not about competition for a fixed pile of resources, which once exhausted, brings the game to a halt. It is a complex game in which patterns of resources used shift all the time according to price and the development of new technologies, which in turn could alter an economy's comparative advantage. China's integration into the world economy will require careful response and adaptation from both the developed and developing economies. But it is no cause for panic.

China's outstanding economic performance over the past two decades is no guarantee of her future success. The Chinese leadership is facing profound challenges, as it seeks to balance robust economic growth to keep improving the nation's living standards with painful structural reforms. Continued economic liberalisation will create more unemployment and potential social unrest in the short run. The Chinese leadership must also grapple with income inequality, which on every identifiable dimension has increased sharply since reform started. Last but not least, China is suffering from significant environmental deterioration, which, according to the World Bank, is generating substantial excess mortality and morbidity.

Critics often argue that China has replaced Japan as the most common source of trade disputes with the US. But those who point the finger at China's large trade deficit with the US and mounting foreign reserve accumulation as evidence for foul play by China shutting her domestic market and keeping her currency artificially low are missing the point. At the time Japan had her record-setting trade surplus with the US, she also had a massive trade surplus with the rest of the world. However, China's global trade surplus in recent years has been quite small because her surplus with the developed markets has largely been offset by her trade deficit with other Asian economies. Further, China has a deficit on her services account and its foreign income account, so that her current account, a better reflection of her overall external balances, is in a relatively small surplus (less than 2% of GDP).

It is true that China has the largest bilateral trade surplus with the US among all her trading partners. But this is not because of closed Chinese markets. It is because of China's emergence as the world's major production base for labour-intensive manufacturing goods. Global exports of foreign-invested companies in China have grown from US$300 million in 1995, when they were only 1 per cent of China's total exports, to US$340 billion in 2004, when they comprised over half of China's total exports. Most of the foreign direct investment (FDI) in China originates from Hong Kong, Korea, Taiwan and more recently Singapore, where rising labour cost has driven manufacturers in these economies to relocate production to lower-cost production bases, notably China in recent years. What this means is that China has become the last stop in the global production chain before end products are shipped to other markets. Many goods that were formerly made and exported directly from the rich Asian economies to the developed markets have been made in and exported from China in recent years.

As a result, China has rapidly displaced the exports of many Asian economies in third markets like Japan, Europe and the US. Since the mid-1980s, China has displaced Taiwan and Korea as the major supplier of footwear to the US market. She has also displaced Hong Kong, Taiwan and Korea as the key supply sources of toys, games and sporting goods.

A similar transformation has been underway for some time in some consumer electronics products and appears to be underway in information technology (IT) hardware, like personal computers, notebook computers, monitors, scanners, PC servers and personal digital assistants.

However, it is crucial to note that China's production of IT hardware is based on the import of high value-added parts and components, almost all of which are made within the more advanced Asian economies, in which the developed world has invested. China's production of liquid crystal display monitors, for example, is based largely on liquid crystal modules imported from Japan, Korea or Taiwan. Thus, even as China displaces other Asian sources of supply of end products in third markets, at the same time she is emerging as a huge market for high value-added parts and components made mostly in Asia. This results in a surge in intra-regional trade, where China imports a large amount of parts, components and electronics assemblies from other Asian economies in the process of running large bilateral deficits with the region. She then exports the end products to the developed markets, racking up a trade surplus with them.

Those who are worried about China sucking in all the foreign capital at the expense of the rest of Asia should note that the global shift in manufacturing to China will start to wind down in the coming years so that strong FDI inflow to China will end. So China is facing the same economic challenge as her Asian neighbours in attracting foreign investment. In particular, foreign investors are looking to relocate service industries after the first wave of cross-border investment by the manufacturing industry from developed to developing nations to cut costs. While China is the main beneficiary in this first wave of transnational FDI movement, there is no guarantee she will succeed in attracting foreign capital in the future, if she fails to come up with a new economic strategy.

Globalisation and structural adjustment of the services industry suggest that multinationals and big companies will scramble to outsource their service businesses to cut costs and raise their competitive edges. If China fails to beef up her services industry fast enough to match this next wave of FDI relocation, she faces a risk of losing out to competitors such as India and even the Philippines.

In a nutshell, China is not invincible and not a threat. Her economic ascent presents both opportunities and challenges for the global economy. Although the Mainland's national income was only 4% of the world's total in 2004, it contributed more than 10% of global economic growth. Further, China's foreign trade volume, less than 6% of the world's total, contributed about 12% of global trade growth. Arguably, the Middle Kingdom's participation in the global division of labour and absorption of labour-intensive manufacturing has in effect promoted the upgrading of industries in many other economies. In particular, China's rapidly expanding trade volume has become a major engine of growth in Asia because of the imported capital goods and parts and components used in processing her exports. China has also become an increasingly important market for American firms, as can be seen in the rise in American exports to China since 2001, when China entered the WTO.

On the other hand, China is inflicting a significant competitive stress on producers of labour-intensive manufacturing goods. Many, especially in Asia, have adjusted by investing in China in manufacturing facilities to take advantage of China's low labour costs. But this, in turn, has resulted in a loss of employment and investment at home. More advanced Asian economies like Taiwan, Korea and Singapore face the challenge of continuing to move up the technology ladder into the production of higher value-added, more sophisticated and capital-intensive goods.

Although China is displacing some production in the US, the impact is far smaller than many have stated. Production of footwear, toys, apparel and sporting goods largely moved out of the US to other production bases in Asia a long time before they migrated to China. The US economy adjusted to the loss of these jobs years ago. Thus, the China bashers are using old news to misdirect the China debate. The story is the same with respect to most IT products. The bottom line is that those who see China as an economic threat, with the potential of triggering another Asian crisis, should look at the hard facts and think again before jumping to a conclusion.

Notes

Introduction

1 See chapters 3–5 in Chi Lo, *The Misunderstood China: Uncovering the Truth Behind the Bamboo Curtain*, Pearson Prentice Hall 2004.

1 The New China Threat

1 Brunei, Cambodia, Indonesia, Laos, Malaysia, Myanmar, the Philippines, Singapore, Thailand, Vietnam.
2 Relationship or connection deals.
3 This is simply national income accounting identity, where GDP is equal to the sum of consumption, investment, government spending and net exports. The last item is total exports net of imports so that at any given level of imports, a rise in exports adds directly to a country's GDP.
4 Economic hard-landing refers to the situation when GDP growth slumps from positive to negative as a result of the government's harsh economic tightening measures.
5 For more details, please see chapter 4 in Chi Lo, *The Misunderstood China: Uncovering the Truth Behind the Bamboo Curtain*, Pearson Prentice Hall 2004.

2 A Conspiracy Theory

1 The MTEs include Korea, Taiwan, Malaysia, Indonesia, Singapore, the Philippines and Thailand. Hong Kong is excluded from the group because it is really part of China, with 90% of its exports routed to and from China as re-exports to the rest of the world.
2 For more details on this argument, see chapter 8 in Chi Lo, *When Asia Meets China in the New Millennium*, Pearson Prentice Hall 2003.
3 Empirical evidence shows that this is also the level of income where consumption begins to shift quickly from basic necessities to discretionary spending.
4 The issues of China's manufacturing threat and competitiveness are dealt with in Chapter 8.
5 Unemployed refers to out of work completely, while underemployed means insufficient work – typically defined in developed economies as anyone who works less than 40 hours a week.
6 The Asian Tiger economies include Korea, Hong Kong, Singapore and Taiwan.

3 The Outsourcing Threat

1 The Association of Southeast Asian Nations (ASEAN) consists of ten countries: Myanmar, Vietnam, Thailand, Laos, Cambodia, Indonesia, Malaysia, Brunei, Singapore and the Philippines.

4 The Next Asian Crisis: Made in China?

1. Under China's de facto fixed exchange system, capital inflow will lead to a surge in domestic liquidity. This is because capital inflow tends to push up the renminbi (RMB) exchange rate as the demand for RMB exceeds supply in the foreign exchange market. But to keep the exchange rate from rising, the PBoC has to sell RMB (i.e. increase RMB supply), thus increasing domestic money supply as a result.
2. When foreign capital flows in, swelling the foreign reserves and forcing domestic money supply to expand (see note 1), the PBoC sells government bonds (thus taking in cash) to absorb the increase in money supply. This operation is called 'sterilisation' and is commonly used by central banks to offset the impact of rising foreign reserves on domestic money growth under a fixed exchange rate system.
3. Experience in the emerging markets shows that major economic dislocation would happen when an economy's current account deficit goes above 5% of GDP for a sustained period of time.

5 The Next Asian Crisis: Self-inflicted?

1. Non-financial public sector debt includes liabilities of the central government, government agencies and non-financial public sector companies.
2. This is gross debt, which includes primarily bonds issued against assets of the Central Provident Fund (CPF). The picture is quite different on a net basis. Singapore's fiscal reserves were estimated at some 230% of GDP in 2003, more than enough to cover the gross debt.
3. China's budget deficit is about 3% of GDP by official estimates. But it is much higher if off-balance sheet spending and hidden debt items are included.
4. The HKD has been pegged to the USD at an exchange rate of HK$7.8 per USD since 1984. The currency link, as it is locally known, is seen as a major factor in dragging Hong Kong into a 6-year deflation spiral after the 1997–1998 Asian crisis by denying the HKD to depreciate along with the regional currencies.
5. For example, see 'Fiscal Vulnerability and Financial Crisis in Emerging Market Economies', Occasional paper 218, IMF, 2003.
6. Private sector analysts estimate that Asia's sterilisation debt burden ranges from a hefty 37% of GDP in Taiwan and 34% in Singapore to 5% in China and 4% in the Philippines in early 2004.
7. For example, see Chi Lo, *When Asia Meets China in the New Millennium*, Pearson Prentice Hall 2003, pp. 26–30.
8. Conglomerates in South Korea are known as *chaebol*.

6 The External Stresses

1. The current account includes merchandise trade plus other overseas payments and receipts, such as travel, foreign income, and interests and dividends.
2. Any one of the components of net national savings (personal, corporate and government) could be negative if it is dis-saving.

7 The Real Danger Isn't Another Crisis

1. Except the Chinese renminbi, the Hong Kong dollar and the Malaysia ringgit. The renminbi has been unofficially pegged to the US dollar since 1994, while the Hong Kong dollar has been pegged to the US dollar since 1985. The ringgit has been pegged to the US dollar since 1998 when the Malaysian authorities wanted to suppress exchange volatility resulting from the Asian crisis.
2. See note 2 in Chapter 5.
3. China, Hong Kong, India, Indonesia, Korea, Malaysia, the Philippines, Singapore, Taiwan and Thailand.
4. Currently, only 3% of the 3.2 million-strong working population pay over 60% of total salary tax and just 1% of Hong Kong firms pays 60% of total profit tax.
5. Insolvency is defined as a situation when a bank has a capital–asset ratio of less than 8%, as required by the Bank of International Settlements.
6. The solvency issue may be relevant to regulators in a developed economy for deciding whether to step in and save a bank from collapsing. Typically, they will only save a solvent bank that is suffering from temporary liquidity problems. An insolvent bank will be allowed to fail, with safety measures, such as deposit insurance, to help minimise the shock to the financial system.
7. China's close capital account forbids short-term portfolio flows. Her foreign debt totalled US$220 billion in 2004, compared to US$610 billion in foreign reserves. This means China would have more than enough reserves to repay foreign creditors if they were to withdraw all at once.
8. Short-selling is an investment strategy where an investor borrows a security, such as a bond or a stock, and sells it to the market, hoping to buy it back to cover his/her position when the price of the security falls in a short period of time.
9. China's pension debt is the present value of promised future payments to existing pensioners. The estimated size of the pension depends on many assumptions, and a small change in these assumptions could make a big difference. To estimate the debt, one needs to make assumptions on the pensioners' life expectancy, the long-term growth rate of average wages, inflation and discount rates. That is why there is such a wide range of estimates (45–75% of GDP) for the size of China's pension shortfall.
10. Under the 1973 Multifibre Agreement, developed markets in Europe and the US limited the amount of apparel imported from developing economies. The end of the quota system has opened the garment trade among WTO members and allowed companies to freely source from the cheapest suppliers.

8 What China Threat?

1. But of course, the point is that if there were no such inertia, China would have moved even faster up the global economic league.
2. Mr Guo replaced Zhang Enzhao, who resigned as chairman of the China Construction Bank in March 2005 after a kickback scandal.

3 Huijin Investment was set up by the central government in December 2003 as a special purpose state-owned commercial vehicle to manage the US$45 billion injection to the Bank of China and the China Construction Bank as part of the bank recapitalisation effort.
4 The purchasing power parity, or PPP, measurement adjusts for relative inflation and exchange rates between economies. It states that the exchange rate between two economies should equal to the ratio of their price level of a fixed comparable basket of goods and services. Thus, when a country's domestic price level is rising faster than the other (i.e. it is experiencing higher inflation), its exchange rate must depreciate to keep the purchasing power between the two economies constant. The basis for PPP is the 'law of one price'. In the absence of transportation and other transaction costs, competitive markets will equalise the price of an identical basket of goods in two economies when the prices are expressed in the same currency. Thus, PPP calculation compares China's GDP with those of the other economies on a like-for-like basis.
5 South Korea, Taiwan, Hong Kong and Singapore.
6 Association of Southeast Asian Nations. It consists of 10 countries: Myanmar, Thailand, Laos, Vietnam, Cambodia, Indonesia, Malaysia, Brunei, Singapore and the Philippines.
7 A country has an absolute advantage in producing a good when it can make more of that good with each unit of input than another country. A country has a comparative advantage in making a good when it has lower opportunity costs of making that good than its trading partners; i.e. when it can forgo less resource to make that good than its trading partners. It is not necessary to have an absolute advantage in order to have a comparative advantage. Gains from trade depend on comparative advantage but not absolute advantage.

Bibliography

Andersen, Jonathan, 'How I Learned to Stop Worrying and Forget the Yuan', *Far Eastern Economic Review*, December 2004

Asian Development Bank, 'Risks to the Outlook for Development Asia', *Asian Development Outlook*, 2004

Aziz, Jahangir and Christoph Duenwald, 'Growth-Financial Intermediation Nexus in China', IMF Working Paper, WP/02/194, November 2002

Bhwagwati, Jagdish, 'The Muddles over Outsourcing', *Journal of Economic Perspectives*, Fall 2004

Callen, Tim, Marco Terrones, Xavier Debrun, James Daniel and Celine Allard, 'Public Debt in Emerging Markets: Is It Too High?', *World Economic Outlook*, IMF, Chapter 3, September 2003

Fishman, Ted, *China Inc.: How the Rise of the Next Superpower Challenges America and the World*, Scribner, 2005

Fullbrook, David, 'Thailand's Booming Economy Stokes Irrational Exuberance', *South China Morning Post*, 20 January, 2004

Henning, Richard, Michael Kell and Axel Schimmelpfening, 'Fiscal Vulnerability and Financial Crisis in Emerging Market Economies', IMF Occasional paper 218, May 2003

Holland, Tom and Michael Vatikiotis, 'Asian Financial Union – Thinking the Unthinkable', *Far Eastern Economic Review*, 8 April, 2004

Ikenson, Daniel, 'Threadbare Excuses: the Textile Industry's Campaign to Preserve Import Restraints', Cato Institute, October 2003

International Monetary Fund, 'The IMF's Response to the Asian Crisis – a Fact Sheet', January 1999, found in http://www.imf.org/External/np/exr/facts/asia.htm

Irwin, Douglas, *Free Trade Under Fire*, Princeton University Press, 2003

Jensen, Bradford and Lori Kletzer, 'Tradable Services: Understanding the Size and Scope of Services Outsourcing and Its Impact on American Workers', Institute for International Economics, October 2004

Jones, Sidney, 'Terrorism in Southeast Asia, More Than Just JI', *Asian Wall Street Journal*, July 2004

Kagan, Robert, 'The Illusion of Managing China', *Washington Post*, 15 May, 2005

Keliher, Macabe, 'Dragon Seizes Market Share', *Asia Times Online*, 10 February, 2004

Lo, Chi, 'Fiscal Vulnerability and Financial Crisis in Emerging Market Economies', Occasional paper 218, IMF, 2003

Lo, Chi, *When Asia Meets China in the New Millennium – China's Role in Shaping Asia's Post-Crisis Economic Transformation*, Pearson Prentice Hall, 2003

Lo, Chi, *The Misunderstood China – Uncovering the Truth Behind the Bamboo Curtain*, Pearson Prentice Hall, 2004

Ma, Jun and Fan Zhai, 'Financing China's Pension Reform', paper presented at Harvard University Conference on China's Financial Reform, September 2001

MacTeer, Bob, 'China is Too Big to Ignore', Federal Reserve Bank of Dallas, 22 May, 2000

Mandelson, Peter, 'Building Europe's Relations with a Rising China', *Asian Wall Street Journal*, 7–8 December, 2004

Morici, Peter, 'The Danger of Adopting a Soft Approach to China', *Asian Wall Street Journal*, 8–10 July, 2005

North, Douglass, *Understanding the Process of Economic Change*, Princeton University Press, 2005

Pettis, Michael, *The Volatility Machine: Emerging Economies and the Threat of Financial Collapse*, Oxford University Press, 2001

Rodlauer, Marhus and Wanda Tseng (eds), 'China Competing in the Global Economy', International Monetary Fund, 2003

Samuelson, Paul, 'Where Ricardo and Mill Rebut and Confirm Arguments of Mainstream Economists Supporting Globalisation', *Journal of Economic Perspectives*, Summer 2004

Schell, Orville, 'Let China Play the Game, Too', *South China Morning Post*, 8 July, 2005

Sharma, Shalendra, *The Asian Financial Crisis: New International Financial Architecture: Crisis, Reform and Recovery*, Manchester University Press, 2003

Tseng, Wanda and Harm Zebregs, 'Foreign Direction in China: Some Lessons for Other Countries', Transcript of Economic Forums and International Seminars, IMF Auditorium, 2 May, 2002

Wang, Yan, Dianqiang Xu and Fan Zhai, 'Implicit Pension Debt and Transition Cost in China: the Pension Reform', World Bank Policy Research Working Paper, 2001

Wong, John, *China's Economy and the Asian Financial Crisis*, World Scientific Publishing Co., 1998

Zakaria, Fareed, 'Does the Future Belong to China', *Newsweek*, 19 May, 2005

Index

Absolute advantage   174–5, 197
Administrative measures   82, 84, 96
Aggregate profits proxy   98
Asia Pacific Economic Cooperation (APEC)   181
ASEAN   2, 6, 10, 25, 27, 38, 50, 51, 169, 180, 194, 197
ASEAN Economic Community (AEC)   25
  problems   30, 31
ASEAN Free Trade Area (AFTA)   30
A-share market   78
Asia growth model   23
Asian crisis   1, 2, 12, 21, 29, 59, 84, 86, 88, 89, 90, 95–8, 100, 102, 107–09, 118, 127, 133, 136, 137, 139, 143, 145, 174, 179, 183, 186, 195, 196
  cushions   65–73, 95, 134–42
  external shocks   111, 122
  next crisis   63, 84, 85, 93, 96, 102, 110, 111, 122, 128, 183, 193
  trigger   62–5, 92, 111, 122, 128, 134, 142–50, 183, 186, 187
Asian Development Bank (ADB)   8, 85, 91, 93
Asian Monetary Union (AMU)   187–8
Asian production chain   50–1
Asian Tigers   36, 38, 64, 168, 169, 170, 173, 176, 178, 194
Asset bubbles   84, 86, 95, 103, 104, 111, 117, 118, 119, 120, 124, 128, 186

Balance of payments (BoP)   54, 92, 93, 95, 96, 100, 138, 142, 170, 171
Balance sheet mis-matching   138

Bank recapitalisation   87, 89, 90, 91, 148, 149, 160, 197
Banking crisis   145–8
Banking reform   160–2
  vision problem   162
Baosteel   63
Basic balance   93, 171
Big Four   145, 148, 160, 162
Bigger-is-better strategy   185–6
Bilateral trade pact   10, 31, 56
Boom/bust growth   1, 11–13, 16, 17, 142, 143
Bubble   74, 81, 84, 86, 95, 103, 104, 111, 117, 118, 121, 124
Business cycle   122, 142

Capital account convertibility   143, 173
Capital controls   15, 80, 81, 95, 96, 113, 143
Capital flight   171, 186
Capital market reform   150
Central Provident Fund (CPF)   195
Chaebol   186, 195
Cheap currency policy   124, 165, 178
China as growth source   6–9, 23, 65–73, 127, 190, 192–3
China labour shortages   32–5
China shock
  global markets   11, 17
  oil market   12–13
China reform
  most rapid liberalising economy   181–2
China threat
  boom/bust growth   1, 11–13, 16, 17
  car industry   4
  conspiracy theory   19, 25–8, 39, 40, 84
  demand threat   6–11, 19, 23–5

China threat – *continued*
 exaggerated 189
 external discipline 68
 geopolitics 13
 growth threat 167–70
 industry espionage 5–6
 internal politics 1, 13–17,
 investment threat 170–4
 manufacturing threat 174–80
 perception 2, 30, 133, 157, 183
 political lies 46–51
 real estate bubble 81, 84
 semi-conductor industry 4–5
 supply threat 1–6
Common Effective Preferential Tariff (CEPT) 31
Communist mindset 162
Comparative advantage 23, 36, 39, 44, 49, 51, 52, 151, 166, 167, 174, 176, 180, 186, 190, 197
Competitive advantage 32, 38, 66, 68, 157, 166, 167, 186
Competitive myth 163–7
 low-wage trap 163
 unit labour cost 164–5
Contingent liabilities 89, 90, 91, 93, 140, 141, 149
Core competence 183, 185–7
Creative destruction 2, 44, 54, 68, 143, 158, 181
Credit risk management 143
Cronyism 97, 102, 103, 104, 107, 109, 110, 112, 187
Currency arbitrage 139
Currency link 88, 89, 195
Currency mis-matching 138
Currency risk 137, 138
Current account deficit 56, 84, 86, 95, 99, 111, 117, 122, 132, 133, 134, 137, 195
Current account surplus 93, 95, 96, 99, 122, 134, 141, 173, 191
Cut-throat competition 163, 164

Debt-deficit crisis 90
 indicators 92
Debt-deflation spiral 118, 119
Debt-to-GDP ratio 86, 89, 91, 140, 141

Deficit-to-GDP ratio 86, 141
Deflation 74, 88, 118, 119, 120, 131, 141, 187, 188, 195
Deleveraging 138
Demand management policy 83
Demand supply mis-match 144
Demand threat 6–11, 19, 23–5
Destructive destruction 184
Devaluation 137, 165
Development model 180–1
Diminishing returns 45
Disinflation 131
Dollar crisis contagion 126
Dollar problem 125

Economic efficiency 42, 54, 64, 67, 98, 112, 157, 158
Economic hard landing 11, 15, 194
Economic soft landing 14
Economies of scale 4, 22, 176, 178
Election cycle 13
European Monetary Union (EMU) 187, 188
Excess foreign borrowing 138
Excess foreign reserves 85, 93
Expenditure-switching 176
Export-led growth 21, 49, 92
Externalities 166–7
External shocks
 Foreign direct investment (FDI) 112–14
 terrorism 128–31
 US dollar crisis 122–7
 US fiscal deficit 115–17

Fertility rate 116, 129, 130
Financial contagion 61, 93, 96, 104, 126
Financial liberalisation 77, 79, 83, 114, 143, 147, 162
Financial suppression 143
Fiscal deficit 85, 86, 96, 111, 112, 130, 131, 132, 133, 141, 142, 195
 bank recapitalisation 87, 89
 China time bomb 148–50
 contingent liabilities 89–91

Fiscal deficit – *continued*
  public spending 87–9
  US time bomb 115–17
Fixed asset investment 14, 74, 82
Fixed exchange rates 86, 95, 124, 136, 137, 138, 139, 195
Flexible exchange rates 99, 136, 137, 141
Floating rural population 33
Foreign direct investment (FDI) 6, 26, 35, 111, 171–4, 177–8, 191, 192
  the dark side of 112–14
Foreign exchange intervention 81–2, 92, 93, 95, 120, 124, 138, 139
Forwards market 147, 174
Full currency convertibility 173–4
Fundamentals vs bubble 73–80

Gains from trade 44, 49, 54, 175, 176, 197
Giant sucking sound 65
Global labour arbitrage 41, 48
Global supply chain 57, 167, 191
Globalisation 41, 48, 55, 64, 121, 153, 181, 192
  hypocrites 56
Great Depression 119
Growth threat 167–70
Guanxi 4

Hollowing out 1, 41, 44, 53, 55, 59, 189, 190
  Southeast Asia's fate 183–5
Hot money 93–5, 134
Housing affordability 76
Housing reform 75, 76, 79
Housing Responsibility System 181
Hub-and-spoke arrangements 10
Hu kou system 78

Import coverage 136
Import elasticity 123, 125
Import penetration 25–6, 65
Inflation 12, 12, 16, 34, 59, 60, 74, 79, 84, 88, 96, 118, 120, 132, 143, 188, 196, 197

Integrated production model 41
Intellectual property rights 166
International division of labour 121, 151, 193
International Energy Agency (IEA) 13
International labour arbitrage 40, 41, 48
International Monetary Fund (IMF) 28, 86, 91, 104, 108, 138, 140, 181, 195
International trade
  positive sum game 52
  structural change 19, 21, 23–5, 40
Inter-provincial competition 63
Interest rate liberalisation 162
Interest rate parity 139
Intra-industry trade 176
Intra-regional trade 20, 192
Investment threat 170–4
Invisible costs 27
IT bubble 21, 28, 44, 88, 96, 177

Jobless economic recovery 121–2

Keiretsu 185, 186
Koomin Bank 101
Korea Inc. 100–02
Krung Thai Bank 104

Labour arbitrage 40, 41, 45, 121
Labour immobility 44
Labour productivity 2, 42, 43, 48, 53, 54, 58–60, 121, 130, 164–7
Laissez-faire 89
Law of comparative advantage 151
Law of diminishing returns 190
Law of one price 197
Liquidity 80, 90, 95, 118, 120, 124, 195, 196
Loan maturity mis-match 138
Low-wage trap 163

Managed float exchange rate 139
Manufacturing Performance Institute (MPI) 63–4

Manufacturing threat   174–80
  FDI flows   177–8
Market mechanism   82, 83
Mercantilist policy   181
Middle class   21–2
Monetary base   81
Monetary union   188
Moral hazard   97
Moral suasion   83, 84
Mortgage market – China   77
Multi-fibre Arrangement on Textiles (MFAT)   133, 151, 152, 153, 154, 196
Multilateral free trade agreements   10
Multinational corporations (MNCs)   184
Multiplier effect   121

National Congress, China   14
National income identity   194
Nepotism   106
New economic paradigm   157, 183
Next Asian crisis   1, 63, 84, 85, 93, 96, 102, 110, 111, 112, 128, 183, 193
  China trigger   62–5, 142–50
  cushions   134–42
  external shocks   111, 131–2
  inherent problems   97–100
Non-performing loans (NPLs)   90, 145, 146, 147, 148, 162
North American Free Trade Agreement (NAFTA)   58

Oil crisis   111, 132
Opportunity cost   39
Organisation for Economic Cooperation and Development (OECD)   58
Original Equipment Manufacturers (OEMs)   46
Outsourcing   69, 121, 151, 152, 156, 190, 192
  hollow-out   53
  misguided debate   46–51
  myopia   44–6, 59–60
Overheating   74, 84

Paternalistic capitalist model   105
Pearl River Delta (PRD)   32, 35, 62
Pension puzzle   149
People's Bank of China (PBoC)   15, 80, 81, 82, 83, 84, 147, 162, 195
Policy mistakes   17
Portfolio flow   93, 95, 111, 112–14, 120, 134, 196
Post bubble economy   118, 119, 121, 141
Product cycle   38–40
Productivity   2, 42, 43, 45, 48, 53, 54, 58–60, 121, 130, 132, 144, 151, 164–7
Protectionism   41, 44, 46, 55, 56, 57, 59, 132, 133, 150, 151, 153, 155
  forcing a China threat   155–6
Public debt   86, 89, 148, 195
Purchasing power parity   168, 197

Qualified Domestic Institutional Investors (QDII)   143, 174

Real estate bubble   81, 84
Real exchange rate   188
Reflation   120
Reform inertia   101–02, 158, 185
Regional integration   20, 187–8
Renminbi   15, 81, 136, 148, 167, 196
  full convertibility   173–4
  intervention   195
Replacement rate   128, 129
Reserve requirements   15, 82
Return on capital   190
Return on labour   190

Short selling   147, 196
Specialisation   2, 42, 44, 51, 54, 151, 174, 175, 176
Stagflation   132
State-owned enterprises (SOEs)   2, 82, 143–7, 149, 150, 159, 162
Sterilisation   81–2, 95, 96, 195
Structural reform
  China, the most rapid liberalising economy   181–2
  communist mindset   162–3

Structural reform – *continued*
  deficiency 22, 23, 85, 97–9, 104, 127
  external discipline 1, 2
  labour productivity 2, 42, 43, 48, 53, 54, 58–60
  portfolio inflow distortion 112–14
  reform inertia 101–02, 158, 185
Subsistence wage 34
Supply threat 1–6
Surplus labour 33, 145

Taiwan Semiconductor Manufacturing Co. (TSMC) 4–5
Temasek 105–06
Terms of trade 180
Terrorism 111, 115, 117, 128–31, 142
Thaksinomics 28, 102–04
Too-big-to-fail 89, 145
Trade deficit 119, 122, 180, 191
Twin deficit 111, 132

Undervalued currency 94, 97, 124, 133, 137, 139, 141, 178
United Nations 129, 130
Unit labour cost 164–5

Urbanisation 71, 73, 78, 79
Uruguay Round 154
US dollar crisis 111, 117, 122–7, 132
US–Central America Free Trade Agreement (CAFTA) 155
US-centric global economy 119, 124, 127
US current account deficit 56, 84, 111, 132
  correction 124–6
  global impact 122–7
US fiscal time bomb 115–17

Value-added 4, 9, 36, 37, 38, 45, 50, 51, 67, 71, 151, 160, 163, 164, 166, 176, 185, 192, 193
Voluntary Exports Restraints (VER) 55

Wealth destruction 119
World Bank 78, 91, 107, 181
World Trade Organisation (WTO) 1, 2, 4, 7, 16, 56, 57, 58, 144, 154, 157, 181, 189, 191, 193, 196
  car industry in China 4
  external discipline 1, 2